No Man Can Serve

Two Masters

Small Print Edition

The true story of a man whose
Purpose in life was changed by God
From Gathering Garbage to Saving Souls

Charles B. Moore IV

With

Philip Mark Ames

Foreword by Jimmy Draper

Preface by Kaye Dunn Robinson

DEDICATION

This work is dedicated to my Lord Jesus Christ, who not only gave me salvation but also the real promise of an abundant life. To Him I am grateful for my bride, my wife, my Judy, my lifetime companion who has willingly followed and faithfully accompanied me as I have obeyed His call. To her also I dedicate this work, and to our four grown children: Judy Anne, James, Cal, and Charles V.

Charles Beatty Moore IV
April 13, 2019

The Authors

Charles Moore is a man who, after years of gathering wealth for himself, was led by God to give it all away and begin a ministry that would eventually lead to the saving of more than three million souls by Jesus Christ, whom they received as their Lord and Savior.

This ministry began on both sides of the Blue Ridge Parkway in the mountains and valleys of Western North Carolina during the first three months of 1968 while Charles and his wife Judy, having just completed two years of seminary training in Fort Worth, Texas, and four months of missionary orientation in Black Mountain, North Carolina, were waiting to begin their missionary assignment in Costa Rica.

The activities of those three months were ordained of God and were crucial to the success of their work for the rest of their lives. After fifty years of ministry, this Christian couple now resides in the Southwestern United States.

While visiting his friend Bob in San Diego in November of 2016, Philip Mark Ames met Bob's friend Al, who introduced him by phone to his friend Charles, who was on his way to the airport to fly to Lima, Peru. When Charles returned to San Diego about two weeks later, he telephoned Philip, who had returned to his home in Pennsylvania Amish country.

Charles had learned from Al that Philip had previously written and published several books based on the Bible. Charles asked Philip if he might be interested in helping to write his autobiography; he then proceeded to tell him some of that story. About an hour into that monologue, Philip interrupted Charles and said, "You had me at Glorieta."

Books by Philip Mark Ames

Realization of Prophetic Visions, 1975; *The Realizationist View of Eschatology*, 2014; *Jesus Christ Revealed I, II, III*, 2016; *The Time-Telling Prophecies of Daniel*, 2013, 2017; *The Olivet Oracle and the Apocalypse*, 2019

FOREWORD

The history of Christianity has been punctuated by remarkable reports of the mighty hand of God that came through the witness of faithful believers. We can recall incredible narratives of God's hand throughout the history of the Jewish nation and the early Christian movement. Down through history there have been powerful manifestations of God's Presence and Power! We are all captivated by those descriptions of things that can only be attributed to the activity of God Himself.

This book records one of those ministries that defy imagination and understanding. Only the anointing that comes through the very hand of God can account for the ministry of Charles and Judy Moore through the witness of what came to be known as "Christians Sharing Christ." These pages read like the 29th chapter of the book of Acts! No other explanation can reveal the depth and the simplicity of this ministry.

Charles Moore's father was a hard-working man who founded and controlled several significant businesses. From refueling military aircraft to one of the strongest sanitation companies in the Southwest to transportation, construction, leasing and restaurant companies, he never ceased to succeed in business. He was active in local and statewide politics and well known by elected officials from Texas to Washington, D.C.

Growing up in such a household resulted in Charles becoming very familiar with many elected officials, and brought many friendships from among the political elite. His commission in the United States Army brought him into the military as a 2nd Lieutenant.

In his home town of El Paso, Texas, he met the earthly love of his life—Judy Sandusky, a beautiful coed at Texas Western College. Her hometown was Odessa, Texas. Their love affair has now lasted through more than half a century of marriage and ministry. He will say with emotion and energy, "After Jesus, my greatest love is Judy." Together they have travelled their incredible road, as recorded in these pages.

When he was 24 years old, his father died, and he was placed in charge of eleven corporations from Maine to Florida and on to California. His success in business saw him blossom into an outstanding businessman and a very wealthy man. This is an important point, because the day came when his obedience to the Lord Jesus Christ led him to abandon all business interests and literally give away his assets. That began an incredible journey of faith for Charles and Judy that continues to this day.

I will not detail his journey for him. These pages are his report of the ministry the Lord entrusted to Him, and of the mighty power of God that has attended each day of this ministry. Read these pages with blessing and excitement as you walk the path with Charles and Judy through the many decades of their obedience to God.

Jimmy Draper
President Emeritus of "LifeWay"

PREFACE

For several years, my late husband Ron Dunn was for Charles Moore a mentor, pastor, confidant, and personal friend. He also served on the Board of "Christians Sharing Christ." What a joy it was to have Charles, Judy and their children as members of our church in Irving, Texas.

During that time Charles taught a men's Sunday School class and was further involved in the church as time allowed. Whenever they would return from a foreign mission, Charles and his family would worship and fellowship with us.

God's providence ordained that our lives be woven together through the years. I have always considered Charles a dear friend; but it was Ron who was able to spend time with him, calling him on days he was in town and inviting him for breakfast or lunch. They could often be seen sharing the Word, talking about what God was doing in their lives, praying together and encouraging each other during difficult days.

Charles shared with me the other day how he and Ron wept together when Ronnie, our 18-year-old son, took his own life after a long battle with a Bi-Polar illness.

Charles was also an encourager to our second son, Stephen. One time he invited Ron and Stephen to accompany him on a trip to Costa Rica. It thrilled us that this could be a tremendous influence on Stephen's young life.

Those were wonderful years of revival at our church in the early 1970's. God was teaching all of us so much. In those early years, Ron and I had been convicted that we had not given God Lordship over our finances; we then committed ourselves to getting totally out of debt and learning how to give by faith, giving exactly what God was telling us to give. Little did Charles know that God used him to teach Ron one of his very first lessons in giving: start with a little baby-step.

Some years after losing Ron, I was courted by Dan Robinson; he had also lost his spouse. Our home is now in North Carolina. Dan and I were privileged to have lunch with

Charles and Judy here a few years ago. We again heard Charles express the desire of his heart, his passion for the Lord, his passion for prayer and his passion for evangelism. You can't read the CSCC newsletter each month without knowing that he and his Judy are one, and willing to endure, at any cost to their personal well-being, whatever is necessary to reach lost souls for Christ.

When God's hand is on a man, there are trials and triumphs in his life. I remember when Charles was struggling with such horrendous health issues and in such pain that he was actually despairing of living and was asking us to seek the Lord on his behalf. That particular battle passed with time and the prayers of his friends. But it seems that since then Charles has never been without physical pain, even with surgery after surgery. God perfects our faith through difficult days; and we learn a lot through the tears.

As you walk with Charles through this book, you will be encouraged in your faith. God is always looking for a man whose heart is firmly fixed on Him and who will continually trust Him for what He wants to do with his life. We questioned at the time why the Lord led Charles to divest himself of all earthly wealth and power. This involved multiple companies and millions of dollars he had inherited. But if God has spoken, it is not for us to question what He is doing. God had taught Charles at a young age how to live in poverty or in wealth. He had a specific plan for his life.

God put in his heart a love for the down and out, from the bridge people in Costa Rica to the people who lived on the garbage dumps of Pamplona Alta in Lima, Peru. In the world's eyes, he doesn't have much materially. But, O the riches he has stored up in the lives of men, women and children that will welcome him to Heaven's gates.

—Kaye Dunn Robinson

ACKNOWLEDGMENTS

There are literally hundreds of dear ones who have influenced and impacted my life. Were I to begin listing them, I would unavoidably leave out some very special people despite my best effort. So I will name only a few here.

You will read how my heavenly Father gave me eternal life through His Son on August 30, 1958 (Romans 10:9-10). He is my first love. Then, two months later, I fell in love with my second love: Judith Frances Sandusky, "my Judy." I am in the 61st year of knowing and loving my Savior, and the 61st year of loving my Judy. During these many years my Lord and my Judy have been faithful, loving and good to me.

My Lord gifted Judy and me with four uniquely special children for which I am truly thankful. Each has given us a loving grandchild. I am proud of them all; and they continue to bless me in many ways to this very day.

I am grateful for my father's influence on my life. By precept and example he taught me to be honest in all my dealings; to be truthful in all my statements; to be faithful in all my obligations; and to be loyal to all my friends. Because of him these values have molded my character.

Three men—Dr. Cal Guy, Dr. L. Nelson Bell, and Pastor Ron Dunn—were brought into my life one at a time, when I most needed their knowledge, wisdom, and understanding in order to fulfill God's purpose for my life and ministry.

The power-packed 104 verses found in the book of Philippians have been a continual source of strength in my difficult times.

I also received inspiration from the book *Goforth of China*, which revealed how trials and hardships could be used to glorify our Lord in ways that we might never comprehend while here on earth.

And thanks to my long-time dear friend Jay Wegter who painted the picture for the cover of this book.

Charles B. Moore IV

No man can serve two masters....Ye cannot serve God and mammon.
—Matthew 6:24 KJV

CONTENTS

INTRODUCTION

"Why don't you write a book?"

That's the question I've often heard after answering the other question I have been asked over and over in the last half century, a question that rarely elicits a short answer: "Why did you give away all your multiple millions in wealth and take your wife and children to Central America where you had to sleep on the floor for two months?"

Sometimes other questions follow, such as, "What was it like to be thrown into jail in the red light district of San Jose, Costa Rica?" or, "Why did you turn down an opportunity to serve in the administrations of two U.S. Presidents?"

I was a very rich young man when I first met and campaigned with a future President of the United States of America. I was sixteen years older when I helped develop the strategy that got Ronald Reagan elected to that high office, which he held successfully for eight years. In the intervening years I had given away all my wealth, including several million-dollar corporations, in order to serve the Lord Jesus Christ in the poorest of the poor communities of Central and South America.

Before Jesus used me and my wife to begin a ministry that has resulted in the salvation of more than three million souls, I had hobnobbed with the rich and famous in the business and political world of the 1950's and 1960's.

Among those who counted me as their friend were State Governors and U.S. Senators as well as people like Eddie Rickenbacker, the highly decorated WWI flying ace and General Manager/Board Chairman of Eastern Air Lines; Bill Lear, builder of the Lear Jet and inventor of the

1

autopilot for airplanes; and Admiral John Dale Price, the father of naval aviation.

Although I did not turn my back on my friends, I did turn my back on my wealth. Some have asked me why I gave up millions of dollars—and control of eleven corporations—when Judy and I were called by God into missionary work in Latin America. The short answer is, "I fell in love with Jesus."

This is the story of one man and his wife who found out what Jesus can do in the lives of two people who are totally devoted to Him. You will read about the miracles we saw in lives changed from utter hopelessness and helplessness to meaningfulness and hope and joy. As you read this book please recognize that Judy's love for her Lord and for her husband made her willing to leave a life of luxury, and willingly take her small children to another country where they would begin their schooling. You will also see how multiple times she has willingly followed me into difficult circumstances as I have obeyed God's leadership in my life. Because of Judy's intercessory prayer life, she has often known what God was leading us to do before I knew.

You will see how God provides when no one else can. You will experience vicariously the persecution as well as the victory that comes to new Christians, and old, who put their faith on the line and depend on the promises of Jesus Christ. You will see for yourself how an ordinary Christian can be transformed from living for himself among lukewarm churchgoers to putting his life completely in the hands of the One who said, "I will never leave you nor forsake you." You will see what it means to be in the center of God's will and to make a real difference in the lives of countless souls who would have been eternally lost if you had remained in your comfort zone.

Over the years, I have meditated on all that Judy and I have experienced; and that second question I have often been asked has kept coming back to me. By 1972, I had begun considering the possibility that perhaps our story should be preserved in a book, and made available for others to read. But I did not feel qualified to write the book myself; I was a speaker, a preacher, a missionary—not a writer.

Sometime in that year, I found myself on an airplane, sitting beside Bill Glass, the former All-Pro football player for the Cleveland Browns. In our conversation, I mentioned that I was looking for someone to write our biography. He said, "Write it yourself. If someone else writes it, the book will glorify you instead of the Lord." Bill knew whereof he spoke; he had already written several books including his own biography. And in my own reading of more than 300 biographies, I have seen the truth of Bill's words.

Having become convinced that I needed to write the book myself, I passed up a couple of opportunities for having it written by some well-known Christian authors. And, for better or not, that decision has delayed the writing of it until now when, with help from a friend, I am writing this book in my 80th year.

When I was a child, I could not have known that God was already preparing me for the most important work I would ever do, the work of leading lost souls to Christ and teaching them to win others by the Name and Power of Jesus. It all began for me in a little southern town. My father was a "self-made man" who borrowed money to start his own business. But God's hand was on him even then. His great grandfather had been a minister of the Gospel; and God does not forget.

Chapter I
Life on the Rio Grande

> *When I was a child, I spake as a child, I understood as a child, I thought as a child: but when I became a man, I put away childish things.*
> —1 Corinthians 13:11 KJV

James Wilson Moore (1797-1873), originally from Pennsylvania, was the first Presbyterian preacher west of the Mississippi River, and the first pastor in Little Rock. Various memorial plaques—on view in Presbyterian churches throughout Arkansas—recognize James Wilson Moore as the patriarch of Presbyterianism in that state.

IN LOVING MEMORY OF
THE REVEREND JAMES WILSON MOORE
ORGANIZER OF THE FIRST
PRESBYTERIAN CHURCH
IN ARKANSAS AND
WEST OF THE MISSISSIPPI RIVER

PRESENTED BY
MARTHA AND CHARLES B. MOORE III

My great, great grandfather, James Wilson Moore, had a son named Charles Beatty Moore, who fathered two sons: Ralph Guild Moore and Henry Moore, each of whom named his son for their father.

Henry's son was born first and was therefore Charles Beatty Moore II. Ralph's son, my father, was named Charles Beatty Moore III; he was of course a grandson of Charles B. Moore (I) and a cousin to Charles B. Moore II. In March of 1939, I was born Charles Beatty Moore IV, in Texarkana, Arkansas.

When I was 18 months old my parents divorced. My 7-year-old sister Evelyn Anne stayed with our mother, who later married an Army officer. To him and my mother was born my half-sister Carolyn.

Meanwhile, my father took me to live with him on the American side of the Rio Grande. Spaniards had called that settlement Villa del Rio (Village by the River). When we got there it was the small city of Del Rio, Texas. Villa Acuña, a squalid little village of dirt-poor native residents, was across the river in the state of Coahuila, Mexico; it is now known as Ciudad Acuña.

Del Rio and Villa Acuña

We lived in a large house north of the Rio Grande, the care of which my father entrusted to a Mexican maid who could not speak  English. She was married and had several children who lived with her in Villa Acuña. Monday through Friday, she worked at our house. She had her own room at one end of the house; at the opposite end I slept with my father in his bedroom. My father was a very successful business man and politician; he spent a lot of time away from home, and I spent a lot of nights crying myself to sleep in his big bed by myself.

As the Director of Public Relations for the Sheriffs' Association of Texas, as well as a Texas State Representative, my father was often out of town for weeks at a time. So, until I was nine years old, I was taken under the wing of my father's maid from across the river. Since Maria spoke only Spanish, I learned that language like a native Mexican.

Every weekend, Maria would ride the bus across the river to her home in Villa Acuña. There she would stay with her family until Monday morning when she would return to our home in Del Rio. If my father was not home when she left on Friday, she would take me with her. There I would sleep on wooden slats in a mud-floor hut. I always enjoyed playing with Maria's children when I was there.

Because her family home had no running water, I would bathe and swim with her children in the dirty Rio Grande, which received sewage from both towns. I consider it a miracle from God that I survived my childhood. I also believe that even then He was preparing me for my life's work by exposing me from an early age to the experiences of extreme poverty, although I was a son of American wealth.

The memory of living on the weekends in Mexican squalor must have given me a burden to reach the lost among the poorest of the poor in the masses of Latin America. The mud floor and plank bed of my childhood was repeated many years later in the abject poverty of Costa Rica and El Salvador, where in each place my wife and I willingly slept on the floor for up to two months while beginning our missionary work in those countries.

In his gracious wisdom God required me to learn Spanish as a toddler. I had to, so I could be understood when I asked the maid for something to eat. Here in the twilight of my life I can see how God began preparing me for a unique ministry in Latin America. For that ministry, I had to be bilingual and to have the presence to speak to thousands in large meetings. Part of my preparation involved my father's political campaigns. Speaking Spanish at an early age without an accent made me a capable campaigner for my father when he ran for the Texas House of Representatives, and later when he ran for the Texas Senate. During each election cycle I would often sing one of the two songs that I knew in Spanish and make a speech in Spanish on behalf of my father's candidacy.

When I was five years old my father had to make an extra-long trip to the Panhandle of Texas. He didn't want to leave me behind for that lengthy period of time; so he hired a 12-year-old Mexican boy named Paco to travel with us and stay with me during the day. One night we went to a restaurant and Paco was told that he had to go around to the back of the building to eat. To this day I admire my father's convictions as he said, "If he can't eat with us then we will not eat here." Until my father's death, he continued to be the single most important influence in my life. I remember many of the moments in which I saw and heard my father model the honest, respectful and well respected lifestyle that seemed to be his by nature. He was known and loved by great and small, rich and famous, as well as some who had next to nothing.

El Paso and Roswell

When I was nine years old, my father and I moved 425 miles northwest to El Paso, where he remarried and I finished grade school. When I was ten, he became the manager of El Paso International airport. He kept that job for five years. When I was twelve, his second wife Martha gave birth to my half-brother Richard.

My father was not content to just have a job. He was a real entrepreneur. One of his corporations was Moore Service Bus Lines, Inc. with one over-the-road operation and two city operations.

Among the other corporations he founded and controlled were: Moore Service, Inc., which refueled military aircraft at many facilities throughout the United States; Moore Sanitation, Inc., which provided garbage disposal for cities and military bases; CF&T Transportation, Inc., operating in five states; Moore Construction, Inc.; Aviation Acceptance Corporation; U. S. Sonics, with a plant in Dallas and another in Warner Robins, Georgia; Great Western Leasing Corporation; and MWK, Inc., operating four restaurants in two states, including one at "Six Flags Over Texas" in Arlington, between Fort Worth and Dallas.

I began high school in El Paso. But after my freshman year my father sent me to a military school in Roswell, New Mexico, where for the next three school years I lived in the barracks. New Mexico Military Institute (NMMI) is the only state-supported military college located in the western United States. It was patterned on the West Point Military Academy in New York and has been called the West Point of the west. While I was there, I even had to memorize the "West Point definitions." Some of the disciplines I learned there have stayed with me all my life, such as making my own bed every morning, a chore that becomes more difficult with each passing year. NMMI included a three-year college preparatory high school and a two-year junior college.

7

During my summers in El Paso, my father put me to work at one of his garbage-collection companies. He was preparing me to take over all his corporations. But he did not want me to learn our businesses from the ground up; he wanted me to start below ground and learn from the basement up. At the age of 15 I made several lengthy trips alone driving different kinds of trucks from one of our operations to another. Those trips included going from El Paso to an ordinance depot west of Salt Lake City, and from El Paso to Kingsville, Texas.

At 16 I learned how to operate a D8 bulldozer, and worked digging and covering a sanitary landfill with dirt.

At 17 I literally picked up garbage for 3 months. I carried a large cardboard box (which had been used to ship washing machines or dryers) to the back of a house and dumped household garbage into it. Then with the heavy dripping box on my shoulder I carried it to one of our garbage trucks on the street. In the afternoon after work I had to change my filthy clothes in our washroom before I could go into our home. At 18 I drove a truck and trailer from northern New Jersey to El Paso and flew back to Philadelphia to pick up one of our oil trucks and drive it to Dallas. In ten days I traveled more than 3,000 miles behind the wheel of a truck.

Years earlier, my father had borrowed $20,000 and used it wisely to build successful businesses in several states, becoming a multi-millionaire in the process. Now he was teaching me the value of wisdom, honesty, and hard work. How grateful I am to my heavenly Father that I was raised by a man like my earthly father. If my father told me one time he told me innumerable times, "Always tell the truth, pay your bills, and be loyal to your friends and whether you are rich or poor you will be happy."

I am proud to say that I have never known a man of more honesty and integrity than my father. A few vignettes in no particular order must suffice to paint a partial picture of the man I admired and cherished throughout my youth.

My father had been in politics since the age of twenty-one when he was elected City Councilman for Texarkana, Arkansas. His political connections provided me with many opportunities for meeting and spending time with people of fame and influence. Governor Price Daniels named my father a Special Texas Ranger. I still have an authorized replica of his Rangers badge on my desk.

When I was seven years old my father and I went to see former Vice President John Nance Garner who had been FDR's vice president for two terms. He lived in my father's House district. My father and I sat with Vice President Garner on his back porch drinking iced tea, where I listened to these two men, whom I considered to be giants, telling stories and laughing.

Early in his political pursuits, my father held a State political office along with Jim Wright, who later became the speaker of the House of Representatives in Washington, D.C. Years later, on my father's coat tails, so to speak, when I was visiting Washington, I had the privilege of dining with Congressman Wright at the House Restaurant (which was open only for Congressmen and their guests).

On another occasion, again because of my father's contacts, I had the opportunity of having breakfast with both John F. Kennedy and Lyndon B. Johnson with fewer than 15 people present.

When as a teen I was going to take a trip to New York City, my father told me that if I had any difficulty cashing a check, I was to go to a branch of the Chase Manhattan Bank and have the teller call Roland Irvine's office and tell his Secretary that there was a young man trying to cash a Texas check who said his father was a garbage man. I did as my father had directed and immediately my check was cashed. Roland Irvine was a Vice President of Chase Manhattan Bank.

It was some years later, after having retired from the New York bank, that the same Roland Irvine came to Texas and with my father and two other men—Jack Love and Texas governor Allan Shivers—established the Texas State Bank in San Antonio, with himself as its first president.

On several occasions Bill Lear and his wife were in our Texas home. He was the developer of the Lear jet and the Lear autopilot. One night as he was flying into El Paso he had the airport call my father and tell him that his plane would land itself because Bill was sitting way in the back seat. My father and I rushed out to the airport not knowing what to expect.

A frequent guest was Captain Eddie Rickenbacker, a prince among men, and one I greatly admired. His influence on my life motivated in me the desire to serve my country. Captain Eddie, as we called him, had been awarded the Congressional Medal of Honor for his service in World War One. He had been called the "Ace of the flying aces" during that war.

One evening my father and I met Captain Eddie's airplane and as we were walking towards the terminal a man with his five- or six-year-old son asked me, "is that Captain Eddie Rickenbacker?" I replied that it was and he said, "Do you think he would mind me introducing my son to him?" Knowing how gracious Captain Eddie was I said, "Not at all." This man had been serving on a small island during WWII when the plane Captain Eddie—as a civilian passenger—was aboard, had to ditch in the Pacific Ocean. He told the decorated war pilot that when that occurred, he and his buddies had violated standing orders and had kept their searchlights on in hopes that Captain Eddie and the men on his life raft would see the lights and make it to safety. Captain Eddie hugged that man, which I am sure greatly impressed his son.

In preparation for his retirement, Captain Eddie called my father from his home in New York City in 1963 and asked him to help him buy a ranch in the hill country of Texas. Because my father was a man of his word he knew other men in Texas who also were men of their word. He called one of those men who happened to be a County Sheriff in the hill country. They communicated back and forth for two days until the sheriff told my dad that he had found the property that Captain Eddie needed and that it could be purchased at an excellent price. It was near the tiny town of Hunt, in Kerr County.

Based on the sheriff's word my father called Captain Eddie, who asked my father if it was a good price for the property. My father replied, "Yes" and Captain Eddie said, "Tell him I will put a check in the mail today." Without ever having seen it, he purchased that 10,000-acre ranch based on my father's word. Five years later, the Rickenbackers donated that ranch to the Boy Scouts.

I still treasure the letter Captain Eddie wrote to me upon hearing of my father's passing. I quote here the first paragraph of that letter, written on Eastern Air Lines stationery, of which corporation he was still Chairman of the Board.

"My dear Charlie: I was terribly shocked by your letter of December 18, covering the untimely passing of your dad on August 1, 1963 and, though belated, I hasten to offer my deepest sympathy to you and other members of your family in this great loss."

Other men of fame that, with my father, I met in my youth included R. G. LeTourneau (a devout Christian who is considered to have been the world's greatest inventor of earthmoving and materials-handling equipment, and was the founder of LeTourneau University in Longview, Texas).

Another was U.S. Army General Matthew Ridgeway (who in April 1951 replaced General Douglas MacArthur as the commander of the United Nations forces in Korea and the Allied occupation forces in Japan). I also met numerous other generals and several admirals.

One admiral stands out above all others: Admiral John Dale Price, who many consider to be the father of naval aviation. He gave my stepmother a string of genuine pearls that he brought back from Japan. Those pearls are now cherished by my daughter.

I am proud of my father, whose picture hangs on the wall of the House of Representatives in the Texas State Capital in Austin; mine is there too, as a mascot.

By example, my father taught me bearing, tact, and aplomb; my last three years of high school at NMMI taught me self-discipline. Each of these has been of significant value in my relationships with others, including my meetings with foreign dignitaries and American politicians.

I begin college

Having proved myself on the football field at NMMI high school, when I graduated I was presented with a full-ride two-year football scholarship to the NMMI junior college, where I could start playing football in the first semester. My father urged me to accept it because no other college would recognize my abilities; and I knew that without that football scholarship, not only would I have to pay for my college education, but the only way I could make the team would be to try out as a "walk-on" and prove myself all over again. Still, I turned down that scholarship in favor of four years at Texas Western College (TWC), which would later become the University of Texas at El Paso (UTEP).

Knowing my love for football, Dad said I could not even try out for the Texas Western football team as a walk-on until I had made my grades for one year. With that stipulation, he almost persuaded me to return to NMMI just so I could begin playing on the football team right away. As time would eventually tell, I made the right decision; I am thoroughly convinced of that.

At the end of summer in 1957, I began classes at TWC. During my freshman year I also worked in merchandising and display for my father's merchandise brokerage company. As a fraternity pledge, I foolishly focused on everything but the classroom. Both semesters of my freshman year I was voted best pledge of my fraternity; however, my poor grades put me on scholastic probation. Because of that I had to attend summer school before starting my sophomore year.

My summer school classes were scheduled for early morning. I spent the rest of each day driving a garbage truck for one of our companies. That did not leave time for much of anything else.

Things piled up on me that summer. Scholastic probation had removed my opportunity of playing football and prevented me from being an "active" fraternity member; and to top it off, I lost a girlfriend to a fraternity brother. All this drove me into periods of deep introspection.

Chapter II
Major Changes

> *For I was my father's son...he taught me also, and said unto me, Let thine heart retain my words: keep my commandments, and live. Let not mercy and truth forsake thee: bind them about thy neck; write them upon the table of thine heart: So shalt thou find favour and good understanding in the sight of God and man.* —Proverbs 4:3-4; 3:3-4 KJV

First: I met my Jesus

All that summer, I continued to think about my ex-girlfriend. She had Christian parents who treated me well and always had a way of lifting my spirits. On Friday, August 22, when I was feeling very down, I stopped by to see them. While they were talking with me, their daughter informed me that she had a date with her new boyfriend that night. Then, to my surprise, she said that she would break that date so she and I could go out for a soda.

I really thought I was making headway when she offered to do the same thing again the next night. But as we were drinking our sodas this time, it became clear that her only motivation was to lead me to her "Lord and Savior" Jesus Christ.

After taking her home on the second night, Saturday, I climbed the stairs to my room and in the darkness knelt beside my bed and asked God's forgiveness for my sins, and asked to receive His son Jesus Christ as my Savior and Lord. My life was changed forever.

The next morning I attended a church where I had been only once before. The pastor, Dr. William Herschel Ford, preached on the Ten Commandments and specifically the first two (Exodus 20:1-6). He explained that "Thou shalt have no other gods before me" meant that it is a sin to have anything in your life that is more important to you than God. I realized that football, fraternity, and girls were all definitely more important in my life than God.

On Sunday, August 30 of 1958, I went forward in that same church to make a public profession of my faith in Jesus Christ. That was when I fell in love with "my Lord and my God" (John 20:28). He

13

is and always will be my "First Love." Knowing Jesus does make a tremendous difference in a person's life; I can attest to the truth of that statement.

Second: I met my Judy

That same Sunday morning a beautiful young lady went down the same aisle to transfer her membership from her home church in Odessa, Texas. Judy Sandusky had just arrived to begin her freshman year at Texas Western College. Later that same day, Judy and I actually met for the first time at an ice cream social on the college campus.

Two weeks later, I joined two car loads of college students on a weekend-mission trip, traveling 200 miles south to Chihuahua, Mexico. The two days that we spent there brought me face-to-face with several indigenous Tarahumara natives. Their poverty and avoidance of eye contact caught my attention. As we were driving back to El Paso I made the statement to the group that I believed God wanted me to become a missionary to the Tarahumara natives in the Barranca de Cobre (Copper Canyon) of northern Mexico. That was in September, 1958, and although I never followed through on it, that desire to reach those Native Americans for Christ seems to have precipitated my strong affinity for all the indigenous people that I have known throughout Latin America.

Many Christians have a verse that impacted their lives in the first days of their knowing Jesus. My verse was James 1:22, which says, "Be ye doers of the word and not hearers only deceiving your own selves." This was the first verse that I memorized and after 60 years it still reminds me that God's word is my rule and guide. I remember that in the 1950s and 1960s many churches boasted that God's word was their rule and guide. Sadly, during the half century since then, I have seldom heard that phrase uttered in any venue or by any individual.

After Jesus, my greatest love is Judy. We had known each other for two months as casual friends when God did something special in my life. It was on Halloween night; we both were attending a party and I looked across the room and unexpectedly saw Judy in a new and very different way. My heart almost jumped out of my chest and I knew that for the first time in my life I was truly in love.

It took a little pursuing on my part; but eventually God led this beautiful young lady from Odessa, Texas, to realize that I was truly the right man for her. Judy then agreed to wear my high school ring, a sign we were going steady. But our first kiss didn't occur until more than a month later. I did not want to spoil anything by trying to kiss her too soon. Now, more than 60 years later, with pride and gratitude to my heavenly Father, I can honestly say that after kissing Judy my lips have never touched the lips of another woman. Recently God gave us the blessing of standing together in front of Judy's old college dorm where my car had been parked the night I first kissed the love of my life. Naturally, we kissed again on that same spot.

When Judy and I first talked about marriage, I told her that my father had requested that I not marry until I had finished my four years of college. My God had commanded me to honor my parents. So, out of respect for my father and in obedience to God's word, I would honor his request. Judy and I agreed to get married in June at the end of my fourth year. That was a great incentive for me to apply myself and do well academically for my last three college years. For a young man and woman in love, that was a long time to wait. But we remained true to each other; and our commitment during those last three years of college would end up strengthening our marriage in later years.

During the last 2½ years of college, Judy and I taught a Sunday afternoon Bible school in a very poor area of Juarez, just across the Rio Grande. We were part of a group of college students who crossed the bridge each Sunday afternoon to teach small children about Jesus. We would spread out in groups of 2 or 3 to different parts of that Mexican city. Each location of these Bible schools was in an area where there was no church and in most cases an area of poverty. This was another one of God's ways of preparing us for our future ministry in Latin America.

Remember that my freshman year was a "bust" that resulted in my being placed on academic probation. Accepting the Lord at the beginning of my second year in college would make all the difference in the world in my grades. I received only one D in my last 3 years and that was in accounting. What a difference knowing my Savior made in my life and my college grades. In my last two years of college, I was enrolled in the Reserve Officers Training Corp (ROTC) program.

An event in my junior year was used of God to make a drastic change in my life, one that would eventually lead to great blessings. After doing well academically for three semesters, I was finally allowed to play football as a walk on. But after only a short period of time I sustained an injury. Then, after spending a night in the hospital with my right ankle packed in ice, I was told that I would have to wear a cast for six weeks.

With spring practice approaching I knew that as a junior in college I had to make the team in order to play in my senior year. So one night in the dorm, having worn the cast for two weeks, I took a hammer and a screwdriver and chiseled it off of my ankle. Then for two weeks I played football with a black and blue sprained ankle that required taping before every practice. I remember how each afternoon while the trainer was taping my ankle, he would make clear his opinion of my intelligence. Halfway through spring training, despite the taping, I injured the same ankle again; that was the end of my football career. Several months later I had to have surgery on the ankle.

During the last year and a half of my college days, I owned and operated El Paso International Truck Stop. It was the largest in West Texas and was located on U.S. Highway 80, the main transcontinental thoroughfare from the southeast coast to San Diego, California, at that time.

Three months before graduation I was told that after completing the Provost Marshall Generals' Officers Course, I would be assigned to Arlington Hall Station in Arlington, Virginia, as one of four permanent officers of the day for the Army Security Agency Headquarters. I did not know what kind of a military facility that was. And I do not know whether my dad, with his connections, had anything to do with that assignment; but as it turned out, it was obviously of God.

Judy and I wasted no time once my father's request had been honored. On June 20, 1961 Charles Beatty Moore IV was married to Judith Frances Sandusky. I was one very happy young man. Incidentally, by that time my sister Anne, who was six years older than I, had married and was living with her husband in Fort Worth.

By the time I graduated, I had also completed the ROTC program, I was—in spite of my previous injury—still able to pass the Army physical exam and receive my commission as an officer. Dressed in my U.S. Army class "A" tan uniform I walked up on the TWC stage and received my degree from the president of the college; I took three more steps, saluted an Army Colonel, raised my right arm and swore allegiance to the United States of America; I was then presented with my officer's commission as an Army Second Lieutenant, whereupon I entered active duty in the U. S. Army.

Moments later I kissed my sweet bride as she pinned my gold bars on the epaulets of my uniform.

Third: I served my country

In our new Ford Galaxy, we drove to Fort Gordon in Augusta, Georgia. As Second Lieutenant, Military Police Corps, U.S. Army Reserve, I began my Provost Marshall Generals' Officers Course on August 26, 1961.

Happy young newlyweds

Upon arriving at Fort Gordon, I learned that I was the only one of the sixty-one officers in my basic officers' course whose orders had been cut months before I graduated from college and was commissioned. None of my fellow officers knew where they were to be assigned until one week before their graduation from the officers' course. For nearly three months I had known where I would be serving.

My Arlington Hall Station assignment proved to be a very choice one because each day three courier cars left our military post, headed for the White House. Judy and I arrived in Arlington on October 11, 1961.

Arlington Hall Station housed several Army and Air Force intelligence organizations. It was a top secret facility that did not even have an identifying sign outside. I was one of only five lieutenants on the entire post and was in command of a reinforced platoon of 41 men. There were five generals, more than 50 full colonels, innumerable lieutenant colonels and majors, and nearly 1,000 civilian intelligence analysts who worked in the three buildings on the post.

When I was on duty I was responsible for the security of this important top-secret facility, and in a sense, I was also the City Manager that handled the everyday problems that a small city would experience.

Financially, Judy and I had difficulty living in the Military District of Washington on a second lieutenant's pay. No matter how we budgeted our money, the end of the month meant we would eat peanut butter and jelly sandwiches and a bowl of cereal. A welcome one-time windfall came in the form of a check for $60 (equal to more than $600 in today's money), the final payment on the sale of the truck stop I had personally owned in El Paso.

For entertainment we would go to the Capitol building and sit in the gallery of the House or Senate and listen to them debate. Or we would go in the back gate of Fort Myer, wherein Judy and I would go to the Tomb of the Unknown in the Arlington Cemetery and watch the changing of the guard.

For many years my favorite national monument has been the Tomb of the Unknown, and one of my heartfelt desires had been to "march the Tomb." No officer has been permitted to march the tomb. Only enlisted personnel are given that honor. With great respect I have watched the changing of the guard more than twenty times.

My father had always placed great emphasis on honesty. One evening while we lived across the road from Arlington Hall station, he called long distance from Texas and in our conversation I told him a lie. After we hung up I was filled with remorse.

So I spent money from our limited resources to call him back and tell him I had lied to him. Instead of getting mad he said he was glad that I had called back. One of my cherished possessions is a letter that my father sent me after our conversations that night. He stated that he was glad that I placed importance on telling the truth.

About two months after I began my duty as Officer of the Day at Arlington Hall Station, I began having pain and swelling in the ankle that had been operated on. This was well over a year after the surgery. Subsequent to extensive examinations performed by Army doctors, I was told that I would be discharged from the Army; the term they were using for my discharge was, "pre-existing injury."

During my young and impressionable days at New Mexico Military Institute, I had learned about a fellow Texan named Audie Murphy. He had become my hero. He was the most decorated soldier of the Second World War and had been awarded the Congressional Medal of Honor, just like my other war hero Captain Eddie Rickenbacker. Because of their example and my love for my country I also wanted to be awarded the Congressional Medal of Honor.

I wanted to make the Army my career. So I began what became a six-month legal battle to stay in the Army. Many military personnel were doing everything they could to get out of the Army, but I was fighting to stay in.

My father contacted a Congressman and even hired a very good lawyer to represent me in that legal battle. The lawyer filed several appeals on my behalf. He also flew to Washington for my hearing before the Medical Review Board at Walter Reed Army Hospital.

The Congressman known to my father began writing letters to the Army Secretary requesting him to intervene. But appeal upon appeal was denied; then in August of 1962, I received the final refusal, a letter signed by the Secretary of the Army, Cyrus R. Vance. Had I been allowed to remain in the Army I would have been a Captain during the Tet offensive in Vietnam, a place from which some of my friends never came back alive. Having been on active duty during the Vietnam War, I was eligible to receive funding for school from the GI Bill, which I later used for seminary.

After my discharge, Judy and I returned to El Paso where I applied to become an FBI agent. This was in the wake of the Cuban "Bay of Pigs" fiasco of April, 1961, and just after the beginning of the

Cuban missile crisis, which climaxed in October and November, 1962. The agency was looking for men who were fluent in both English and Spanish; law degrees were no longer a priority.

Despite my medical discharge from the Army, I passed the FBI physical exam, which, ironically, was administered at the very same Army General Hospital at which I had been examined before I was commissioned as an Army officer. I was accepted by the FBI and was scheduled for the June, 1963, class at the Quantico Academy in Virginia. But God had other plans for my life.

Fourth: I lost my father

Four months before I was to begin training at the FBI Academy, my father and my wife were both hospitalized. On the same night and in the same hospital, Judy was giving birth to our first child and my father was being diagnosed with a wide aortic valve; he was told he had less than six months to live. He was gone in five months and nine days. During that time, he cherished his new little granddaughter, Judy Anne.

My father was in his last political campaign when he got the devastating news of his terminal heart condition. It was a month-long runoff election for Mayor of El Paso. But he was able to campaign for only one day. Despite that, he got only 800 fewer votes than his opponent. A total of more than 30,000 votes were cast.

The night of his defeat he said to me, "Charles, we will get you ready to run for office because by not winning I did not make any enemies and because I did not lose by a large margin I have nothing to be ashamed of." In the following year, I would honor his wish by running for office, myself. During the last few months of his life, at his request, I occupied my father's chair as head of our eleven corporations. I did everything I could to fill his enormous shoes.

For two of those agonizing months, he was in the Houston Methodist Hospital under the care of Dr. Michael E. DeBakey and Dr. Denton Cooley, two of the world's most famous heart specialists. Late afternoon each day, I was allowed to speak with my father by phone for only a few minutes. I learned to prioritize those minutes; there was always so much knowledge and advice I needed from him.

When the best doctors could do no more for him, my father was released from the hospital and returned home. Two weeks before his death, my father had come to know Jesus Christ as his Savior. On his last evening at home, he was visited by a good friend who was the president of El Paso Electric Company. During their conversation, my father shared unashamedly his testimony of how he had come to know Christ Jesus.

Charles B. Moore III

The following afternoon, my father suffered a heart attack; I rode in the ambulance with him to the hospital. By the time we arrived, his heart had stopped, he had stopped breathing, and there was nothing that could be done to resuscitate him. My only consoling thought was that he died in Christ.

That same evening, three Christian men went out of their way to tell me that my father had shared his testimony with them and they wanted me to rest assured that I would see him in glory. There is no greater gift than to know that you will see your loved one at the throne of grace.

Chapter III
Christian Business Man

Happy is the man that findeth wisdom, and the man that getteth understanding. For the merchandise of it is better than the merchandise of silver, and the gain thereof than fine gold. —Proverbs 3:13-14 KJV

When my father died on August 1, 1963, I was twenty-four years old. My half-brother Richard was twelve. Our father had left me in charge of his eleven corporations located in several states from Maine to Florida to California. I was suddenly responsible for more than 500 employees. I accepted the challenge and began running those businesses as my father had taught me. Also, because of my name, I easily slipped into leadership positions on the boards of several organizations he had served in.

That's how this 24-year-old kid became more acquainted with the world of business. For years our vice presidents in charge of some of the corporations had called me "Little Charlie." Now, with some difficulty, they began calling me Charles, or Mr. Moore. One of the vice presidents was a retired Air Force two-star general who had commanded more than 26,000 personnel; now he was subordinate to a 24-year-old former Second Lieutenant.

In the world of business, I soon proved to be my father's son, deeply involved in the day-to-day administration of each corporation. I became a micro-manager. And I didn't leave work at the office; I brought it home with me. I was constantly in touch with the corporate vice-presidents and regional managers by phone. The long-distance charges on my home phone averaged more than $400 a month. Several years before that, when I found out that my father's telephone bill at home was in excess of $800 I had flippantly said, "I would never do that." I guess you could say that at this time in my life, I was half way there.

With the success of my corporations, the money was pouring in. And I was finding ways to spend it. We owned a flashy Thunderbird automobile and a 15,676-acre ranch in west Texas; I had twenty top-of-the-line designer business suits in my closet; if I was going to the YMCA for a steam bath and massage I would always wear a suit. Image was important, or so I thought.

Many people believed that I had everything I could ever want. I was a successful young business man who could walk down the street and men old enough to be my grandfather would say to me, "Good morning, Mr. Moore. How are you, sir?" To some, I was the Marlboro man without the cigarette. In the advertisements, the Marlboro man had a white Thunderbird automobile, a white Stetson hat, and a very expensive suit. At that time in my life, I may have been unduly influenced by the allure of status. But I viewed cigarettes with disgust.

Many an afternoon before going home from work, I would visit the El Paso Club on the 18th floor of El Paso National Bank. My father had been the first president of that club, and I was the first president of its young membership (aged 21-35). At this club I would socialize with my peers. I believed that by being the only one that did not smoke—or drink any alcohol—I was witnessing for Christ. How wrong was my thinking!

Once a week, nine wealthy young men of our city would meet for lunch at the club. There we would sit at our special roundtable and pridefully discuss our recent successes. My position of wealth and influence gave me an ideal platform to testify of salvation through Christ. But not once did I ever witness to one of those men about the love of my Savior. One day one of them took his two young sons to the sand hills west of El Paso; there he killed them both, and then killed himself.

To this day I regret not allowing my Lord to use me to lead many of my wealthy friends to Christ. The rich and powerful need Jesus just as much as do the lower class of people who are left out of "polite society." But I used this platform just for my personal gain (Matthew 19:23-26).

Running for political office

Remembering what my father had said about getting me ready to run for political office, I began thinking about running for the Texas House of Representatives. I was still looking for some sense of satisfaction and fulfillment, some greater purpose in life, which I was not finding in business or church or in being a Christian.

Therefore, in February of 1964 I had to decide whether to run as a Democrat or as a Republican. Each party chairman in El Paso

County took me to lunch and tried to convince me to run on their ticket. I even traveled to Austin to seek the advice of a man who had known and respected my father.

Lieutenant Governor Preston Smith and I sat in his suite in the Texas capital building as I listened to him, a Democrat, advise me on how I should carry out my campaign in order to be elected to the House of Representatives as a Republican. Many years later, after he had served as the State Governor, I had an interesting experience in a hotel in Temple, Texas. Judy and I were walking through the lobby on our way to the medical clinic where she was being treated. Across the lobby I heard someone shout, "Hi little Charlie" and turned to see the former governor of Texas, Preston Smith.

The Republican Party in the State of Texas was in its infancy. But in 1964, a young man from Midland announced his intentions to run as a Republican for the U.S. Senate; and a younger man from El Paso announced that he would run as a Republican for the Texas House of Representatives. Both of these men recognized that they would have a very difficult campaign in a state where being a Democrat almost always was tantamount to being elected.

I for one felt that I could best represent the people of El Paso, and remain true to my character, as a Republican. At one venue in my race for the House of Representatives I spoke on the same stage with Presidential candidate Barry Goldwater; he was the keynote speaker.

I campaigned day and night for 8 months while continuing to run my businesses using a mobile phone beside my desk in the bus. At that time there were only 12 mobile phones in all of West Texas.

On three different days, from early morning until late at night, I shared my bus with George H. W. Bush, the young Republican from Midland who was running for the U.S. Senate. When he came to campaign in El Paso, he found that I was the only full-time Republican candidate in the area. And since I had my own campaign bus with a telephone in it—of which he made full use—campaigning together was only logical. George had been the Midland County Republican Chairman; I had been involved in campaigns helping my father get elected to office.

On one of the several occasions that we campaigned together, George was accompanied by his wife Barbara. When both candidates were invited to speak at a Young Republicans monthly meeting, we knew that there would be a limited number of people present. The venue was a very small basement room under the Pancake Cottage (one of my MWK restaurants). The podium was at the center of the head table, which could seat only four. The club president and George sat on one side of the podium; Barbara and I sat on the other.

When George had finished speaking and I was being introduced, Barbara leaned over and quickly told me a very funny story. Seconds later my introduction was completed and with my mind still distracted by that story, I stood up to speak. To say the least, the few minutes that I had been given were not used as effectively as they could have been.

After the meeting was over I went to Barbara and told her she had played a dirty trick on me. I told her that George, of course, had been given twenty minutes because he was running for a statewide office; however, I had only six minutes, of which the first two or three had been spent getting my composure after her story. She broke out into one of her tremendous laughs and we both laughed together.

1964 Campaign picture
Overlooking El Paso from Scenic Drive

Barbara Bush's humor helped George reach Texans who were somewhat skittish of his northeastern "Yankee" upbringing. Over the years I have had the privilege of seeing how Barbara's influence has made President Bush more like a native Texan. George and I did not happen to see each other again for 16 years, and that was only briefly at an airport when he was running against Ronald Reagan in the Republican Presidential Primaries.

The word "fatigue" best describes what it was like to campaign 10 to 12 hours a day while simultaneously managing my corporations. Exiting my campaign bus in a different neighborhood each day, I personally knocked on more than 15,000 doors visiting the homes of registered voters. One night I fell asleep leaning against our door while saying good night to the campaign staff.

I racked up 33,000 miles behind the wheel of my bus during that political exercise in futility. At that time I owned four bus lines and 67 buses. On the back of my campaign bus I had painted, "Driver of this bus is Charles B. Moore Candidate for Place 4." After the election I reluctantly had my campaign bus repainted, the seats put back in, and had it returned to a bus route.

My campaign bus

The night of the election our friends who had helped us in our campaign were sad and dejected by my defeat; but God in his omniscience had another plan for Charles and Judy Moore, and we were happy. To cheer up our friends, we took them for a late night dinner to the most exclusive steakhouse in the city.

During the campaign I had come to recognize that it would be difficult to win, and to be an effective Representative on Capitol Hill in Austin, without compromising my convictions. I will never forget the day that I lied to a wealthy oilman just to receive his support. Coming out of his office I felt very dirty.

With hindsight I can see how God used the votes of Hispanics to defeat me because He had a plan that one day I would be preaching the message of salvation to Hispanics throughout Latin America. As a Republican I handily won every Anglo precinct but overwhelmingly lost the Hispanic vote.

1964 was the year of Barry Goldwater vs. Lyndon Johnson, when every Republican candidate in Texas was defeated. I have often said, "Praise the Lord I ran as a Republican, because if I had run as a Democrat I most assuredly would have been elected."

Having lost that election, I resumed my search to find joy and fulfillment—a journey that would not be concluded until the following year in Glorieta, New Mexico. But in 1964, I had no idea what lay ahead. I was still myopic, if not blind, in regard to the Lord's plan for my life.

Back to business as usual

The day after my defeat Judy and I were back to looking for that elusive thing that could fill our needs and make us happy. Some might ask, "How was it possible that you and Judy were not happy and fulfilled? You had so much!" And it's true, we did. I'm sure in many ways we looked like a happy young Christian family.

Besides our family's corporations and my annual salary, equivalent to more than $300,000 in today's money, Judy and I personally had lucrative investments. It seemed like everything we touched turned to gold. We had paid $8.32 an acre for our ranch; by 1965, having made significant improvements, we could have easily sold it for $30 an acre.

We already owned one airplane (I had begun flying lessons at the age of ten). And now I was initiating the purchase of a Riley Rocket, a twin engine aircraft that would cruise at 300 miles an hour at 20,000 feet. I also came very close to buying a P51—a World War II fighter plane. Having done due diligence, I was in the process of starting a charter airline. Our first aircraft was to have been a DC-3 or a 4-engine Viscount.

I was in negotiations with Ford Motor Company to take over one of their dealerships on the border between Texas and New Mexico. I sold used garbage trucks to Mexico. The Mayor of Juarez, Mexico, was my partner in manufacturing wooden Coca-Cola boxes which we shipped to Los Angeles. I was even preparing to invest in a potentially very lucrative silver mining operation in Chihuahua, Mexico. All this was in addition to what I had inherited from my father.

In 1964, with Jimmy Peticolas, a childhood friend, I had started two wholesale and retail gun stores. In less than a year we grossed nearly $400,000 with an astounding profit margin. We were the largest distributor of weapons and ammunition between Dallas and Los Angeles. Many of our customers were from Mexico and Central America.

With my partner in the gun store

For some reason, I had the idea that if I could work at making Moore Sanitation the largest garbage-collecting corporation in the United States, I would finally find fulfillment. Eighteen months later—after having flown 250,000 miles on commercial airlines and in my own aircraft, getting new contracts for that corporation—I saw that dream come true.

Already, at twenty-five years of age, I was working on contracts in places such as Israel, Mexico, and the Philippines. But when I had finally reached my goal of having that corporation become the largest of its kind in the U.S.A. I felt that something was still missing in my life. I was no closer to finding that which I still had not been able to define. I was only older, wealthier, and had more possessions, more "things" to play with.

Moore Sanitation
State-of-the-art garbage trucks

What would be my next goal? Would it be to see that corporation become the largest in the world? At that point in time it probably already was. I began to see the futility of trying to find peace and fulfillment in the things of the world. But, where else was I to look?

I felt that I was living as good a Christian life as anyone in our church. I knew I was a faithful church member who was living a very moral upright life, while loving the Lord to the extent that I knew how. I had come to understand that the Christian life was a life of the do's and the don'ts. I didn't drink, I didn't smoke, and I didn't do other things that I knew I shouldn't do.

At the same time, I did do the things that I should. I tithed. I was happily married to a good Christian woman. Judy and I were very active in our church. We both taught Sunday school and we were in church every time the doors were open, which included Sunday morning, Sunday night, and Wednesday night.

Moore Family Moment

I was Chairman of the Baptist Goodwill Board of Advisers, as well as a member of the Salvation Army Board of Advisers (nearly everyone on each board was old enough to be my father). I was also Chairman of the Juarez missions committee of our church. To top it all off, at the age of twenty-five, I was elected Layman of the Year for Christians in 41 churches in El Paso County, the youngest person to have received this honor. I knew that it was bestowed on me because I was a very active, dedicated, moral-minded, hard-working church member.

But being named Layman of the Year was actually an embarrassment for me. I knew that it was not in recognition of my love for my Lord. There were many less wealthy and less well-known Christian laymen—who were truly in love with Jesus—who should have received that honor.

Chapter IV
Becoming Missionaries

> *But what things were gain to me, those I counted loss for Christ. Yea doubtless, and I count all things but loss for the excellency of the knowledge of Christ Jesus my Lord: for whom I have suffered the loss of all things, and do count them but dung [Greek: skubala = garbage], that I may win Christ....That I may know him, and the power of his resurrection, and the fellowship of his sufferings, being made conformable unto his death.*—Philippians 3:7-10 KJV

By this time in my life it was becoming evident that the "joy and fulfillment" that my life was lacking could not be found in just listening to what my pastor taught each Sunday, or even in my church activity. I felt there was more that I could and should be doing in my walk with the Lord.

A week after we learned that our company had become the largest of its type in the United States, Judy heard that there was going to be a missions conference in Glorieta, New Mexico, near Santa Fe. She asked me if I was interested in going to the conference, and without any thought I said, Yes.

Judy later said that she thought we would never make that trip because the following week I had a conference to attend in California, and she knew I wouldn't want to be away from the office two weeks in a row. She also found out that there were only two pay phones at the conference center and there would be more than 1,000 attendees.

When I heard this, I came close to canceling our reservations because I knew that I could not micro-manage our corporations without the use of a telephone. However, God didn't let me back out. So, with much concern for my businesses, I loaded my little family into our plane and flew to Santa Fe, New Mexico, and the Glorieta Baptist conference center. Our daughter Judy Anne was 2½ years old. My wife Judy was seven months pregnant with our first son, who was to be named James Wilson Moore in honor of my great, great grandfather.

I had asked my secretary, Rachel, to locate suitable lodging. She reserved a nicely furnished cabin with a beautiful view on the side of one of the hills at the conference center. I intended to make this our first vacation in several years. Renting this cabin turned out to be a mistake (or so it seemed) because of the physical strain it put on us, especially me. But, providentially, it made our time something more than a vacation.

Each morning I carried our daughter on my shoulders and held Judy's arm as we walked a "country mile" down to the conference center dining room for breakfast. After lunch I would repeat the trip; however, this time it was uphill. After a short nap I would load up and take my small family down for dinner and the evening conference. During that evening session most of my time was spent dreading the ordeal of climbing the hill back up to our cabin.

Two days into the conference I finally knew we had to move down to one of the dormitory type lodges. It took the remaining five days for me to recover physically. My heavenly Father knew that in my weakness I would be more attentive to His message. God had given me the desire to attend, and He worked things out so that we actually found ourselves at the Conference Center. Now, He was making sure that I would pay attention.

Upon arrival, Judy and I learned that the morning Bible study was to be given by Dr. Charles Culpepper. He was Missionary Emeritus to China. Listening to him speak, I was reminded of a letter I had received from China sixteen years earlier. At the age of nine I recited the Presbyterian Catechism and received a New Testament. My name was then entered in the Presbyterian Journal. Somehow a missionary in China named Elizabeth Lancaster came across my name and wrote me a letter in which she said, "So many of the boys and girls in China do not know about Jesus. I hope you will pray for them and pray for the missionaries who are trying to win the people to Jesus. We need your prayers." It may be that God used Elizabeth Lancaster to plant the seed that eventually grew into my desire to become a missionary myself.

Telling about that letter now reminds me of my great aunt. She told me on several occasions that she was praying that I would receive Christ as my personal Lord and Savior. After she saw that prayer answered, she told me she was praying that I would become a missionary. As I look back over my life, I can see that everything that is successfully done for Christ is first undergirded by the prayers of His saints.

That was a truth that Dr. Culpepper was bringing home to us there in Glorieta. He said that while preaching Christ in China, he had experienced the great Shantung Revival. We heard Dr. Culpepper talk about a deeper relationship with Jesus Christ than Judy and I had ever experienced or even heard of. He described how this great moving of God's Spirit began in the early 1930's when twenty Baptist missionaries gathered for their annual mission business conference in the Shantung province of China. They discussed the fact that their mission was being pressured by the Chinese Communists on the one hand, and by the Japanese army on the other. The missionaries knew that their days in China were numbered, and they were sadly aware of the fact that they were not winning China to Christ.

Dr. Culpepper told how these missionaries began to pray together and to seek the Lord. They recognized that they had only a minimal love for Jesus Christ. They began to confess sins to each other and to the Lord. They began to realize that God required that their lives be holy and acceptable unto Him if they were to reach the masses of lost Chinese for Christ.

In the previous 13 years, their mission had seen only 800 baptisms in a country with hundreds of millions of people. As a direct result of their brokenness, and their willingness to devote themselves to prayer and to confess their sins to each other and to the Lord, they saw a true revival break out in their midst and in many other parts of China. The next year in Shantung Province, without any additional missionaries, money, or new programs, this small group of missionaries saw more than 17,000 people baptized, having received Christ Jesus as Lord and Savior (John 1:12).

As Judy and I heard the messages that Dr. Culpepper gave each morning, we both recognized that we had never known or understood the depth of the Christian life that those missionaries experienced. We began to desire to live a life that was pleasing to the Lord, a life filled with joy, peace, and power that glorifies Jesus Christ.

In considering the things I was learning in Glorieta, I came to understand that even though it had been seven years since I claimed Jesus Christ as my Lord and Savior, I had still been living my life only for myself and my family and not for my Lord. I was sure of my salvation; I believed that, should I die at any moment, I would be in the presence of the Lord. But at the conference center, Judy and I both came to understand what had been missing. We learned about a life of obedience and surrender, a life of dying unto self and living unto

Christ. This life is sometimes called, "the abundant life" or, "the Spirit-filled life" or, "the real Christian life."

At the conference center we made friends with a missionary couple from Colombia, South America, and ate most of our meals with them. They clearly understood that although we were at the mission conference, we were not considering a call to missions. On one of our last days there, we picked up a denominational magazine; on one page, in bold letters, were the words "How Much Do You Love Jesus?" We became enthralled with that article. It was a message on how we are to love our Lord. Both Judy and I read the article twice and we still value that small magazine and the message it contains. It really impacted our lives.

On the last night of the conference it was the custom to give an altar call and invite all that were making a decision to come forward. The choir loft was filled with missionaries from around the world and as someone would come down the aisle one of the missionaries would come down from the choir loft and take that person to a small room in the rear of the auditorium.

That night I knew I had found that which I had searched for in all those different ways. I looked over at Judy and asked her if she wanted to go forward and she almost pushed me out of the pew; hand-in-hand we started down the aisle to the front of the auditorium.

About halfway down I motioned to the man who was our missionary friend from Colombia, inviting him to come down from the choir loft and take us to a prayer room. He already knew that we had not sensed a call of God to go as missionaries. He was the first to start praying. His prayer was filled with emotion.

Then Judy began praying and weeping as she poured out her heart of gratefulness to her loving heavenly Father.

As I began praying, I had a once-in-a-lifetime experience. I was filled with joy because at that moment I was truly talking with my heavenly Father; but along with the joy, I also was suffering great agony. The intense emotion I was feeling made it difficult to speak out loud. For seven years I had known my loving Savior, and for seven years I had placed everything in my life ahead of what He desired of me. In those few minutes I recognized that I had been in love with my fame and fortune, my ranch, my airplanes, my goals, my daughter, my wife, and my Lord in that order.

It was very painful to recognize how little love I had for my Savior; but in that moment I came to realize that I now loved Him in a new and real way, and it filled my heart with joy. Few can understand that my joy came from my new relationship with Christ, and that I had found what I had been looking for in so many different places. I cannot describe the joy that Judy and I found that night at Glorieta. It was overwhelming.

For my seven years as a Christian I had never understood that God wanted me to love his Son more than anything else, even more than my own life. I now realized that I had wasted those years looking for that unknown in football, in the Army, the FBI, my father's businesses, politics, in seeing my company become the largest of its type in the United States, and in my possessions.

I know that there are many today who are searching for that unexplained and unreachable, like I did for those seven wasted years in which I had not yet experienced the reality of Christ's promise: "I have come that you might have life and you might have it in abundance." But during the past half century, both Judy and I have seen the truth of this promise time after time in our lives. The Apostle Paul said it in another way, 'We are more than conquerors through Christ Jesus our Lord.'

The day following that momentous evening, my wife and daughter sat strapped in, in the back of the airplane, as I flew us back to El Paso. That hour was a time of real agony for me. I had heard stories of those who had had mountaintop experiences at conferences or church retreats and I was greatly concerned that I would lose my new relationship with my Lord. I did not want what had happened at Glorieta to be just a mountaintop experience that I would forget in a week or two.

Landing in El Paso produced a horrible feeling. This fear was almost palpable, because I thought that I could not live victoriously in the work-a-day world. Our men helped us load our car with our luggage and they put the plane in the hangar.

As I drove home I called my secretary on our mobile phone and said, "Rachel, don't tell anyone that we are at home and please don't call me. I will see you in the morning." I intended to hold on to this new relationship I had with my Lord for as long as possible. Normally I would have done everything I could to get right to the office and take care of things that had been ignored during my week of isolation from work. My new attitude evidenced what God had done in my life.

That night after Judy Anne had been put to bed Judy and I sat in our living room, each holding our Bible on our lap as we listened to each of the two Christian records we owned. We were greatly blessed as we sat in silence knowing the joy of the presence of our Lord. The next morning as I drove towards my office, I felt I was about to lose the relationship I had with my Savior, as I reentered the business world. I can still remember the exact place on the highway where my concern was the greatest.

Upon entering my office I found an extremely large stack of mail on my desk. On the very top was a phonograph record. It was wrapped and had a letter taped to it. The letter was from Jimmy Thurmond, a dear Christian friend in San Antonio, from whom I had purchased many trucks for one of my businesses. He had written, "Charles, here is a record by a very close friend of ours. I hope it will help you grow in grace."

I looked at the record titled "Crusade Favorites" by Fritz Smith, and saw that there were songs like "More so Much More" and "Fill My Cup Lord." We had not heard those songs before but their titles spoke to my heart. These are songs about an intimate loving relationship with Christ Jesus. It was as if my Lord was saying, "Charles, I did not leave you on the mountaintop in Glorieta. I will always be there for you if you allow me to be your Lord."

That evening Judy and I again sat in our living room and did what we had done the previous night. We now had a third Christian record to listen to, and were blessed by it even more than the ones we had listened to the night before. Sitting in our chairs, listening to this new record, and reading God's word resulted in something very special for me.

That night a few verses of Scripture that I read in the sixth chapter of Matthew changed our Christian lives forever. Let me share them with you now:

> *"Lay not up for yourselves treasures upon earth, where moth and rust doth corrupt, and where thieves break through and steal: But lay up for yourselves treasures in heaven, where neither moth nor rust doth corrupt, and where thieves do not break through nor steal: For where your treasure is, there will your heart be also. No man can serve two masters: for either he will hate the one, and love the other; or else he will hold to the one, and despise the other. Ye cannot serve God and mammon.*
> —Matthew 6:19-21, 24 KJV

The lives that God had changed in Glorieta, New Mexico, would remain changed for we had come to understand God's greatest commandment. Jesus said, "Thou shalt love the Lord thy God with all thy heart, and with all thy soul, and with all thy mind." (Matthew 22:37 KJV)

I now recognized that for my seven years as a Christian my love had been for everything except for my Savior. Right then I made the decision that I would seek to love the Lord with all of my heart, mind, body and soul and that I would pay any price to do this.

Divestitures

That second evening at home I called one of my business partners and arranged for us to meet for breakfast the next morning. After sharing my testimony of what God had done in our lives at Glorieta, I told him I wanted him to buy me out of our guns and ammunition business. He was shocked. We had been close friends since the age of 10 and we always were more concerned for each other than we were for our own selves. He said that it would not be right because we had begun making a very good profit. I had signed a $20,000 note to put my childhood friend into this business. And I had not drawn any money from this corporation. That morning I told him that at any point for any amount he could take my half of the company.

During the next two months, I began selling my family's corporations. I discontinued negotiations I had begun for purchasing the firm of one of my competitors. I backed out of the Mexican silver mine deal—which I later learned would have been a financial disaster. I walked away from a lucrative contract I had signed to purchase property in the area of the Chamizal, freeing the seller to accept a much better offer from another buyer. I did not proceed with plans for the charter airline. Although I was not certain what our future would hold, I knew that Judy and I did not want anything to hinder our love and obedience to our Lord and His word.

In mid-November, 1965, just days before Judy gave birth to our second child, God burdened us both with the overwhelming desire to leave all of the businesses and many of our belongings and go to seminary in January. We had no idea why God was leading us to do all the things necessary to enroll in seminary in a little over two months. We knew that God had not called me to be a pastor; but at that time we understood that was the only way one could become a missionary. Our question was, "God, why are you leading us to seminary? Could it be you are preparing me to be a better Christian businessman and not just a businessman who is a Christian? God, if that is your purpose, then why did you lead us to divest ourselves of our earthly wealth?"

We literally gave away the 15,676-acre ranch to a Christian friend. At that time its market value was about $470,000, or the equivalent of more than $3,000,000 in today's money. And that was just the ranch. We had given away all of our personal wealth. I continued to receive a small monthly allowance from my GI bill, which we'd live on in seminary.

Still, there remained a few of the family businesses that had not yet been sold or otherwise disposed of. I needed to find someone to run those businesses; and I needed to train that person in the next two months, which included the Christmas holidays. Judy and I had to be in Fort Worth to begin classes in the last week of January.

One Sunday I shared with a Christian friend what God was leading us to do and asked him to pray that I would find the right man to run the businesses. He said, "Find a Christian."

To me that seemed like an impossibility. But the next morning as I was shaving, God gave me the name of a man who was a Christian and had worked for our firm for many years. Recently I had sold the last of our four bus lines and he went with the sale as their general manager.

Before I left home that day, I called and asked him to meet me at the El Paso Club at noon. I began our meeting by sharing what God had done in our lives at Glorieta. Then I told him that God had placed his name on my heart to become the head of our family's businesses. His reply was that he needed to talk with his wife and pray with her about this decision. We agreed to again meet at the club three days later.

That Thursday at lunch he told me that he and his wife had prayed about it and knew that it was God's will for him to accept the offer. He told me he needed to give his employer 3 to 4 weeks' notice. Two hours later he called and said his employer said he could resign effective in one week; they had a manager of one of their other bus lines that would assume his position.

One week later we were in my plane flying to visit each operation so he could meet the managers, the mayors, and the overseers of our government contracts. For all of this to happen so effectively in such a short period of time was to me evidence of God's will being done.

39

While I was out of town Judy was at home packing, with a little help from our nearly 3-year-old daughter Judy Anne, who also helped keep our month-old son entertained. Writing this, I recognize just how much "my Judy" went through in doing everything necessary for us to move and change our lifestyle. While I was out flying all over the country introducing the man who would head up our companies, Judy was diligently dealing with everything on the home front.

As you read this book you will see "my Judy" always willing to follow her husband despite the hardships she foresaw. Few men have been blessed with a wife who loves Jesus wholeheartedly and then loves her husband and is willing to pay whatever price that needs to be paid to be obedient to God's will. Her interceding before the Throne of Glory has under-girded every step of our ministry.

How many women would agree to load up a Volkswagen van with 13 dozen disposable diapers, 13 dozen sterilized nipples, and 13 dozen disposable bottles of baby formula along with an eight-year-old daughter, six-year-old son, two-and-a-half-year-old son, and nine-month-old son to travel 2,600 miles through 6 countries to reach the country where she and her husband had been called to serve their Lord? One day we had to travel 537 miles through an area of Mexico where there were no motels or hotels and no hospitals. Leaving at 3 o'clock in the morning we arrived at the Guatemalan border just before dark.

We drank cold drinks and ate cookies and crackers along the way because there was no place where we felt safe to stop and eat. But I'm getting ahead of myself. You will see many more of the blessings God has given to me in "my Judy" as you continue in this book.

Over the past fifty years we have been asked many times what we did with all the wealth we had before our trip to Glorieta. The answer is always the same: "We gave it away." We've been asked why we didn't use it for ministry. We answer: "God led us to separate from that which had been the center of our affection." When asked if I miss any of the things that we gave away, I say I only miss being in the solitude of the ranch where silence was golden.

One question that always hurts is, "Wouldn't it have been smart to put money aside for your children's education?" I answer that I was being obedient to what God called me to do and I fully believe that God has blessed my children more than if I had given each one a million dollars. Many find it hard to believe what we did, and how this action resulted in so many great blessings from God. We are well aware that God calls only a few to give everything away to follow Him, but we do believe that God wants every Christian to be <u>willing</u> to give it all away and to love him more than their families and all material things (Matthew 19:21).

The seminary would be providing minimal living quarters for us. So, as we prepared to move to Fort Worth, Judy and I had to determine what we could take that would fit in our small duplex apartment, the whole of which was no bigger than our living room in El Paso.

We did not want to be a stumbling block for seminary students; so we moved our furniture in the back of a stake-bed truck covered with a tarp. We did this instead of hiring a moving company, even though all of our furniture was some of the best early-American available. That stake-bed truck was used at our Fort Bliss garbage operation, so we can honestly say we moved to seminary in a garbage truck.

At Seminary in Fort Worth

Judy and I felt like we were not really sacrificing anything to obey God. Rather, we rejoiced in knowing we were in the center of His will; and we continued to see evidences of that. In January, 1966, when our little family—our first son, James, was 3 months old—moved 600 miles east to Fort Worth, we saw God completely change our lifestyle. On our first day in the seminary living quarters, our precious Judy Anne said, "Mommy I love our new little house." We had come to rest in the Lord and had learned to be sensitive to how God would lead and how He would bless. And we learned to love the five seminary couples who lived within a stone's throw of our apartment.

Late one afternoon, three weeks after we had begun seminary classes, I received a phone call with some very sad news. The seven-year-old son of a former employee had been run over by a school bus. I quickly made reservations to fly late that night to El Paso to preach little Steve's funeral. As I was leaving our apartment Judy voiced a simple exhortation, "Don't forget about the passenger who will be flying beside you tonight." For more than seven years I had known my Lord but never had I directly witnessed to someone about accepting Christ.

41

Sitting in the darkened airplane cabin, I thought of how my love for Christ had grown, and then God led me to brazenly say to the man sitting beside me, "If this plane crashes, do you know where you will go?" He replied by pointing his finger downward.

Because I was on uncharted ground all I could think of was asking another question. So I asked. "Would you like to go to heaven?" And he said, "Yes." Then I said, "Do you know you are a sinner and ought to go to hell?" And he said "Yes." By that time, I thought, "God, when is he going to say No? This is supposed to be difficult."

A few moments later he repeated after me a prayer in which he asked God's forgiveness for his sins, and asked Christ to come into his life. When we both said, "Amen" he raised up, smiled and said, "Thank you Charles. Thank you Charles."

No one had taught me how to witness to someone about Christ. And no one had taught the 18-year-old girl from college, the ex-girlfriend who led me to Christ. She could not quote a verse from the Bible, but her love for her Savior compelled her to want me to love Him as well.

That night in the sky was the first of many, many times when I have personally invited someone to receive Jesus Christ as Lord and Savior. It is a very rewarding experience.

Upon returning to Fort Worth, one thing that shocked and saddened me was what I heard in conversations of students sitting around a table in the seminary coffee shop. Many talked about their churches and their responsibilities like my fellow businessmen and I had talked about our businesses at the El Paso Club. Friends had told me to be prepared to be disappointed by what I would find at the seminary. But I guess I was really not prepared. In great sadness I found that many "preacher boys" considered their ministry to be a road to fame and wealth.

Three fellow students and I covenanted to pray that God would send a great revival to our seminary. For 31 days the four of us students met every night at 10 o'clock in a vacant apartment, and on our knees we would pray until 1 o'clock or later. Our prayer was simple, "God please send revival to our seminary."

More than two years later, in Costa Rica in 1968, I received a letter from Professor of missions Dr. L. Jack Gray. He joyfully shared that God had honored our prayer time. He said that several students from Asbury Seminary had come to our seminary to share what God had done in the revival that was ongoing in their seminary. Their testimonies were used of God to bring revival in the lives of many students. When one of those students returned to his church, the difference in his life was so great that God used it to bring his wife to Christ. She not only was married to a pastor but her father had been a pastor as well.

Back in 1966 in Fort Worth, God in His love introduced us to Dr. Cal Guy, a man who believed that, by definition, the Christian life is a life of surrender to the Lord Jesus Christ, and obedience to the known will of God. Dr. Guy was the head of the missions department at the seminary; he was also the pastor of a small country church about 20 miles south of Fort Worth. Our great God led us to become members of Dr. Cal Guy's church. At this small church, Judy and I grew in our understanding of God's will for our lives. Because of our love and respect for Dr. Cal Guy, we named our second son in his honor (Richard Calvin Moore was born in Costa Rica in January, 1969).

Through Dr. Guy we met many students and visiting missionaries who were "sold out to God." Their love for the Lord was so evident that we could see God's presence in their lives. One was Miss Bertha Smith. Dr. Guy arranged for us to host a dinner for her in our apartment. She had been one of the missionaries in the Shantung revival in China. Some of the things she said while we were eating were a little hard for me to appreciate. As I was driving her back to the women's dorm she said, "Charles, when you come to the death to self, you will better understand what I have said." Driving the two blocks back to our apartment I was filled with disgust at her insinuation. Hadn't we given up everything to follow God's leadership? So how could she say what she said? At that moment I recognized that self was still very much alive in me.

A few years later in San Jose, Costa Rica, Bertha Smith had dinner with us again. And again she spoke of being dead to self. I will never forget the illustration she used. She said, "When your "self" is no longer alive it is like you're in a coffin and someone passes by to view your remains. They make the statement, 'boy he sure became ugly-looking in his old age.' This will not be taken by you as an insult, for you will be dead. When you are dead to your pride and ego and alive in Christ, let the world say what it may and you will not be offended." This was the life that the Apostle Paul lived and the life that we wanted to live.

In my lifetime I have read more than 300 biographies; one stands out above all others. Rosalind Goforth wrote her husband's biography several years after his death. Its title is *Goforth of China*. Next to my Bibles marked with my notes, I cherish this biography. It greatly influenced our days as missionaries and my love for Jesus. I have never read a book describing the life of a man so dedicated to the Lord as was Jonathan Goforth. Mrs. Goforth tells of a man who loved Christ more than he loved his own life, his wife, his children, and all the material values of life.

Goforth of China became as inspirational a guide to my Christian life as any book that I had ever read. Jonathan Goforth placed little value upon money, as was illustrated by his taking the money which could have been used for an engagement ring for his fiancée and using the money instead for gospel tracts. He told her that if she married him, she would have to consent to God being first and her being second in his life. This was only a small illustration of his devotedness to Christ and his being obedient to the calling of Christ on his life (Luke 14:25-35; 18:28-30).

At the age of 76 and blind, in the last 6 months of his life, Jonathan Goforth spoke nearly 100 times to the Presbyterian churches of Canada and the United States, pleading with them to turn from modernism back to the gospel. In 1983, as the Chaplain of Christian Heritage College (now called San Diego Christian University), I had the privilege of meeting the youngest of the 11 Goforth children. Five had been buried in China. Mary Goforth Moynan was gracious enough to have lunch with my family. Judy and I took all four of our children out of school just so they could meet a daughter of a man whose life and testimony had so greatly influenced their father.

For me to be in the right relationship with my Lord is not a statement that can be made today and be expected to be true tomorrow. For me to be in God's will is a day by day, hour by hour and minute by minute effort upon myself to love Christ and to bring every thought into subjection to Him (2 Corinthians 10:5).

While at seminary in Fort Worth, Texas, in 1966, I began searching for what God wanted me to do after graduation. I was sure that He had not called me to pastor a church. In fact, going to seminary did not mean that Judy and I would go into full-time ministry. We knew only that we both wanted to be in the center of God's will for the rest of our lives.

The more we read the Bible, the more we saw that God's greatest desire was that each Christian should love God with all their heart, all their soul, and all their mind (Matthew 22:37). When I began pondering this truth while thinking about how much I loved our two small children, I decided to graphically demonstrate what this meant.

I vividly remember placing our three-year-old daughter on one knee and our four-month-old son on my other knee and with all honesty saying through tears, "God, I love you more than these two precious children that you have given me. If you were to take them from me right now, I would still love and serve you."

This emotional experience showed me that at that moment I did love the Lord with all of my heart, soul, and mind. This gave me a foundation that would help me to be obedient when the Lord would lead me in ways that could put my family in possible danger or have them live with much less than other families.

During our first year at seminary we looked into the possibility of going to Limuru, Kenya, or Fortaleza, Brazil, where I would be able to serve as a missionary pilot. We had by then begun to realize that God wanted us to be involved in some way in missionary work.

Eventually, the missions board decided that, to utilize my God-given ability to speak Spanish, and my extensive business experience, we would be commissioned to go to Lima, Peru, where I would serve as the business manager for 26 Baptist missionaries. As a prerequisite, we would go to Costa Rica to attend language school for one year.

Before beginning our second year of seminary, we heard from my childhood friend, Jimmy Peticolas, to whom I had given the opportunity of buying my half of our business partnership. He expressed how difficult it had been to make important decisions during the past year without consulting me. For that reason he wanted to go ahead and buy me out.

He and I agreed that for my half he would pay me $250 a month for three years. We both knew that I could have been receiving more than $1,000 a month without having sold my share of the corporation. That $250 each month supplied a major part of our young family's subsistence once we arrived in Costa Rica. Before passing away several years ago, my friend told me that after he made the last payment of $250, his business rapidly began to fall apart. He said, "I should've kept on sending you $250 a month."

Almost two years to the day after Judy and I had gone forward at Glorieta to commit our lives to the will of God, we were commissioned as missionaries by the Foreign Missions Board of the Southern Baptist Convention.

At the time of our commissioning

Before that commissioning service took place, we had packed everything we still owned into two wooden crates to be stored in Fort Worth until we arrived in Lima, Peru.

Judy and I were informed by the missions board that before going to Costa Rica, we would need to attend mission orientation classes in North Carolina. Our assigned schedule called for us to depart from North Carolina in December and arrive in San Jose, Costa Rica, just before Christmas in 1967. Language school would begin there in January, 1968.

Missionary Orientation

A week after our missionary commissioning service Judy and I, with our two small children, drove to Ridgecrest Christian Conference Center, near Black Mountain, North Carolina, to begin a four-month missionary orientation.

There were ninety-three missionaries and ninety-five children living close together on two floors in hotel-type rooms. We ate all of our meals together. We had from 8 to 10 hours of class each day Monday through Friday; sometimes there were classes on Saturday. We learned the basics of phonetics and speed reading, how to help in a breach-birth delivery, how to adapt to a different culture, how to teach our children using correspondence courses, as well as many other practical things.

For five years, both in El Paso and in Fort Worth, I had been active in Gideon Camps. So it was natural for me to associate with the Gideon Camp in Asheville, North Carolina. Gideons are known for loving the Lord and loving His word, and distributing Bibles far and wide. But to be a Gideon you cannot be an ordained minister.

Many of the men at orientation were ordained and were preparing to go to a foreign country as church planters. Those men might expect to be invited by local churches to preach in one of their Sunday services. Naturally, during the four months of orientation I was never invited to preach. As a layman, up until that time I had preached fewer than a dozen sermons.

The closer we came to the end of missionary orientation the more I recognized that I personally was not prepared spiritually to become the eight-hour-a-day business manager for the twenty-six missionaries in the country of Peru. I recognized that I had learned very little of God's word at seminary. And most importantly, I recognized that I needed to begin praying for my family. We would be facing the ordeal of living out of three foot lockers (trunks) for one year in Costa Rica, and then adapting to the culture and customs of another country (Peru) where we would live for three years.

I was absolutely certain that God was leading me to do something that was outside of the norm. He laid on my soul the

47

assurance that His will was for us to stay behind to spend time in prayer and the study of His word. But the very mention of delaying our arrival in Costa Rica for three months sent shock waves through the leadership of the Foreign Missions Board. They insisted that we start language school in the first trimester, not the second.

Many believed that we were questioning our call to missions. No matter what I said, they could not be convinced otherwise. The foreign missions board said that if we stayed behind and didn't go on like everyone else we would be taken off salary. They didn't know us well enough to understand that such a threat would not dissuade us; we knew how to live resourcefully with limited money. Even our beloved former pastor and dear friend, Dr. Cal Guy, was against us delaying our departure.

For a short period of time Judy also felt that we should go on to Costa Rica with the others. Because our conference center was within three miles of the home of Billy and Ruth Graham, everyone had read or was reading Billy Graham's authorized biography by John Charles Pollock. I had already finished reading it and now Judy was reading it.

When she had put it down for a moment, I picked it up and opened it to where her bookmark was. It was on the last page of a chapter; my eyes fell on the passage where Ruth had continued insisting that she and Billy should go to Tibet as missionaries (Ruth had lived in China for many years with her missionary parents). Billy is quoted as having said to Ruth, "Was it God's will that we marry?" Ruth answered, "Yes." Then Billy said, "I am the spiritual head of our house and we are going to stay here in the United States for me to preach." You know the rest of their story.

Judy had been observing me read the last page that she had read, and when I raised my eyes to look at her, she said, "We are going to stay here." In the rest of our story, you will see some of the many blessings that resulted from that decision. The two of us in one accord and one spirit stayed behind; we did not go to Costa Rica for language school until the second trimester of 1968.

Meanwhile, we decided to fly back to Texas for one last Christmas with family members before our intended four years out of the country. We could have easily located a temporary place to rent in Texas, but we chose to return to Western North Carolina, where we knew a few people from the local Gideons Camp.

We wanted to spend the next three months in North Carolina because we believed that we should protect our testimony. We felt that by staying there, where we knew only a handful of people, the true purpose of our delayed departure for Costa Rica would be understood. God's grace is always evident when your desire is to obey the "still, small voice" of the Holy Spirit.

Before taking off for Texas, we thought it best to locate a place where we could live once we got back. But finding a suitable rental in Western North Carolina in the winter time is well-nigh impossible. Even so, by the grace and providence of God we were able to meet the wife of a retired Presbyterian pastor who owned a cottage in Black Mountain a few miles east of Asheville. He was away serving as an interim preacher down in Savannah, Georgia. His wife happened to be visiting their summer cottage located high up on the side of a mountain with a view overlooking the Billy Graham home across the valley.

This gracious Christian woman told us that they had never rented their cottage to anyone with children, and would really rather not. However, after seeing our two little ones she agreed to let us rent it for the 3 months.

God had now provided us a mountain cottage with a beautiful view. It was 500 yards from our nearest neighbor. In the basement was a complete pastor's library. Available for my perusal were numerous books by outstanding authors, as well as some of the best Bible commentaries. These would help expand my knowledge and understanding of God's Word. His grace is always sufficient. With this place secured, we left for Texas.

Chapter V
Christians Sharing Christ

> *Let him know, that he which converteth the sinner from the error of his way shall save a soul from death, and shall hide a multitude of sins.*
> —James 5:20 KJV

Upon returning to North Carolina early in January, we settled into our mountain cottage in the middle of a snowstorm. Although I had not been asked to preach during the four months of missionary orientation, I thought it best to set limits on the number of times I would preach each week for the next three months. I set these limits when I had not received even one invitation because, as a necessary discipline, I planned to allocate time for prayer and the study of God's Word.

A few days after we got settled in, a Gideon brother called and invited me to speak on Monday evening, January 29, at the West Asheville Baptist Church. The occasion was a quarterly meeting of Baptist Brotherhood and Women's Missionary Union (WMU) leaders and pastors. About 250 would be present.

Meanwhile, in early January I was invited to speak at the Montreat Presbyterian Church and to the Montreat College. The pastor of the church was my friend, Dr. Calvin Thielman. While I was there, he introduced me to Dr. L. Nelson Bell, with whose testimony I was already familiar; later I would read his biography, *A Foreign Devil in China*. Dr. and Mrs. Bell had been Presbyterian missionaries in China for many years. Their daughter Ruth was now married to Billy Graham, whose home I could see from our rented cottage.

Almost immediately Dr. Bell took me under his wing. In less than three months he taught me so much about the Christian life and being a missionary. Each morning after his quiet time, like clockwork he would call me and I would spring out of bed to answer the phone, "Good morning Dr. Bell."

Many mornings Dr. L. Nelson Bell would invite me to come by his home where we would talk about winning the lost world to Jesus.

One morning I was in his basement office when he received a call from Dr. Carl Henry who was resigning as editor of *Christianity Today*. Dr. Bell and Billy Graham had been responsible for the creation of this monthly periodical. I heard Dr. Bell discussing with Dr. Henry the idea of asking Dr. Harold Lindsel to become the new editor.

A short time later it was announced that Dr. Lindsel had accepted the position. *Christianity Today* is still one of the world's most respected Christian publications.

The Real Preaching Begins

January 29 came and I was prepared for my speaking engagement. The message that God gave me to preach that night was one that might have resulted in my being "run out of town on a rail." I spoke very clearly and bluntly about why God had not blessed their churches and the churches of Western North Carolina. After the service was over eleven pastors came up and invited me to come to their churches and preach the same type of message. I took their information and said I would call them within the next two days. That night as I drove back to our mountain cottage, I pondered what God wanted me to do.

The next afternoon I began calling the pastors. I told each one that I would come if I could preach on Friday and Saturday evenings, and Sunday morning. All but one of the pastors agreed to those conditions. This was added confirmation that God had done something very special that Monday evening.

Only one of the eleven pastors asked me how much remuneration I wanted for preaching in his church. He explained his question by saying that they did not have anything in their budget for such a meeting. Because of that question, which led me to believe that this pastor's concern was money, I put his church at the bottom of my list; I would preach my last series of meetings there on our last weekend in Western North Carolina. For two months I dreaded preaching in his church.

God immediately began using me in phenomenal ways. I was preaching in a different church each weekend on Friday and Saturday nights and Sunday mornings. That left each of those Sunday nights open for me to accept preaching opportunities. Also, almost every night of each week God arranged for me to preach to churches and men's groups. I was blessed with the opportunity of preaching in the morning chapel at three Christian colleges. Revivals broke out in churches; pastors regained their zeal to glorify Jesus; laymen became soul winners; and I received more invitations to preach than I could accept. But always in the back of my mind was the dread of preaching in the church where the pastor's concern was money.

Hitchhiker

As you can tell, during the three months we were living in that cottage on the side of a mountain in Western North Carolina, my schedule was hectic. But only one time did I miss an appointment, and that was because God had ordained a different type of appointment for that time slot. I was in the right place at the right time for God to use me in the life of a seventeen-year-old hitchhiker.

At 3 o'clock in the afternoon I was headed to our cottage in Black Mountain some twenty miles away. Passing through Asheville, I saw on the side of the highway a young man holding his thumb out trying to get a ride. All he had with him was a guitar in a case. Without any doubt God led me to stop and pick him up. His name was Bob Burgin. He had run away from home and had been living by playing his guitar and singing in the Asheville bars.

Because opportunities for performing had dried up, he decided to head to Nashville and try to make a living with his music there. He said he had been standing on the other side of the highway for more than an hour hoping to get a ride. He then decided to cross the highway and spend only fifteen minutes trying to get a ride which would take him back to his home in Hickory, North Carolina. God had me miss my appointment so that I could pick up Bob during those fifteen minutes before he would have again crossed the highway to go farther away from his home.

As we were driving those 20 miles to Black Mountain, and toward his home in Hickory, God gave me the joy of leading him to Christ. Immediately, this seventeen-year-old runaway's countenance changed. His new-found joy in Jesus was visible. I decided to take him to the bus station in Black Mountain and buy him a ticket to Hickory, which was about 70 miles farther east. We had a great time talking about the Lord during our wait for his bus to arrive. Saying goodbye was difficult, but we had talked about seeing each other at the feet of our Savior in glory.

Having been a Gideon for five years I knew I could call a Gideon brother in Hickory who would meet the bus and take Bob to his home. That Gideon, who was a pharmacist, met the bus and one of the first things Bob said was "I have been wondering what made Mr. Moore so different and now I know; it was Jesus." When Bob and the Gideon arrived at his parents' darkened home, the Gideon expected to let him out of the car and say goodbye; however, Bob insisted that he go in and meet his parents and tell them that he had given his life to Jesus.

Josh Dockerty

Because I had not scheduled appointments for Sunday evenings, I was able to accept invitations for that time slot on short notice. One Sunday night God gave me the wonderful blessing of getting to know Josh Dockerty. I had been invited to preach to a gap church in the mountains north of Asheville. A gap Church was where the Baptists and the Methodists worship in the same building on alternate weekends. Both the Baptists and the Methodists had agreed to have a joint meeting on a Sunday evening and invite me to preach.

Sitting on the front row before I was called on to preach had become standard for me. That night it resulted in one of the greatest blessings of my life. Let me explain. Sitting in a wheelchair across the aisle from me was a severely disfigured, almost grotesque, man in his late thirties. This man would bless me like few men in my life have blessed me. Before introducing me to preach, the pastor called on Josh Dockerty to pray.

I will always remember Josh talking to our heavenly Father. How can I explain the exhilaration of knowing that my loving God was present and having a personal conversation with this man seated beside me? I could almost hear God answering Josh. Josh reinforced my belief that prayer is talking to God.

The blessing of Josh's prayer carried over into the message that God gave me for the people of this gap church. After the service, the pastor asked if I would like to go with him to take Josh home. How could I deny the opportunity to be with Josh a little longer? It was extremely difficult to get Josh out of the church and into the front seat of the pastor's car, and even more difficult to get him out of the car and across a muddy front yard into his tar paper shack.

This one room was home to Josh, his elderly mother, and seriously retarded aunt. A rope with two Army blankets divided the room. As we had driven to his home, Josh told me that he had lived up in the mountains many miles from the nearest road and at the age of

28 he saw a car for the first time. He had moved down to live with his uncle and it was because of the uncle's love for Jesus that Josh learned to read using his uncle's Bible.

Matters of the Heart

While driving home one night after preaching, I felt like I was having a heart attack. I checked into the emergency room of the Memorial Hospital in Asheville. Everything proved negative but they gave me a shot and told me that I could not drive home. I called a dear friend, the pastor of the First Baptist Church of Swannanoa, a small town between Asheville and Black Mountain. He graciously came and drove me home. Subsequently, if I were to eat anything before preaching, I would have indigestion during the sermon.

Late one Sunday night in my quiet time, God made me aware that time was fleeting and that I had only a few more weeks before Judy and I would be leaving North Carolina and traveling to Costa Rica. It seemed as if my Lord was trying to tell me that there were so many more laymen in Western North Carolina that needed to hear the message of love for Jesus and understand that they could have life and have it in abundance.

My speaking schedule was almost full and I didn't know how I could reach many more than those to whom I was already scheduled to preach. For more than a week I was burdened with the fact that we had only a few more weeks to minister to the laymen of Western North Carolina.

I recognized that literally thousands of the Christian men in that area were satisfied just to be "saved" and they did not have any idea that the Christian life can be filled with joy and purpose. I continued praying until one Sunday night during a time of prayer I knew that the Lord wanted me to rent the Asheville city auditorium for a series of three meetings.

All I knew during those wee hours of the morning was that God was laying on my heart the burden for reaching many more Christian men in Western North Carolina with the message He had given me. Early that morning before I left my home, I called the manager of the Asheville city auditorium and made an appointment to see him at 10:30. En route I stopped by the home of a Gideon who I knew was a prayer warrior. I asked him to pray for the meeting and that God would provide a way for me to rent the auditorium.

Finding out that the name of the manager of the auditorium was "Mr. James" caused me to remember two verses from the Bible: James 1:5 says that if we lack wisdom we are to ask God and He will give it to us in abundance; and James 1:22 had been my favorite verse for years. It was always a constant reminder to me of how I was to live. "Be ye doers of the word and not hearers only, deceiving your own selves." I recognized that both of these verses applied to what I was planning on doing when I arrived at the auditorium.

Mr. James told me that the auditorium was completely booked for the next two years. Undaunted, I told him the dates of the weekend that I wanted to rent the auditorium. He thumbed through his schedule book and found that Saturday, Sunday, and Monday of that weekend had recently been canceled. I then asked, "How much will it cost to rent the city auditorium for three days?" He said it would be $504. I agreed to that amount; then he said a $100 deposit would be required.

Because we were no longer receiving a salary from the Foreign Missions board our bank account balance was down to $122. I made out the check for $100 and gave it to him. He did not realize, nor did anyone know, that the rental deposit had nearly depleted our account and that we had no expectation of receiving any more funds for several weeks.

From the office of Mr. James I called one of my Gideon brother's and told him what I had done. He expressed much surprise and said he needed to call some of our Gideon brothers and we needed to get together for lunch that day. I can clearly remember that I had no idea of how to proceed next. I was only being obedient to God's leading, and He had led me to secure the city auditorium with our last $100.

The Upper Room

Six Gideons and one pastor met with me that day for lunch. The oldest and most respected of the group said, "Charles, we had an evangelistic meeting in the city auditorium one time, and it took us 14 months of planning and $13,000. This time we have less than a month before the meeting will take place!" I said, "Bert, God told me to rent it and He didn't say anything about filling it."

At that first luncheon we decided we needed to meet on Wednesday two days later. There was a dining room on the third floor of the S&W cafeteria which would hold nearly 100 people. This became known as our "Upper Room." During the next three weeks an ever-increasing number of Christian men would meet in that third floor "Upper Room" to eat and pray.

I insisted that we take no collection during the meetings at the city auditorium, by faith allowing God to provide for expenses. Someone suggested that we put some type of bucket on the front of the platform so that anyone who wanted to help could put money in it. We also agreed that no mention of money would be made from the podium.

We all agreed that we should not do any extensive advertising campaign; however, one brother had a small article placed in the Asheville newspaper. All of us who met three times a week in our Upper Room were greatly blessed—even if for some reason we could not have had the meetings in the auditorium. These godly men all agreed with what God had burdened my soul to do. The meetings at the city auditorium were to be a time for Christians from Western North Carolina to stand up in front of a group and testify to the joy and victory that they had in their relationship with Christ.

One day at lunch the issue of what to call these meetings came up. Several names were suggested. Then someone said that what we intended to do would best be described by the phrase, "Christians Sharing Christ" and we unanimously agreed on that name. No one at that time could have imagined that the work of "Christians Sharing Christ" would lead to more than three million people being won to Christ and receiving salvation in His name.

Most of those men that met three times a week in the Upper Room have finished their earthly course. The full extent of the harvest resulting from the work God gave them to do will not be known until we all join with them around the throne of glory.

Waynesville

Shortly after we had begun those Upper-Room prayer-and-planning sessions, I had occasion to speak in Waynesville, a city some distance west of Asheville. Early Monday morning I left our cottage home for the lengthy drive to Waynesville. I was to speak to a large number of pastors at their once-a-month morning meeting. Driving west, I picked up a hitchhiker and had the privilege of leading him to Christ.

I arrived at the meeting place very tired from all the services that weekend. So I told the pastors, "I don't have the strength to preach a message this morning; so let me sit down in a chair and share a few things with you." God in his love for those pastors used me that morning in a truly unexpected way. As I was speaking, pastors got down on their knees to pray. Some were weeping loud enough for all of us to hear. What a glorious thing it is to realize that God doesn't need our wisdom or our strength to bless others.

On my lengthy trip home I again picked up a hitchhiker. I presented the claims of Christ but was disobedient to the leading of the Holy Spirit; I lacked the faith to believe that the second hitchhiker in one day would accept Christ. So I didn't invite him to do so. To this day I deeply regret my quenching the Spirit by not leading that young man all the way to Christ Jesus.

After meeting with those Waynesville pastors, I began receiving calls inviting me to preach in their churches. Timewise, I was able to accept only one invitation for a Sunday night service. A lot happened that Sunday night in Alan Creek Baptist Church.

This was one of the first times for me to see God's Holy Spirit mightily bless a church with a truly great revival. Before I tell you what God did in that church, I want to tell you what happened earlier that afternoon as I started on my journey to Waynesville.

I had eaten lunch with my wife and our two small children, and we had hugged before I got into our car to leave. Exhaustion had become a very real part of my life. As I drove away from our mountain cottage I felt led of the Lord to stop by Dr. Bell's home to very briefly discuss some of the developing details of my renting the Asheville city auditorium for the series of "Christians Sharing Christ" services.

Normally I would park in the back of his home and go in the back door. But this being Sunday and my seeing a car parked in front on the street, I decided out of respect that I would knock on the front door. Dr. Bell graciously answered the door and I walked in only to find after he closed the door that I was standing face-to-face with Dr. Billy Graham. Turning and looking into the rest of the living room I saw several members of the Bell family. I had walked in on a birthday party for Dr. Bell's son-in-law, a medical doctor. I tried to make a polite exit but Dr. Bell would not hear of it.

With Billy Graham sitting right beside me I looked straight at Dr. Bell and for fifteen minutes discussed with him the series to be held in the city auditorium. Billy listened intently and interrupted our conversation only once as he asked, "Is the pastor of the First Baptist Church of Asheville supporting your meeting?" I told him that I had personally spoken with the pastor, and that he had used the excuse of being too busy to help us get the word around to the laymen of his church. By Billy's reaction I felt that he had expected that answer.

When I had left and was driving towards Waynesville for that Sunday night service, I remember thinking, "There I was sitting beside Billy Graham, one of the Christian men that I most respect, and I spent all of my time talking to Dr. Bell and completely ignoring Billy." Dr. Bell and I spoke almost every morning and I visited his home many times. But then, as I drove on towards Waynesville, I recognized that my meeting that afternoon with Dr. Bell solved important problems, and it was more important to do that than for me to spend time getting to know Billy better.

When I arrived at Alan Creek Baptist Church in Waynesville, Pastor Carl Presnell and I met in his office. One other man joined us; his name was Ken Best. The three of us knelt in prayer. That afternoon we saw what North Carolinians call "praying the white throne of glory down." This is their way of saying that we saw lightning and heard thunder as the three of us in one spirit talked to God about that evening's service.

The service itself began at 6:30 with standing room only in an auditorium that would seat several hundred. By that time in that part of the state, people would drive great distances to attend a service where I was to preach. What Christians in Western North Carolina were seeing was God's love and His desire to bless His people. There is no way I can glory in myself because God gave me the message every time I stood up to speak. I never knew what I was going to say until I started to preach. That is not to say that I made no preparation; actually, I studied the Word day and night; so when I stood up to preach, God's Word flowed out of my mouth. God used those words for his glory. If people were convicted and blessed of God, then it was God who received the honor and glory. How grateful I am that the Lord taught me to never accept any of the glory; it all belongs to Him.

My lengthy time of Bible study and prayer was in the middle of the night. As God would speak to me during those periods of time He would give me His thoughts and words for His people in Western North Carolina.

That evening in Waynesville I must have preached on Galatians 2:20, for a fifteen year-old girl who had come forward asked if she could say something on the microphone. I gladly gave it to her and she said, "When brother Moore asked us if we were living for Christ, I thought I was; and then when he said, Are we dying daily to self for Christ, I again thought I was; but when he said, Are you

58

taking up the cross daily and following Jesus, I recognized that I'm not doing that and the rest of you hypocrites in this church are not doing it either." Out of the mouths of babes! God mightily used her exhortation.

That night's invitation lasted until well after 11 o'clock. Some people would come forward and throw their cigarette packs on the floor; others would cross the auditorium to embrace someone and ask for forgiveness; others came forward and openly testified to the entire congregation of sins that they had committed that had hurt the testimony of their church. The pastor and I alternated standing at the microphone during the invitation. During my breaks I would lie down on the carpet in front of the first row of pews.

At the beginning of the invitation I said, "If any of you do not like the length of this invitation, or do not like what you are seeing God do, then please quietly slip out of your pew and go home, for God wants us to be in one accord and one spirit asking Him to bless us individually with the convicting power of his Holy Spirit." It was well after midnight when I said goodbye to pastor Carl Presnell.

The following Sunday morning Carl announced to his church that he believed they were ready for an evangelistic meeting. He asked everyone to stand up who felt that they should have an evangelistic service that same Sunday night. He told me later that no one remained seated. He called an evangelist who lived in Western North Carolina and asked him to come that evening and preach an evangelistic message. Because many accepted the Lord that night they continued nightly evangelistic services for more than two weeks, during which time every night at least fourteen people gave their lives to Christ.

The experience of that church is a living testimony to what God will do when His people become holy, acceptable unto Him, and are willing to allow God to be the Lord of their lives and the Lord of their church. More than a year later in Costa Rica, God would bring the name of Pastor Carl Presnell into my mind. On a Sunday morning as I was shaving, God burdened my heart to pray for Carl, then again God reminded me to pray for Carl as I was driving to a church where I was to preach. My prayer just prior to preaching was a prayer of intercession for Carl. After the service I no longer felt a burden to intercede for him.

That afternoon I wrote Carl a letter and told him that I had prayed for him not knowing what his need was that Sunday morning. Several weeks later I received a reply. Carl said that on that very

Sunday morning he was barely able to finish giving the invitation before he collapsed behind the pulpit from a high blood pressure attack.

Only God knows why He gave me the opportunity to intercede for my dear pastor friend, and only He knows why he honored my prayers. Carl and I will know when we get to glory who accepted the Lord during the invitation that he almost could not complete.

The City Auditorium

In Western North Carolina, the Upper Room meetings continued until Friday, the day before the "Christians Sharing Christ" services were to begin on Saturday. That last Friday, the meeting was attended by more than 60 laymen and one black pastor. That pastor, Reverend Wesley Grant Sr., was a sure-fire man of God. With a heart full of gratefulness he prayed saying, "Thank you Lord, because I haven't seen this many laymen on their knees praying in my life."

We had spent exactly $100 in advertising. That went for a small brochure that was distributed to churches. I quote here from the last two paragraphs of that brochure.

"As plans for these Sharing Services were being carried out, Charles has been speaking to laymen at every opportunity. Over 5,000 people in this area have been stirred and challenged to search their own hearts.

"Charles Moore would be the first to say that this is not his meeting, nor is it the meeting of any group or denomination. Everyone involved is praying that it may truly be the Lord's meeting, as Christians share Christ."

For each day of the gatherings, several persons needed to be selected and invited to share their testimonies. Also, we all felt that we needed someone to close each service with a challenge.

These three persons needed to accept that responsibility before the first day's service began, so they would be prepared. I felt that the selecting of all the participants and closers should be done by the members of the planning committee who lived in the area and knew the locals. But those committee members encouraged me to select the participants and to either close each meeting myself, or choose those who would present the closing challenge.

At first I refused because I knew that the meetings were not mine; God had ordained them. But no matter how hard I tried to convince them that they should be the ones to choose the participants and to find the person to voice the challenge each day—a man or woman who had a testimony that would glorify God—they insisted that I make those selections.

You have to remember that Asheville, North Carolina, was not my home; I had been out preaching in their churches for less than two months. Nevertheless, after much prayer, I agreed to accept their commission. I would be the one to assign the challenge to qualified individuals.

God led me to give the challenge the first night. For the Sunday afternoon challenge, I chose my friend Dr. Calvin Thielman, pastor of the Montreat Presbyterian Church. I felt that the last night's challenge was the most important; I asked my beloved friend and mentor Dr. L. Nelson Bell, to handle it.

I would of course need assistance in selecting those who would share their testimonies, I wanted their life experiences to demonstrate to every man and woman in Western North Carolina that Christ came to give them life and to give it to them in abundance; and that He wanted their love and total commitment to his will. The first person that came to my mind to testify to the reality of this was Josh Dockerty. The testimony of Josh was a highlight of these meetings.

He told us that he had prayed, like Paul, to have his thorn in the flesh removed; but he quickly added, "One day soon I will have a body better than any of you have now!" He said that, because of his condition, he had a full schedule of preaching opportunities at health care facilities throughout Western North Carolina. Then with authority he asked, "What are you doing to allow God to use you for his glory?" How I look forward to seeing my dear brother Josh in glory.

Sunday afternoon Mr. James, the manager of the auditorium, went up to one of our men and handed him my $100 check. He said, "I never cashed the boy's check because I never thought that this would happen." He also said, "Because you all have not caused us to have to clean up after you, I am dropping the charge from $504 to $354."

The three "Christians Sharing Christ" meetings, where dozens of Christians shared their faith in Christ Jesus, had an average attendance of close to 1,000 people and cost less than $500 total, including advertising.

The real reason that all of this occurred, and was so greatly blessed, lies totally at the feet of our Lord. God used us, and blessed many through us, because He had transformed the lives of two young people—who had been in love with the things of the world—into young people who loved Jesus more than they loved their own lives. When you give Him all you have, He will give you all you need.

The Last Church

That much-dreaded final Friday night of March came when I was to speak at this unknown church. As I prepared to leave the cottage, our sweet five year-old daughter Judy Anne came to me crying and said, "Daddy can't you stay home and eat with us tonight?"

With a heavy heart I put on my overcoat and went out into the late March snowstorm to get in my car and drive to an anticipated spiritually cold church. As I drove over the Blue Ridge Parkway, I asked the Lord to give me the freedom, if there were only a few in attendance, to cancel the Saturday night service. I would tell them that I was physically exhausted and needed to be with my family. In my prayer I made sure that God knew that more than anything I wanted to do His will but I was only asking Him a favor.

Driving into the parking lot, I saw that the snowstorm had blown over a large tree and the electric company was trying to repair the electric lines into the church. My first reaction was, "Glory, the service has been canceled." However, as I entered the large, extremely beautiful, sanctuary I saw that it was lit by many large ornate candelabras. That night less than forty were in attendance, which was an uncommon number for any of my meetings.

As I started the long drive back across the Blue Ridge Parkway I realized that I had not told them that I would not be back the next night. By that time I was driving in an almost blinding snowstorm. Again talking to my heavenly Father I asked him to let it snow so much that the church would have to cancel the following night's service. Then I quickly added, "Not my will but thine be done."

Upon awakening the next morning, I literally rushed to the window to see how much snow there was on the ground. My great God had stopped the snowstorm and there was now a bright sun that was melting all that I had seen falling the night before. That evening as I drove to the Biltmore Forest Baptist Church, I knew for a certainty that instead of my saving the worst church for last God had saved a church and a pastor that, more than any of the others, needed what He had given me to preach.

The auditorium was full that night, a big difference from the previous night. That night, for the very first time, I preached the message from John 21:15-17. "Peter do you love me?" "Yes Lord I like you." "Peter do you love me? "Yes Lord I like you." "Peter, do you really like me?" "Oh Lord you know that at least I like you." At this point Peter's life was transformed, for he fell in love with his Lord and only because of this experience did Peter join the 120 in the upper room.

Because my messages were not about re-dedication but about falling in love with Jesus I did not give an invitation at the evening services.

At the conclusion of the sermon no one moved or left the auditorium. I didn't know what to do. As I walked down the center aisle everyone in the pews pressed inward. They all seemed to be trying to shake my hand and many began sharing what God had done in their lives that night. This was the only time in more than 50 years of ministry that I have seen this happen.

As I was driving back to our cottage I recognized all that the adversary had done to try to keep me from being used of my heavenly Father in that church. Not thinking of the velocity of my car I was pulled over by a North Carolina Highway Patrolman. Sitting in his car I admitted that I had been speeding and briefly explained that I had come from a church service where God had mightily blessed. Instead of giving me a ticket he challenged me to watch my speed. I said thank you and extended my hand to shake his hand. His response was, "Don't thank me; but I will shake your hand."

The remainder of my drive home was filled with praise to my great and loving heavenly Father, thanking Him for allowing me to see Romans 8:28 fulfilled that night in my life. "We know that all things work together for good to them that love God, to them who are called according to his purpose." But the story does not end there.

The next morning, the Sunday service was also greatly blessed of God. The invitation did not finish until well after 1 P.M. Because so many people came forward to testify, I felt compelled to turn my back to the congregation while standing on one side of the platform. This meant that I was looking into the faces of a large number of weeping choir members, until I closed my eyes.

The reason for turning, and closing my eyes, rather than looking at what was happening during the invitation, was to make sure that I would not be guilty of trying to accept any of the glory; it all belonged to my heavenly Father.

63

After everyone had left, the pastor led me to his office and as he closed the door behind us he turned around and with deep sobs he reached out and hugged me. He said, "Charles you do not know that I had decided to leave the ministry and return to selling insurance." My great and loving God did a mighty work in this dear pastor's life.

Six months later, through shortwave radio, I was able to talk with him from Costa Rica. He told me that in those six months they had baptized 26 people. In the entire previous year they had baptized less than a handful and most of them were children.

The experience with this dear pastor reaffirms that which I need reaffirmed from time to time. If we truly love our Lord and we truly desire to do his will, He will use and bless us beyond anything we can imagine.

For His Glory

In just over two months I had preached 68 times; and despite the fact that the services were not evangelistic, 137 people gave their lives to Christ.

During our three months in Western North Carolina God allowed us to develop a solid prayer base for our ministry. By the time we left for Costa Rica we had seventeen widows and old maids who promised to faithfully pray for us each day. Most of these ladies were at least seventy years old and one had been in an iron lung for twenty-two years. Kathryn Bryson prayed for us every hour of every day until she went to be with her Lord.

With all of my heart I believe that God honored the prayers of those godly women, which allowed us to see more than 5,000 accept Christ in our Costa Rican Upper Room in the first two years of our ministry.

Those women who prayed truly stored up their treasure in heaven, for the ministry that began at that time is still being used in mighty ways to glorify the name above all names, Jesus.

Judy and I left our beloved Western North Carolina on April 1, 1968. Before we caught our afternoon flight, a group of men who had been involved in the "Christians Sharing Christ" planning meetings met with us in the Upper Room at the S&W cafeteria. Many of them brought their wives for this time of sharing a last meal and praying together.

We didn't eat much of what was on our plates as we were recalling all those testimonies we had heard at the "Christians Sharing Christ" meetings in the Asheville city auditorium.

**Dear friends who attended
our farewell gathering**

One of the many statements made that afternoon has served as a guidepost for my ministry. Edna Phillips, the mother of Kathryn Bryson who had lived in the iron lung for 22 years, summed up the reason why God so greatly blessed our CSC meeting. She said, "The reason God blessed the meeting was that he received all of the glory." I learned that if I am to see God mightily bless any ministry He and He alone must receive all the glory.

Chapter VI
Beginning in Costa Rica

*To the weak became I as weak, that I might
gain the weak; I am made all things to all men, that I
might by all means save some.*
— 1 Corinthians 9:22 KJV

MEXICO 1968

It was April, 1968; America was entrenched in the Viet Nam
war. Judy and I, with our two little children, were on our way to Costa
Rica for language school. En route, we deplaned and spent two nights
in a Mexico City hotel. A high-ranking official of the North
Vietnamese government was also staying there. I felt moved to

witness to this man; but despite all my efforts he was not ready, or willing, to receive Christ.

Our young family arrived in San Jose, Costa Rica, on Friday, April 26, with our suitcases and three footlocker trunks. We expected to live out of these until our scheduled arrival in Peru at the end of the year.

We settled into the accommodations provided by the missions board conveniently located close to where we were to take our classes. On the third day after our arrival in Costa Rica God gave me the opportunity of preaching a thirty-minute message in Spanish. How blessed was I to hit the mission field running!

Culture shock is common for missionaries arriving in a foreign country for an extended stay, with the language barrier being a large part of it. But that was not as big a problem for Judy and me. While in college we had for 2½ years done weekend missionary work in Juarez, Mexico; also, while in the business world we employed a maid who could speak only Spanish. This especially helped Judy to become more familiar with that language; she had not spent her early years with a Mexican maid as I had, and she was not totally fluent in Spanish.

But language is only one part of culture shock, and we were not immune to some of the other aspects. A letter from Judy to family and friends, written three weeks after we arrived in Costa Rica, best describes some of the culture shock that we did experience.

May 1968

Greetings from San Jose, Costa Rica. The Moore family arrived in this lovely, and in some ways unlovely, country on Friday, April 26, 1968, to begin one year of Spanish language study. By 1969, we trust to be on our way to Lima, Peru, as missionaries under the Southern Baptist Foreign Missions board where Charles will work as business manager for the mission there.

This fourth week of primavera (spring), which is distinguished by the daily afternoon rains, finds us in our 3rd week of language study. Our weekdays begin at 5:45 AM (Do you believe that?) Our classes are from 7:30 AM to 11:50 AM, with a chapel service, in Spanish, at 9:15 AM.

Costa Rica has made many fleeting impressions on us in 3 weeks. They are fleeting because they so soon become a part of what we expect. We would like to share some of these, which are still fresh on our minds, with you.

SIGHTS:

<u>Smiling Ticos</u> – *The Costa Ricans are very amiable and quick to become friends. It is customary, especially among women, to kiss cheeks when greeting for the first time, and always.*

<u>Growing Fence Posts</u> -*how beautiful it is to look at the mountains out in the countryside and see the farmlands, neatly divided by straight rows of tall trees. The farmers put green fencepost in the ground, and before too long they have sprouted and leafed out into growing trees.*

<u>Tall Flowering Trees</u> -*blossoms of periwinkle blue, lacy pink, and vibrant red-orange topped the tallest imaginable trees in some places. The parks and cemeteries, however, are virtually treeless.*

<u>Houses</u> - *Neatly painted in many bright colors and they almost glisten in most cases.*

SOUNDS:

<u>Buses and Trucks</u> - *Crowded with people, loud and rickety; many are more than 20 years old.*

<u>A Little Niño</u> - *James, our 2 ½-year-old, crying loudly and broken hearted each morning as Daddy, Mommy and sister 5-year-old Judy Anne leave for school.*

<u>A Loud Parrot</u> - *Who lives next door and wakes us quite early with "O'la. Que tal," the Tico hello.*

<u>Raindrops</u> - *on top of tin roofs. All but the most elegant mansions are topped with tin.*

SMELLS:

<u>Fresh Mountain Air</u> - *Wonderful, away from the main streets, which are filled with carbon from worn-out buses.*

Papaya - A fruit which smells like rotten oranges, but could compete with cantaloupe for flavor. Judy Anne has the habit of holding her nose as she eats it.

Open Drainage Canals - Where wastewater runs beside all the main streets

FEELINGS:

At Home - Seeing a welcome sign with 16 of our fellow missionaries at San Jose's El Coco airport to greet us.

Homesickness - longing for family, friends, and an English-speaking church service.

Frustration - At a task so great, not knowing just where to plant our feet in the ground in a new place of work.

Yearning - To feed the obvious spiritual hunger written on the faces of countless people.

Encouragement - When an opportunity presents itself to share Christ with one; and there are many such opportunities daily, even at our own doorstep.

Discouragement - Our disappointment in people: A maid, who is a Christian national but isn't quite working out; fellow missionaries whose feelings can't help but be on their sleeve sometimes, when so far away from home. The daily trip to the post office can be either discouraging or encouraging, depending on whether or not your letters are there.

So many more impressions could be listed. It is obvious that not all would be positive. But when the going seems toughest - and it isn't easy here, back in school with language school study, etc. the Lord always gives such personal and living comfort. Such as---

One blue day when the Scripture reading was: "Weeping may endure for a night, but joy cometh in the morning."

Or, one homesick Sunday when, after observing a blind beggar on the street, Judy Anne, "Mommy, wont it be nice when that man gets to heaven? Jesus will make him be able to see then."

Or, on one discouraging day of language study when Judy Anne asked to pray, and did so in perfect Spanish.

Or, on numerous occasions when spirits are low and James reminds us that it's "mine turn" to choose a Bible verse to read at the table.

Or, when we're the most tired of hearing and speaking only Spanish, going to chapel one day and singing a chorus like this one:

Written by Jorge Dias, language Institute Professor:

Yo tengo un hogar-	*I have a special place-*
Mas arriba del sol	*Much higher than the sun*
Que Cristo Jesus	*That Jesus Christ*
A mi me prometio	*Has promised to me*
Yo tengo un Hogar-	*I have a special place*
Muy cerca del Senor y Dios	*Very near my Lord and God*
Donde podre pasar feliz	*Where I'll spend happy time*
La eternidad	*eternally*

The people here are receptive, and the opportunities are great. But, we are reminded that it is so in every walk of life--yours as well as ours.

Pray with us as we seek the Lord's will for our time here in the "Garden of the Americas."

Charles and Judy Moore

San Jose, Costa Rica, C. A.

In Judy's letter, you saw that early each morning there was an emotionally difficult time for the four of us. Little James had to be left with an elderly Costa Rican maid with whom he could not communicate. Saying goodbye to our son each morning was a painful way to start our day.

At the end of our first trimester at language school, the director was greatly perplexed. He had a student who was very fluent in Spanish but knew absolutely nothing about grammar. During our second trimester, I spent one hour a day with a language-school teacher who tried in vain to teach me all the Spanish rules of grammar. I still lean toward the Tex-Mex "rules" I learned as a child on the Rio Grande.

Before I fill in some of the details of our extra-curricular missionary activities, let me tell you of an unusual summertime mission of mercy that God drew me into. It was a genuine life-and-death experience, the memory of which sometimes haunts me to this day.

Volcano

On Monday afternoon, July 29, 1968, two men from the American Embassy in San Jose invited any missionaries with vehicles to join their team in the first search and rescue effort for survivors on the western side of the eruption of Arenal, a volcano that had been dormant for more than 900 years. Other teams would approach the eastern side. Three of us volunteered our vehicles and quickly found three other missionaries, one for each vehicle, to go with us as we followed the four-wheel-drive Embassy vehicle to a heart-rending experience at a distant location.

Arenal volcano was in the North of Costa Rica; it took us five hours to reach La Fortuna, a small village very close to the western side of that volcano. By the time we got there, it was already dark. We decided to begin immediately to evacuate all those who could be in danger from a second eruption.

By midnight each of our vehicles was completely loaded with people and their belongings. To get them to safety we had to cross the fast-flowing San Carlos River. It was about two blocks wide. My vehicle was a two-wheel-drive Volkswagen van; it was not heavy like the other three vehicles.

So we decided to send two four-wheel-drive vehicles across first and have the third one follow my light boat-like van across the river. Only by God's grace did we not float down the river to a certain death. What saved us was the weight of our twelve passengers with all they owned. The motor of the old Volkswagen van was in the back and the air-intake vents were high up on either side. As I began to cross the river with its rocky bottom, water almost blocked my entire view through the windshield.

Keeping the pedal to the metal created a wake that directed the water away from the engine; and by God's grace we reached the other side of the river giving thanks to God for His hand of mercy.

We left our human cargo at Villa Quesada and after a short nap, just before sunrise, we headed back up to the side of the actual volcano to see if we could find any survivors. However, we had decided that my old Volkswagen van would have a difficult time traversing the paths that we knew we would have to take to reach the small villages that had been in the path of the volcanic pyroclastic flow.

We had agreed to take with us the superintendent of highways for that area. Two Willis Jeeps with 55 gallon drums of diesel had left our base of operations during the night, headed for La Fortuna, where they would wait for Superintendent Castro to direct their effort at burning the carcasses of the dead animals. There was concern that if they were not burnt various diseases could result.

For the two-hour drive, the superintendent and I had a very pleasant conversation as he told me of his plan for the next month—to board a banana boat and travel to Seattle to see his two sons who were attending different universities. I can too vividly remember the prompting of the Holy Spirit for me to lead this man to Christ. But each time, I quenched the Spirit, as we continued talking about everything but my Savior.

When we arrived at La Fortuna, which was the closest undamaged community to the volcano, the superintendent transferred to one of the Willis Jeeps that were waiting with their barrels of diesel fuel. He and I said goodbye at that time.

5' diameter tree after first eruption

While the two Jeeps with the diesel fuel for burning animal carcasses were somehow delayed, the three-car group I was with went on ahead as we started our journey into the area that had already been destroyed by the volcano.

We were tasked with searching for human survivors. We slipped and slid along cow paths until we came over a rise and were shocked to see what one can only imagine would have been seen in a battlefield of the First World War. What had once been an area of lush vegetation and trees more than 100 feet tall was nothing but a flat dirt field with nothing standing and nothing that was green.

Finally we had to stop and leave our four-wheel-drive vehicles, to continue our search on foot. We saw many dead cows whose skin had been burnt off of them; but we were not able to find any humans. Some distance away we saw the very small cone of the volcano. There were fumaroles of smoky gas coming out of a volcanic vent. Not being aware of what to expect before a volcano would erupt, we ignored this telltale sign.

**View of volcano thirty minutes before
deadly second eruption**

Eventually, we recognized the futility of our search and we started our lengthy walk back to our vehicles. We reached them at noon and decided to eat our lunch: long salamis and hard rolls of bread.

At the small river called Tabacon, we stopped to wash our hands; two of us took off our shoes to wade in the river. It was I who then suggested that we stay beside that river to eat. I believe it was in the Providence of God that someone said, "No, let's go on out." So we began the arduous drive back toward Fortuna.

Washing in river 15 minutes before second eruption that killed six near this spot

After leaving the river, we started up a 300-foot-high hill. Being in the first of the three vehicles to reach the top, I saw the two Willis Jeeps, with my friend the superintendent, coming toward us; they were going toward the volcano. They cautiously passed us to go down the hill we had just ascended.

The first two of our vehicles started down the other side of the hill; then we stopped and got out to wait for our third vehicle, the Embassy wagon, which was delayed while passing the two Willis Jeeps. Standing in the mud awaiting our third vehicle, we saw it clear the hilltop and begin down toward us. Just then, we heard two mighty roars like the sound of a 155mm howitzer.

Looking back across the terrain we had just traversed, we saw a pyroclastic flow parallel to the ground; then looking up we saw a volcanic cloud that an airline pilot flying nearby reported to be more than 30,000 feet high.

Our three vehicles were protected from the pyroclastic flow, which had spread outward from the volcano for more than seven miles along the ground; we were saved by the 300-foot hill. But the men in the other two vehicles, including my friend the superintendent, were burnt alive within 300 feet from where I had washed my feet and suggested that we stay and eat lunch.

Pyroclastic flow from second eruption; small hill provided cover.

These facts are well documented by original pictures that I have in my possession, and by a report made by the Smithsonian Institution's Department of Small Lived Research. In his investigation, one of their research analysts spent two hours looking at our pictures and asking me numerous questions.

There were 87 people killed in the two eruptions of the Volcano Arenal. By God's grace my life and the lives of the others who were in our three-car search and rescue team were spared. But I cannot forget the two hours I had spent with the Superintendent of Transportation. Nor can I erase the memory of quenching the Holy Spirit when I knew He wanted me to lead this man to Christ.

In the first eruption of Arenal on July 29, 1968, there were 81 souls that were burnt alive as 700°F gases traveled laterally across seven miles at almost the speed of sound. On the next day, while we were there, six more were burnt alive by the same type of eruption. One of those was my friend the superintendent; the other five were acquaintances we had made in La Fortuna.

Back to Sharing Christ

Judy and I, from our first days in Costa Rica, had a great desire to see everyone come to know our Jesus. Because we could converse in Spanish we were able to lead many Costa Ricans to Christ. But our evangelistic zeal did cause problems with a few missionary language-school students. Our language-school next-door neighbor explicitly told me, "Do not witness to our maid because we do not want any problems."

Javier Obando

Thief on a motorcycle came to know Christ

The sovereignty of God is shown by the way we are able to see his grace at work in our lives. God blessed me in a marvelous way when he allowed me to lead Javier Obando to Christ. He was my first son in the Lord in Latin America and he was to become one of the greatest soul winners I have ever known.

This God-ordained relationship started one day when I was having the back seat of our beat-up 1961 Volkswagen van welded to the floor. While the repair was underway, this 18-year-old boy came up to me and started a conversation. Javier was the youngest of 21 siblings and he earned his living by selling marijuana to bus drivers.

We bonded almost immediately. He was gregarious and highly motivated, though not always in the right direction. But he would always listen. He began visiting our home regularly. During each visit, Judy would offer him something to eat or drink; he would refuse every time.

One evening I was in our carport conversing with Javier when the Holy Spirit got through to him. Finally, right then and there, he gave his life to Christ. Javier and I went into the house to share the good news with Judy. After the excitement, he said, "Doña Judy would you give me a glass of milk and a piece of bread?"

Two days later he asked me if I understood why he had not accepted any food or drink from Judy before. Then he explained that all along his intent had been to steal from us, and that it would have been a disgraceful thing to receive something from us and then steal from us. After receiving Christ, the "honorable young thief" wanted to steal no more.

During my more than 50 years of ministry I have never led anyone else to Christ who within a month led more than 30 other people to Christ. The change in his life was so evident that he attracted his family and friends, causing them to ask what had happened. His life and his explanation were enough for most of them to want to receive Christ themselves. Day or night Javier would look for me, bringing with him someone who was ready to accept Christ. Javier had clearly explained the plan of salvation and all I needed to do was ask them if they wanted to pray with me. I continued encouraging and exhorting Javier to go ahead and pray with the ones he had led to Christ, but for some reason he wanted me to do it.

Late one night I turned off any light visible outside so that nothing would give evidence that we were still awake. Judy and I were lying on our bed reading and the doorbell rang. Immediately I knew that it was Javier bringing someone for me to pray with. That same night in our living room, the young man he had brought prayed to receive Christ. His name was Jaime Valverde. We had a time of rejoicing and then I told Javier, "The next time you bring someone to me like this, I am going to say, 'I don't a speaky Spanish.'"

Undeterred, he went on to lead hundreds more to Christ, including all but three of his brothers and sisters. Thinking back, I wonder, how could I have been so exasperated at his bringing someone to me who wanted to receive Jesus, even if it was nearly midnight?

Javier with wife and firstborn

God blesses those who receive and love His son, and Javier was a great example of this. God gave me the opportunity of officiating at the wedding of Javier and his beautiful bride Olga.

They quickly became like a son and daughter to Judy and me. My counseling with Javier had two parts. I helped him grow in God's grace and I helped him become an astute businessman who, because of his love for Jesus, was known for being a man of integrity.

He started his own business with the main purpose of using it as a means of reaching the lost and of providing an inheritance for his three children. He was well known throughout Costa Rica because he would combine his sales efforts with the showing of evangelistic movies in bars, or on a sheet on the outside of a building, in remote areas of the country. He had gone from selling marijuana to bus drivers to becoming a wealthy and reputable Christian businessman, selling remanufactured products. If an area of the country was accessible by his truck then Javier had been there to evangelize and to sell his products, in that order. Judy and I consider his three grown children as our grandchildren.

Several years ago, my beloved brother Javier went to be with the Lord, and I had the blessing of preaching his funeral service. More than 1,000 attended, most of whom were his children in the Lord. Neither he nor I have ever had the need for anyone to motivate us to win the lost to Christ; so Javier and I had wonderful times together leading people to Jesus.

The Crusade Experience

Great things had begun happening in Costa Rica shortly after we had arrived there. Twelve pastors would come to our home every Wednesday for lunch and prayer. We would have a lengthy season of prayer asking God to bless Costa Rica and each of the churches that were preaching the gospel. In his prayer, one of these pastors said, "Thank you Lord that for the first time in my life I have been able to pray for the missionaries."

Many good things happened in the lives of all of us because of these prayer meetings. Through the prayer time of our group God began burdening my heart to preach to the lost in Costa Rica. This would put in motion circumstances that would change our lives dramatically.

Because of my fluency in the Spanish language, I was not required to continue language school past my second trimester. But Judy needed to complete the year, upon which we were expected to leave Costa Rica and move to Lima, Peru, where I would become the business manager for the 26 missionaries there.

In 1968, the leadership of the Southern Baptist Convention decided that every Southern Baptist Church in the western hemisphere would have a one-week evangelistic crusade. It was called the Crusade of the Americas.

That year there were 18 Southern Baptist churches in Costa Rica. One of them was pastored by a man who attended our weekly lunch and prayer meeting. He had also been attending our weekly evangelistic meetings that were being held in a downtown parking lot (more about those meetings later).

This pastor asked if I would preach the crusade in his church. I explained to him that I had never preached an evangelistic crusade; but he insisted and I finally agreed, with some strong conditions. The church was not to publicize the crusade like all the other churches had been doing. I said that they were to pray for three specific things.

They were to pray for their own lives, that the lost would see Jesus in them. They were to pray for their church, that it would be in one accord and one spirit and there would be no unconfessed sin. Then I asked them to pray for their pastor and for me that during the crusade we would be hidden behind the cross of Calvary. There were six weeks before the beginning of the crusade and I challenged all the members to dedicate their lives to God in prayer.

This pastor's church was to be the 18th and last church to participate in the "Crusade of the Americas" in Costa Rica. Most of the other 17 churches worked very hard to gather a crowd and to try to win many to Christ. They rented the services of trucks with loudspeakers to publicize their Crusades; many designed and printed flyers that they distributed to hundreds of homes around their church; they even paid for radio spots to announce their Crusades.

By the time those 17 churches had completed their Crusades, six people had accepted the Lord. There had been 119 evangelistic services resulting in only a handful having received Christ.

The Crusade at the last church was to begin on a Sunday evening. That morning I preached a message to the church. I challenged all the church members to begin praying for those who would accept Christ that night. I told them that the service would begin at 7 o'clock on the dot and no one would be allowed to come in after that starting time (beginning on time is not customary in Latin America). I then told them that the invitation would be completed by 7:30 on the dot.

80

The most important thing I said that morning was that each of them did not need to listen to my sermon because it would be an evangelistic message intended for the lost. I challenged them to pray for each one in the service that had not received Christ as their Savior.

We had previously trained some of the church members to serve as spiritual counselors to the lost souls who came to Christ during the Crusade. That night and every succeeding night the meeting began with a very brief greeting from the pastor, two verses of a hymn, and the pastor reading a portion of God's word.

This was followed by my preaching a 15-minute sermon that concluded at 7:30 p.m. The first night 38 people came forward to receive Christ and at the conclusion of the extended crusade 122 had accepted Christ.

I believe God mightily blessed this church—and did not bless the others the same way—for one reason. There was no one in this church who could try to share the glory that belonged to God. No one could take pride in having designed the handouts; no one could be proud that they knocked on 100 doors; and no one could be proud that they helped pay for the radio spots or the trucks with loudspeakers. And most of all, I could not accept even a little bit of the glory because the sermons I preached were difficult even for me to understand. The salvation of souls was entirely a work of the Holy Spirit.

More often than not, man's programs, plans, efforts, and wisdom only get in God's way. Within a month 90 new Christians were baptized, and the church doubled in size. In six months they had built a new place of worship, without going into debt. That building is still in use today.

Here in Costa Rica we saw God use us to glorify the Name of His Son in the same way we had seen Him use us in North Carolina. When I was not required to attend language school any more, we felt led of God to move to the opposite side of town; we were truly grateful for this opportunity to live in the midst of the lost souls we hoped to reach, thus increasing the effectiveness of our testimony.

We would no longer be surrounded by many language-school students and missionaries who spent much of their time fellowshipping with each other. We knew that we were to redeem the time while we were in Costa Rica so we needed to be as closely as possible associated with the people of this country.

We found a nicely furnished house that the Foreign Missions board agreed to rent for us. It was a block and a half from the closest house of prostitution and amazingly only two blocks from the building where our "Upper Room" would be located for the next 31 years. We lived in this home, several miles from the nearest English-speaking missionaries, for the next six months. It was located on the edge of a five-square-mile area containing 50,000 people and no evangelical church and only one Catholic Church. This was exactly where we wanted to be, in the midst of humble people of poverty. "Blessed are the poor in spirit."

Early each morning, I would drive Judy through the heart of the marketplace across the breadth of San Jose to the Spanish Language Institute and then return to pick her up at 12 noon.

Daily, God allowed me to see men with open running sores and prostitutes with extended stomachs. God broke my heart and burdened my soul to reach these people with the message of salvation. They were people who had no hope of having even one good meal a day, or of sleeping in a bed at night; so I knew that a message of salvation in Christ Jesus would provide each of them with hope. But, how was I to reach them?

Preaching in a parking lot

I began trying to find a parking lot in the middle of the red light and market district that would let me rent space that I could use to preach to the thousands the message of Jesus. One young man who managed a parking lot said he would rent his lot to me between 11:30 a.m. and 1:30 p.m. every Tuesday. Later I would be blessed with the privilege of leading this young man to Jesus.

Our second hurdle was to find a sound system we could attach to the battery of our 1961 Volkswagen van. This was no easy task, but by God's grace we were able to obtain exactly what we needed, which would allow us to preach and be heard for half a block in each direction. With excitement, we preached our first message and were greatly blessed to see more than thirty men and women come forward in that small parking lot to make their profession of faith in Christ Jesus.

Immediately across the street from our parking lot was a house of prostitution with three large round windows. During the first three weeks women would shout vulgarities from these windows; but from the fourth week on, the windows were filled with women who were silently listening to the message of Christ and who would break out in applause as people would go forward at the invitation.

Parking lot preaching

It was glorious to see the poorest of the poor hear the message of salvation and come forward. We had pastors and laymen who counseled every new Christian. Many Tuesdays we saw more than fifty people give their lives to Christ. Beginning with the first Tuesday, I invited the large number of pastors that helped us in the counseling to take their turn at preaching. One layman, Carlos Muñoz, volunteered. He worked at a Christian book store and took time off work to preach in that parking lot; more about him in the next chapter.

All the pastors turned me down. But they were more than willing to do the counseling. It was not until later that I learned the reason they were reluctant to preach, and what it would take to change their mind.

Jail Time

On the fourth Tuesday I was arrested by two Guardia Civil, or policemen, and taken to jail and placed in a holding cell. Claudio Rojas, a godly language-school teacher had been on hand each week helping to counsel the new Christians. When I was arrested, he said, "I want to go with you Carlos."

So, Claudio and I were locked in a cell filled with six semiconscious drunks lying on the floor. In only 10' square it was hard not to step on the other occupants. There was no light and only a small gap in the top and the bottom of the steel door. To this day, I can

83

remember the stench in that small drunk tank. Excitedly Claudio asked me, "Don't you feel like Paul and Silas must have felt?" I replied, "No," for I had not thought of their Philippian jail experience. Then one of us said, "I hope we don't have an earthquake."

During the nearly three hours that we were in the cell I was taken out twice. The first time, a police Lieutenant told me in no uncertain terms that I should not be preaching in that parking lot. I explained that I knew the laws of Costa Rica and I was not violating any law by preaching in a space that I had rented.

When I was returned to the cell Claudio said, "I thought they were going to let you out and leave me here." I assured him that I would never leave him there, no matter what.

Sometime later a guard returned for me, and again took me to the angry Lieutenant who handed me a phone and said, "The Major wants to speak with you." He repeated what I had already heard and I repeated what I had told the Lieutenant. The Major became furious and said he was going to send a car to pick me up and take me to the penitentiary. Because of the time that Claudio and I had spent praying together inside of that filthy cell, I was able to boldly tell the Major, "Okay go ahead, and I will call the American Embassy."

Upon hearing that, the major slammed the phone down and I was returned to the cell. A short time later Claudio and I were released. As we came out to the street it took us a moment to adjust to the bright sunlight; then we saw five pastors across the street. They had been there the whole time, praying for us. We had a joyful reunion and a time of thanksgiving prayer to God for what He had done.

The next Tuesday the same pastors and several more were in line volunteering to preach. What had changed from the first three weeks when they had refused the offer to preach?

Several years ago, looking back on that time, I came to understand what Paul meant when he wrote in Philippians 1:14 "And many of the brethren in the Lord, waxing confident by my bonds, are much more bold to speak the word without fear."

It was a true blessing to see the excitement of these pastors as they preached in the parking lot for the first time. While this was a blessing it also presented me with a problem. By giving them my time to preach I was left thinking that I needed to find another parking lot to rent so I could preach.

The first Tuesday after I was arrested, a man in civilian clothes came up to me and asked, "Hermano Carlos, do you remember me?" I said, "Of course, you are Corporal Guillen; you arrested me last week." He said, "Brother, did you recognize that I waited to arrest you until after you gave the invitation?" I replied, "No."

Corporal Guillen then told me what God had done in his life. First, he told me that he had arrested me on orders from the major; then said that he was a member of the Calle Blanco Bible church. He said he had gone forward in his church that Sunday to tell the story of having to arrest me, and then confessed to the whole church that he felt ashamed that it was a North American that was preaching to his fellow Costa Ricans. He said he told the church that he was going to begin reaching the lost for Jesus. I told the Corporal that if he knew any other Christian policemen that needed to get right with the Lord, he should tell them to come and arrest me the next week. The two of us then had a good laugh.

Peru can wait

How could any man who was being led by God, was seeing dozens of lost souls accept Christ each week in a parking lot, and was being used mightily in churches, settle for being a business manager in Peru, even if it was for other missionaries?

Before we knew it, Judy and I were quickly heading toward the third time in our lives when God would lead us to do something that all our most respected friends, who loved the Lord, would oppose. Our first time was when we were led of the Lord to give everything away and go to seminary, and the second was when God led us to delay our departure for Costa Rica and stay in North Carolina, where God opened the door for me to preach 68 times in just over two months.

God in his marvelous grace has always had a way of drawing my attention to what he is planning to do in my life. Judy and I agonized in prayer over what we should do. We communicated with our loved ones in the United States what we believed God wanted us to do.

Like the previous two times when God led us to do something that seemed to many to be illogical, every person whose advice and counsel we valued gave us many reasons why our thinking had to be wrong. This time they all told us that we needed to go on to Peru. One said, "If you are with the Foreign Missions board and one of your children becomes sick the Board will fly them back to the Mayo Clinic for the best care possible." Another said, "How are you going to live?"

85

When we had "prayed through" and knew that it was God's will for us to stay in Costa Rica, we asked the Foreign Missions Board for permission. They sent the three that were in our immediate chain of authority to Costa Rica to meet with us. We met one evening in the nicely furnished home that they had rented for us.

The Assistant Executive Secretary of the Foreign Missions Board told us that we needed to go on to Peru where I was to be the business manager for the Peruvian mission, or we needed to return to the States where I should complete my seminary education and pastor a church for two years. Given the choices, God made it very easy for us to decide what to do. We told the three men that in order to be obedient to God's will for our lives we would have to resign from the Foreign Missions Board and stay in Costa Rica.

We were told that they would pay the rent for only two more months for the storage of our belongings in Fort Worth; we would have to deal with the Board's business manager from that point on. We were surprised to later find out they wanted us to reimburse them $3,000 for our travel expenses to Costa Rica, our rent, and our salary. If Doctor Cal Guy had not written a strong letter stating that they should consider that money as an investment in winning Costa Rica to Christ, we would have had a sizable debt.

That evening Judy and I, and two of the three from the Foreign Missions Board, wept. The two wept because they had known us personally for some time, and they knew from their own experiences what we would face trying to live by faith.

A Physical Death and a Spiritual Revival

Monday night, January 14, 1969, was an exciting night for our little family. I was by Judy's side for the birth of our third child. Cal was born in the Clinica Biblica de San Jose, Costa Rica, and was named for our former pastor and seminary professor Dr. Cal Guy; it was a joyful but exhausting experience not only for Judy but for myself as well.

Returning from the hospital I found Miguel, a deacon of a large church in Alajuela, waiting on our porch. I did not invite him in. As we stood out front, I spoke sternly about the seriousness of his actions within his church. It was well-known that he was a gossip and had been causing division in the congregation.

That Monday evening, already emotionally spent from our third child's birth, I was very blunt with him. I told Miguel that I was

86

beginning a series of meetings in his church on Thursday night, and that on that night I expected him to come forward in the church to confess his sins and repent of his actions. I told him that if he didn't, I would confess his sins for him to the whole church.

When I said these things to Miguel, my mind was preoccupied with the homecoming of Judy and our newborn son Cal. That might explain why those words were not in the front of my mind when I began preaching in his church, which was in the third-largest city of Costa Rica. Buses coming from San Jose stopped for passengers right in front of that church. On that Thursday night, when the first of the series of meetings was held, God led me to preach on Ananias and Sapphira (Acts 5:1-11).

While preparing for my sermon, I was not thinking about what I had told Miguel. Arriving at the church I found there were less than 20 people in an auditorium that could easily seat over 200. With no thought of Miguel, I said, "Before God can bless this church there may need to be a death." I was speaking of the importance of the church being in one accord and one spirit before God would bless them. An example was when Israel could not win battles until Joshua had severely dealt with the sin of Achan (Joshua 7:13).

The next morning early, I received a call from the pastor who told me that Miguel had been shot to death at three o'clock that morning on his way back from taking his wife to the bakery where she worked. The pastor said, "What should we do?" I responded with, "Why are you asking me?" He said, "You preached on Ananias and Sapphira last night." I had no answer and my first thought was, "What hath God wrought?" and then, "Father, have thine own way."

A few hours later Miguel's wife called and asked if I would officiate at his funeral that afternoon. Today I can only remember mixed feelings. I recognized that God loves His church and that with the removal of Miguel, the church could begin to reach the lost in their community.

That night, Friday, nearly every seat in the church was full. Remember the night before, there were only twenty present, but now the church was in one accord and one spirit. Miguel had been unrepentant and God would not bless until he was removed. A short time later I found that Miguel's sin was much greater than being a gossip.

The one who committed the murder was Miguel's neighbor. He was never arrested and brought to trial because it was known that Miguel the deacon had sexually assaulted the murderer's daughter.

For the years that we lived in Costa Rica, after that incident, that church had a positive testimony and a good and fruitful ministry in their city. Years later, the pastor of that church invited me to go with him high up on the slopes of one of the volcanos to preach to a small community of 15 homes. We were in the first vehicle to make it up the muddy roads at the end of the rainy season.

All the Christians were gathered together in the home of a farmer who had only one arm. You could tell that his handicap had limited his small family's income. Their small house had mud floors and wood slat beds which reminded me of my youth when I would ride the bus across the Rio Grande to Mexico with our family's maid.

In the meeting house, there were no seats, and the two windows and two doors were filled with Christians eager to hear the word preached to them. It had been five months since the last preacher had visited this small community. In the middle of the group that was packed into this home, there was a very elderly lady whose face would make someone think she had walked with God.

When I finished the hour-long sermon, I was about to say my goodbyes when a man pulled on my jacket and said, "Give an invitation." I had believed that all that were there were born-again Christians. I said, "All of you who want to make a public profession of your faith in Jesus Christ come in." No one moved but the elderly woman standing right in front of me. As she shuffled forward I rejoiced with her and all those whose faces were lit up with joy.

This 88-year-old woman made known to the world and to a surprised Charles that she had come to know the Lord in the rainy season and was then making known to the world that she knew Jesus as her Savior and Lord. As we were getting in the four-wheel-drive vehicle to leave, it looked like they were preparing to have a fiesta. To this day, I believe she is the oldest person I have ever seen make a profession of faith in a service where I have preached.

A Place to Live

We knew that we had a very short time to find a much less expensive home to rent. The only monthly income we had was the $250 from my former business partner. Decent homes for much less money were to be found only in areas farther away from the center of San Jose.

We found an unfurnished house for rent on the outskirts of San Jose. Various missionary friends gave us a kitchen table with 4 chairs, a metal-frame baby bed for Cal, and two collapsible lightweight aluminum cots, one for each of our older children, aged four and six. Another friend gave us a hot plate. This is all the furniture that we had for the next two months.

For two months Judy and I slept on the floor, for six weeks we didn't have a stove, and for seven weeks we didn't have a refrigerator. Judy and I remember those days as being filled with joy, for each day we knew we were in the center of God's will. This is how we began our lives as "Independent Missionaries."

Eventually, a very dear missionary friend, who to this day continues to be a wise counselor and strong supporter of our ministry, gave us a bed. We rejoiced in his gift only to find that the bed was infested with fleas. For days, we put every imaginable flea powder on the straw mattress but continued to be bitten by the fleas.

One morning Judy and I knelt beside the bed and asked God to remove the fleas, which He did almost immediately. What a mistake to not have gone to God first.

Recently, the friend who gave us the bed filled with fleas jokingly said he got it at a flea market. In the 1960s, and especially in Costa Rica, American style "flea markets" did not exist.

After we had moved into our "new home" I received an unexpected invitation. A man who had witnessed my arrest in the parking lot, turned out to be the Colombian team leader for an organization then known as Overseas Crusades. His organization invited me to visit their work in Colombia. I responded with a brief trip to Cali, where God let me know that He wanted me to continue working in the red light and market district of San Jose, Costa Rica.

Chapter VII
Our Upper Room

Those things, which you have both learned, and received, and heard, and seen in me, do: and the God of peace shall be with you.—Philippians 4:9 KJV

I kept preaching in the parking lot; but I knew that although we were reaching 30-50 people a week for Christ, thousands more were not being reached. I remembered the meetings in the "Upper Room" in Asheville, North Carolina, where we planned for the "Christians Sharing Christ" gatherings at the Auditorium. I realized that something like that, but on a more permanent basis, needed to begin in Costa Rica. We needed to start the Costa Rican version of "Christians Sharing Christ."

To reach the masses of the poorest of the poor of Costa Rica we would have to find and rent space in a building that was strategically located in the center of the red light and market district.

My dear brother Carlos Muñoz, who worked in the Baptist Book Store, had been the only one willing to preach in the parking lot those first three weeks. We had developed a kindred spirit and we both wanted to reach everyone in the marketplace for Jesus. Carlos and I covenanted together to find a building centrally located.

For more than a month, I would leave home each morning and ride a bus to meet Carlos. From 8:00 until around noon he and I would walk through all the market area, stopping on each corner to pray. We prayed that God would lead us to a building that we could rent in that block. At the same time, we were asking God to use us to win for Jesus all the people that were walking by us.

We must have been a strange sight to see, a tall North American and a short Costa Rican with their heads bowed praying to their Lord. We would go into every store on each block asking if they knew where there was a building we could rent. After the first few weeks, the owners or employees of most of the stores we walked into would greet us by waving their index finger and saying "Nada," which meant that they knew of nothing for rent. The reason we had to keep going every day was that, as soon as a building was available to rent, somebody else would already have rented it. This is what prompted us to look diligently each day for a building that was being vacated.

Bus fares were unbelievably low. A round trip from our home to downtown San Jose cost less than half the value of an American penny. I found it interesting that I would sometimes see old Moore Service buses operating in Central America with our emblem still easily visible.

On a Tuesday morning, I was leaving to catch the bus to meet Carlos to continue our search for a building when Judy said, "Charles we are out of food and I know we don't have any money. I'm telling you this only so that you know."

She had some black beans, rice, and oatmeal for our two older children and she had enough baby formula for our youngest son. She was using a hot plate for cooking, and we would buy a chunk of ice to put in a plastic box we had for keeping food cold. Judy and I were the only ones on this earth who knew that we didn't have any food or money. I fasted Tuesday, Wednesday, and Thursday.

Midmorning Thursday, Carlos and I went into a small establishment and asked if they knew anybody that had a building to rent. The landlady, Señora Elba Mora came out and said she had a second story space for rent. She had been offered the equivalent of $300 and $400 a month but still had not rented it. I asked her to give us one hour to come back with an offer. I made her promise me that she wouldn't rent it before we returned.

Carlos and I went down to an isolated place close to the parada Coca Cola where we could pray in private. When we finished, I told Carlos that I was going to offer Señora Mora $100 per month. He said with excitement, "You heard what she's already been offered; she is going to get mad."

I agreed; but still, God had given me that figure. Keep in mind I was making an offer of $100 a month when our family had no money and no food. But God doesn't make mistakes. The mistakes result when we do not listen to His "still, small voice."

We immediately went back and I said, "Señora Mora, I offer you $100 per month for your second-floor space." She became somewhat agitated just as Carlos had predicted. She repeated the amounts that she had already been offered for the space. Shocked as she was by my offer she said, rather indignantly, "What do you want to use the building for?"

I said in a confident voice, "To preach the gospel of Jesus Christ to the people here in the market." Without a blink of an eye she said "All right, I'll take your offer because I don't want it to be a house of prostitution again, and that's what the others want to use it for."

As I said, my God does not make any mistakes. Judy and I had less than a dollar and if Señora Mora had asked us for any earnest money we would not have been able to rent the building. She told me to come back on Monday, which was the first of the month, and she would have a contract ready for me to sign. I would need to pay her then.   Carlos and I left her business very excited that we had found a building that we could rent, one where we could preach day and night the message of salvation to the thousands in the marketplace of San Jose.

This was Thursday morning and I had to return to her establishment on Monday with $100 so I could sign the contract. God had given me peace beyond all human understanding about our family living with limited food and me without any money. And then God gave me that same peace when by faith I rented the second floor of that building without any money and no anticipated monies to come.

The Lord Provides

As we left Señora Mora's store, Carlos headed for the Christian bookstore where he worked; I walked across the street into El Mercado Borbon, the main market of San Jose. I saw David Cordero, a good friend who attended a church I had preached in several times. He was sitting on the floor with all his vegetables for sale, spread around him. He motioned for me to come over to him where he immediately took out two paper sacks and began filling them with vegetables.

When he graciously handed me the two sacks full of green vegetables, my first thought was, "My God is so amazing. He truly loves my family and me." I then thanked David and ran to catch a bus; I wanted to show Judy how God had blessed us this time.

Let me repeat what I said above, no one on this earth knew that we didn't have any money and that we didn't have any food at home. Our loving heavenly Father knew, and He provided. But the story doesn't end there. You cannot imagine the joy I felt that afternoon as I rode the bus home with green vegetables for my beloved Judy and our children.

An interesting thought came to me from God as I rode home. He reminded me of something the brother of the Lord had written: "You have not because you ask not (James 4:2b)."

Not once during this time of fasting did I believe that I needed to ask my Heavenly Father to provide for me and my family. My mind was always on the fact that He knows how many hairs there are on my head; He knows all our needs. So I felt I did not have to plead with him to provide for us. He says that he loves us more than an earthly father loves his son. But then, I know my heart has been touched when my own sons have asked me for things.

So as I arrived at our home I was totally convinced that Judy and I now needed to actually ask God to provide. My love and I touched our foreheads together and all I said was, "God we are asking in Jesus' name." Oh! What a loving God we serve. Within 45 minutes, our telephone rang three times and the doorbell twice. Each time the phone rang, I literally ran to answer it; I knew my Lord was going to answer our prayer.

The third phone call was from a missionary who had allowed us to use his post office mailbox as our mailing address. He said he had two letters for me, and told me who had sent them. The letters came from two different friends who didn't know the Lord; we did not expect that they would send us money. I said, "Sydney I will pick those letters up from you tomorrow if I can."

When the doorbell rang the first time, I ran to the door only to find a young man who would often come, unannounced and uninvited, to our home at dinner time. I silently asked, "Lord, why did you have him come tonight? You know he eats more than most of the others who come uninvited." I was thinking about how fast those two sacks of green vegetables would be eaten.

Many Costa Ricans would come to our home to see what North Americans ate. They saw that we ate beans and rice, then rice and beans, then beans and rice. Meat was expensive and very tough. We learned to eat a fish from the market that was called whitefish. They called it that so no one would know they were eating shark. But our family enjoyed eating it and considered it a special treat.

There were nearly thirty different kinds of fruit that we could buy in the market. Our little family loved fruits with names like granadilla and mamon chinos. Once a year during Christmas time we could buy a large imported red apple for the equivalent of a dollar.

When the doorbell rang again, it was our next-door neighbor Marco. He was a very dear friend; I had witnessed to him as strongly as I have witnessed to anybody in my life. I had told him, tongue in cheek, that I was going to get a baseball bat and hit him between the eyes to knock some sense into his head so he would accept my Jesus as his Savior.

That night Marco said, "Charlie, do you have any money?" I didn't know why he was asking, and pride got ahold of me. I said, "Marco I don't have any money to loan you." He seemed insulted and said, "Charlie, I have never asked you for money! I'm asking if you have any money!" I said, "No."

He said, "Come on; we are going up to Los Helados Pops and change a bill so I can give you some money." He changed a one-hundred colon bill and gave me fifty colones. In the car, I told him that less than 45 minutes before he came to our door we had asked God to provide us with money, which we very much needed. I said, "Marco, you see, God has used you, a lost man to provide for my family." I was candid with him; I love him like a brother. There were tears in his eyes but he still was not willing to receive Christ.

The next morning, I picked up the two letters that had come to Sydney's mailbox. One of them stated that $667 had been deposited to our bank account in Texas. I was amazed to see that the deposit was made on the same day Judy had told me we were out of food.

Several years later, Marco and his lovely wife Pilar were in our home having dinner. In all that time, I had never thought to ask Marco what had caused him to come over and ask me if I had any money. But that night I asked him. He replied, "I had come home for lunch that day and saw James and Judy Anne playing in front of your home. I told them to go tell their mother that they were going to eat with Uncle Marco and Aunt Pilar. I knew that your family prayed before each meal so I asked Judy Anne to pray. In flawless Spanish, she prayed, 'God, provide some money so that my Daddy can eat.'"

Marco told me something else I had not known; the 100 colones that he split with me was the only money he had at that time. God had used the prayer of a little six-year-old girl to touch the heart of a man—who did not even know Christ—to provide food money for her father. Our God is truly amazing!

With the $667 and what Marco had given me, God provided for our needs. We were able to pay the $100 first month's rent for the second story space that for the next 31 years we would lovingly call our "Upper Room." It would have continued being used to this day as a center for evangelism if the building had not been torn down. In 2001 it was replaced with a modern three-story concrete building.

We were also able to purchase some lumber; and a missionary at the language Institute designed, and helped us build, fourteen benches. Forty-eight years later, my loving Lord allowed me to preach in one of our Costa Rican churches where these same wooden benches were still being used. They have my blood, sweat, and tears on them.

We put up a large sign in Spanish that hung from the outside wall of our second-story space. It read "Cristianos Compartiendo A Cristo." The English meaning was, "Christians Sharing Christ." Under that the Spanish for, "Matthew 7:7 knock, ask and seek."

The Upper Room Ministry

We did not know specifically how God wanted us to use this centrally located Upper Room. We began by renting a few evangelistic films and a projector; and we started showing Gospel films to the people who walked in front of our building, saw our sign, and came in.

Looking out a window of the upper room

Carlos Muñoz with early convert in the Upper Room

For the first few weeks we invited Christian laymen who worked in the marketplace area to come in during their lunch time and join with us in prayer. We asked God to show us how we could most effectively use the Upper Room for His glory.

In God's own timing, a friend in Texas sent us a well-worn Bell & Howell projector, which we put to good use. We had started on a shoestring; and every move we made was, to the best of our knowledge, in the very center of God's will for us at that time.

In 1969 there were fewer than 14,000 evangelicals in all of Costa Rica; God used the ministry of our Upper Room to lead 5,000 people to Christ in the first two years of its existence. Many years later, when I was preaching in a service in Costa Rica, I asked how many in attendance had received Christ in our Upper Room; I was amazed at the number of hands that were raised.

Tragedy and Sorrow

Throughout our lives as missionaries, God has used tragedy and sorrow to keep our hearts soft, and sensitive to the needs of others. Late one afternoon while her husband Ian was in a Bible Caravan in northern Costa Rica, Ann Taylor, a language-school student who was originally from New Zealand, got word to us. She was En route to the Children's Hospital with their 2½ year old son. The Taylors were dear friends of ours. Because of our proximity to the hospital I was able to arrive just after she and her child did. As I walked into the emergency room I saw Ann in a pink dress covered with blood. Beside her on a gurney was her little boy Alan wrapped in a white sheet. He had crawled up onto a shelf and pulled a heavy piece of marble off; it fell on him, killing him instantly.

Ann rushed into my arms and sobbingly said, "God gave him to us and now He has taken him from us."

Dr. Aulden Coble, Director of the Spanish Language Institute took Ann back to her rented apartment and I took the responsibility for little Alan. The normal procedure was for a hospital attendant to rent a taxi to deliver a dead child to the city morgue. I did not want this to happen; so I picked up the body of this precious little boy and carried him to our van. I was accompanied by the attendant. When we arrived at the morgue I carried the lifeless little body in to those who would be responsible for him until the funeral. I did this out of respect for little Alan and because of our love for his parents, Ann and Ian Taylor. I would have wanted someone to have shown the same respect if it were my child.

Saturday morning little Alan's funeral was held in the Spanish Language Institute auditorium. Ian and Ann were 8000 miles away from their nearest family in Australia and New Zealand. Ian stood up before the more than 250 language-school students, missionaries, and Costa Rican Christians and testified to God's grace being sufficient and to God's love being real. He and Ann then stood at the door and consoled each one of us as we left the auditorium. Our God is truly amazing. Judy and I invited them to meet us after church the next day for lunch. We then took them to visit Elizabeth Strachan, who many considered to be the matriarch of evangelical missionaries in Costa Rica. We and Elizabeth wanted to console the bereft parents; but as it turned out, we were all blessed by Ian and Ann.

Sitting in Doña Elizabeth's living room, Ian and Ann said, "Yesterday morning neither one of us felt that we could go to Alan's funeral. But, as we were kneeling beside our bed, God blessed us in such a way that we were able to attend his funeral, and to do the other things that we had felt would be impossible. Today we can say that we would not change anything that has happened in the last four days, if it would cause us to lose the relationship that we now have with our Lord." We knew that they truly valued their new relationship with the Lord more than having their son back.

To this day, I continue being blessed by knowing the reality that all things work together for good to those that love God and are called according to his purposes.

That Sunday evening Ian preached in my stead at the Church in Alajuela. It was one of his first sermons in Spanish. His message came from the first epistle to the Thessalonians where Paul wrote about the future resurrection. Ian stated, "My son is not dead. He is just asleep, and I will see him one day."

In the invitation that followed, a 16-year-old girl came forward to receive Christ. After the service that night, as we drove back to San Jose, we discussed the possibility that God may have used Alan's death to bring that teenage girl to Christ.

The tragedy and sorrow, and the lives touched, and the blessings of God that occurred during those four days were not in vain. Over the last 49 years, God has used them through my ministry to bring comfort and hope to countless others. The testimony of those four days has stood as evidence that God's grace is always sufficient. It brought glory to God and demonstrated that in everything, we should always give thanks.

Necessary Arrangements

Because Judy and I with our young family were not going to be in Lima, Peru, but were staying in Costa Rica, there were things we needed to do other than just find a house to rent.

You recall that in our last days at seminary, prior to going to missionary orientation in North Carolina, Judy and I packed our belongings into two wooden crates that were to be shipped to Lima once we completed language school in Costa Rica. The Missions Board had given us an allowance so we could purchase new appliances and other items to furnish our board-owned Peruvian home.

By short-wave radio, a Peruvian missionary had described the home where we would live in Miraflores, a posh suburb of Lima. They described the home's four bedrooms, living room and den, private office and study, and an apartment for visitors. This home was in an exclusive area of Lima and only one block from the American ambassador's home.

The things we had intended to use in Peru were still being stored in Fort Worth. The Missions Board was paying nearly $50 a month, at a discounted rate, in storage fees. We knew we could not afford to pay the readjusted storage fees. But we did hope that somehow we could keep our personal belongings. There was no way we could pay the cost (more than a dollar a pound) to have our things shipped to Costa Rica, not to mention the high customs fees once they arrived.

Remember, we had little more than $250 a month to live on. Only a few of our friends knew that we no longer received any support from the Foreign Missions Board. We had no known way of either bringing our possessions to Costa Rica or of paying to store them in Texas.

It quickly became apparent that I needed to go back to Texas and sell everything we owned, all that was stored in the two crates. When I asked if she was willing for me to sell everything, Judy replied, "God will take care of it." So, I left our little family in Costa Rica and flew back to Fort Worth prepared to sell everything we owned, including all our wedding gifts. Many of our wedding guests in 1961 had been quite wealthy. So those gifts alone included numerous complete sets of silver, crystal, and china.

The night I arrived in Fort Worth, I was allowed to stay in a missionary apartment at the seminary. Our beloved friend Dr. Cal Guy graciously had arranged that for me.

That night was one of the worst nights of my life. More than a mile I walked down James Avenue, sobbing. I was three thousand miles from the woman I loved, and my three sweet little children; I was preparing to sell everything we owned; I had no one to talk to or pray with; and no matter how hard I tried, I could not take my eyes off myself and look to my loving heavenly father. I felt like I had never been so alone in my life.

The next day at noon I was able to talk to my Judy through the Halo Missionary Net. This was a network of ham (short-wave) radio operators here in the United States that provided for missionaries a means of communicating with their loved ones.

You recall that I had asked Judy if she was willing to sell everything we owned and her reply had been "God will take care of it." Talking to her through ham radio I asked her one more time if she was willing for me to sell everything, and this time she said, "Yes." I broke into uncontrollable sobbing. I had wanted Judy to express her willingness to turn loose of everything we owned, for I had assumed that I was already willing.

At that moment, I realized that I had been considering what was inside of those large crates as an insurance policy. Should one of our children have a serious medical need, selling the contents would make it possible for me to get them to the Mayo Clinic. You remember that one of the reasons our friends had given for us to stay with the Foreign Missions Board was that if one of our children was to get sick the board would pay to have them flown back to "the Mayo Clinic."

That afternoon, after my conversation with Judy on the radio, I went up to the seminary, where I found my two dear friends, Dr. Cal Guy and Dr. L. Jack Gray. Both were missions professors. I could not control my emotions while sitting in Dr. Guy's office. I told them that never in my life had I felt so alone, and yet never in my life was I more sure that I was in the center of God's will.

Dr. Guy said, "Charles, could God be telling you to not resign from the Foreign Missions Board?" I answered him, by repeating what I had just said. Then, Dr. Gray said, "Charles, claim God's promise in Psalm 37:4, 'Delight thyself ... in the LORD; and he shall give thee the desires of thine heart.'" In the twinkling of an eye I had peace. At that moment, I recognized that I should be filled with joy because I was in the center of God's will, and all I had desired was His peace.

That was the day before I was to unpack our crates and sell everything we owned. That evening my sister Anne and her husband Chester returned to Fort Worth from a trip, and took me out to dinner. They graciously offered to pay $20 a month in storage fees so that we could retain our keepsakes.

I put our personal keepsakes into a small wooden crate. Everything else, including unused appliances, furniture, towels, and bedding, I sold to seminary students for less than 25 cents on the dollar. The warehouse company set the monthly charge for our keepsakes at $19.70, just under what Anne and Chester had agreed to pay. This was one of Gods special ways of showing us that He would bless us if we obeyed Him.

The men from the "Christians Sharing Christ" meetings we had held in the Asheville, North Carolina, City Auditorium somehow heard what I was doing; they called Doctor Guy and told him, "We want to pay to fly Charles over here to Asheville to meet with us." So, after I finalized the storage of our small box of belongings, I flew to North Carolina. Meeting with these dear brothers in Christ was a joyful reunion.

We met for lunch in the Upper Room, the third-floor dining room of the S&W cafeteria, the exact same place where we had met to plan the "Christians Sharing Christ" meetings at the City Auditorium. It was now early in 1969.

These dear brothers in Christ said, "We will form a nonprofit organization and we will send what money we receive down to Costa Rica to support you, Judy and the children." They continued by saying, "Between the seven of us, we promise to send you at least $250 a month." We had taken a step of faith in obeying God's leadership; He showed that He honored it by what these men did.

While I was in North Carolina, I traveled from Asheville to Montreat to see my mentor Dr. L. Nelson Bell. I mentioned that I was going to Pennsylvania next, to speak in a church in York that was considering supporting our ministry, and whose pastor was a friend from seminary.

Dr. Bell then called Art DeMoss and told him that I was going to be in Pennsylvania, and suggested that he arrange for me to speak at one of his events there. So when I arrived in Philadelphia I went out to Villanova on the northeast edge of the city. There I spoke to a meeting of the Christian Business Men's Committee (CBMC).

Art DeMoss was well known throughout the United States for his effort to motivate businessmen to let the light of Christ shine through their businesses. He owned a large insurance company and donated much of his wealth to large and small organizations that were making a difference for Christ in education, business, politics, and society as a whole. And personally, Art was a soul winner; according to his daughter Nancy, at the time of his death on September 1, 1979, he had through one-on-one witnessing led 35,000 people to Christ. With him as an example, I became more committed to one-on-one witnessing, myself.

For many years now, I have been trying to witness to every lost soul God puts in my path. As of this writing in 2019, God has used me to personally lead 4,057 people to Christ. It is my hope and prayer that God will use every reader of this book to lead as many souls as possible to Christ before His imminent return.

After returning to Costa Rica and my beloved family, I received evidence that those men in North Carolina were following through with the commitment they had made. I quote here from the first newsletter they sent out after forming the non-profit corporation.

Dear Friend,

Almost every day we meet new people. Some we remember, some we forget, some become a part of our lives and others never affect us. In the spring of 1968 a dynamic young man named Charles Moore began touching the lives of people here in the Asheville area. Some of us first got to know Charles when he did what appeared to be a very foolish thing. He spent his last $100 to reserve the Asheville City Auditorium, although at the time he was not certain what was to take place there. His strong feeling was that it should be a series of meetings carried out by Christian laymen. At the time, Charles knew only a handful of people in Asheville, but he began sharing with us what the Lord had led him to do.

His faith and enthusiasm were contagious and soon we were involved and excited over the possibilities. As we met and prayed, we chose the name "Christians Sharing Christ" and as the days passed the Holy Spirit seemed to be taking a hand in all the preparations. A few weeks later hundreds of people were blessed by three joyful days of Christian witnessing in the City Auditorium.

During the weeks of planning, we had gotten better acquainted with Charles Moore. We learned that he had been a wealthy young businessman in Texas, but had given up all his inheritance to answer God's call to the mission field. At this time Charles was living at nearby Ridgecrest with his young family, completing a phase of his missionary training before going to Costa Rica.

In this brief two month period, Charles had spoken more than 70 times. Thousands of people in the Asheville area heard him preach and almost 200 of them had made decisions for Christ. But now it was time for Charles and his family to leave. He was to attend Language School in Costa Rica for a year, then to go on to Peru as a business manager for other missionaries.

Through letters and tapes, Charles kept us informed of his activities in Costa Rica. Being a native Texan, he had grown up speaking Spanish as well as English, so he was immediately able to begin preaching the Gospel to the local people and to begin sharing with the local ministers. Charles formed prayer groups, study groups, witnessed in the marketplace, held evangelistic services, and has seen hundreds of Costa Ricans make their decisions for Christ.

Charles came back to Asheville in April of 1969, one year after we had first met him, to tell us of his experiences and of a decision he had made. The Lord had provided so many opportunities for him in Costa Rica that he felt, without question, that his ministry was to be in that country.

However, changing his plans and not going to Peru as a business manager meant that Charles was cutting off his support from the Foreign Mission Board. The Board offered him two alternatives. Either he could go on to Peru, or he could go back to the seminary for 2½ years.

Charles saw the risk and knew there would be problems, but he also knew that he must preach the Gospel in Costa Rica! This was a big step in faith; to leave the Foreign Mission Board, with its security, and become an independent evangelist in a foreign country, with no means of support, and with a wife, two children, and now a new baby.

We sent Charles and his family the limited financial support that our small group could provide, and they managed to get by. Charles has always asked more for our prayers than for our money. His hopes for a growing ministry in Costa Rica are very much alive, and the Lord has sent him a teammate.

A brilliant young university student named Carlos Muñoz has been led to join Charles. Carlos had been converted 4 years earlier; he is now 27 years old and married. Those two young men could see the unlimited possibilities of witnessing and ministering to thousands of people, thus encouraging the pastors and strengthening the churches.

Charles, his wife Judy, and their three children have material needs which are barely being met; now Carlos and his wife Martha, who is expecting a baby in November, have joined them. These young families need financial help, as well as prayer support, to continue this ministry in Costa Rica.

In Asheville, our small group, praying for guidance, formed a non-profit corporation with the name "Christians Sharing Christ." We believed that doing this would enable us to channel more support to Charles and Carlos. Any contributions made to this corporation would be tax-deductible. We would have no employees, no office and almost no expenses. At this time, money contributed would be forwarded to Charles Moore, and we have asked Charles to acknowledge each gift so their donor would know he had received it.

Our immediate goal is to provide at least minimum financial support for these two young families, who have dedicated themselves to serving the Lord. Their minimum needs total approximately $500 per month, and we have only one-half of this amount pledged at this time. We are praying that there will be others who will feel led to support them, and will have the confidence to send this support through us.

We hope to send you a newsletter each month with information about Charles Moore, Carlos Muñoz, their families and their ministry.

Frank H. Dorato   Leonard Clayton   Wesley Grant, Sr.

Bert Starnes   Don E. Taylor   William S. Harrison, Jr.

[Original letter included the signatures of these men]

As evidenced by this newsletter, what began in February of 1968 in the Asheville city auditorium and was called "Christians Sharing Christ" was the nucleus of the formation of a nonprofit organization a year later. We never know how God will use and bless what we do when our sole purpose is to glorify His Son.

Chapter VIII
Continuing in Costa Rica

And the things that thou hast heard of me among many witnesses, the same commit thou to faithful men, who shall be able to teach others also.
—2 Timothy 2:2 KJV

We had learned early on that when God called us to do something in His service, He also provided the necessary resources for us to accomplish that work. So we continued to seek His guidance on our use of the Upper Room in the market place of San Jose, knowing that He would supply all our needs.

In the first two years, we saw more than 5,000 professions of faith despite the fact that our invitations were stronger than any other invitation likely to be heard in the United States or Costa Rica. We would tell the people that if they wanted to accept Christ, they should get up out of their seat and come to the front so that we could counsel with them, to make sure they knew what they were doing. We made it difficult because we didn't want anyone to have a false assurance of salvation.

Until the work of Christians Sharing Christ had begun in Costa Rica, there were fewer than 14,000 evangelicals in the entire country; so 5,000 new converts in two years was a truly significant number. It was God who had begun that work through us. He had anointed the market-place ministry right from the beginning.

That was the work He wanted us to do, reaching out to the people who were "down-and-out." We were not focusing on the wealthy people who could financially support a big beautiful church building.

God had given me a burden to reach the unclean and the unlovable in the marketplaces of the world, and He let me experience some of the adversities of that ministry. He allowed me to be pelted with tomatoes, to be verbally and physically assaulted by angry prostitutes, to have my life threatened, to be arrested and thrown in jail for preaching the gospel, and to see Judy and our children have much less than most Americans had. That our God would consider me worthy to suffer for Him, I felt honored and joyful, as did Paul, of whom Jesus had said, "He shall suffer for my name's sake." (Acts 9:16)

The suffering that all of my family went through was not because of vanity or pride on our part, but because we were obedient to our heavenly Father. Recently, Judy reminded me that she and our children never felt that they were suffering; they too were glad to be in the center of God's will.

We continued to see hundreds saved each month; and we were trying to get them into churches so they could grow in grace and knowledge. It is natural and good for a person who has accepted Christ to grow; however, if they do not have the written Word of God, spiritual growth is extremely difficult. Because of this, we started a Bible correspondence course; and for a lengthy period of time, we had more than 800 people in more than a dozen countries enrolled in that course.

God moved in mysterious ways to insure that the work of Christians Sharing Christ continued. We were on a ham radio sharing victories we were seeing in our Upper Room when an American living in Costa Rica broke in and offered to take Judy and me out to dinner; his name was John Livermore. He saw what God was doing through our ministry; so he offered to pay the rent on the Upper Room.

We were extremely grateful to God for this unexpected provision. John faithfully continued making those monthly payments for more than seven years. From that dinner meeting, John eventually began serving on the board of Christians Sharing Christ (CSC); he served sacrificially in that capacity for many years.

One day I stood near the entrance to the Upper Room with a small hand-held counter, tracking the number of people who passed by on foot. I calculated that more than 18,000 people walked in front of that building in an eight hour period.

Within a block and a half of our building, there were 113 houses of prostitution. More than a hundred of the licensed prostitutes in those brothels were girls between the ages of eight and twelve. Every month they were required to have a medical examination at a government clinic. Only rarely would we see these small girls, but we knew they were inside of the buildings that surrounded our Upper Room. The number of prostitutes and brothels was significantly diminished during the time we were ministering in this red-light district of San Jose.

School of Discipleship

Our heavenly Father gave me the joy and privilege of personally mentoring 27 young men in our school of discipleship. Each of these went on to become a preacher and teacher of God's Word, sharing the Lord Jesus Christ with lost souls near and far. Most of these men are still active in several different countries.

Each new CSC team member had to spend nights sleeping on one of our benches, using a newspaper to keep warm; only after six weeks could they sleep in the bunk room with the veterans. Unlike so many others who say they feel called of God, these young men evidenced their call by the price they paid to follow Jesus.

They were trained in groups of six or seven men at a time. These teams were made up of young men from Chile, Peru, Bolivia, Venezuela, and Nicaragua, as well as Costa Rica; many of them had been intercepted by the Lord as they were traveling north to settle in the USA. Upon receiving Christ in the Upper Room, they stayed, were discipled, and became missionaries.

With our first Discipleship Team in the Upper Room

Each highly disciplined and rigorous training period lasted all day every day for seven weeks. From 7 to 11 in the morning, Monday through Friday, I taught them homiletics, ecclesiology and eschatology; and I required them to memorize chapters of the Bible. Judy would have lunch ready at exactly 11 A.M. and we would quickly eat, during which time I taught them dining etiquette. Then, promptly at 11:30 we would get in our Volkswagen van and rush to the Upper Room for the noon service.

One of our first team members was Uriel Hernandez. He served faithfully for many years, for a number of which he led our jungle ministry, as described in the next chapter.

Uriel Hernandez, sharing Christ with two ticos

Each day, each man had a different job. One or two would be out on the street inviting people in; one would get the film and projector ready; one would be preparing to preach; two would be in the small bunk room praying for the service; and two would serve as counselors for those who would accept the Lord in the service.

On Sundays, we had up to seven services beginning at 4 pm; the last service began around 9 or 9:30 at night. There were nights when we would have people getting saved without even showing them a film. When more people would crowd in, another preacher would jump up and preach, and we would have another invitation. This was how God used me to disciple each team.

Coincidences ordained of God

Although we were "independent missionaries" we kept in touch with students and faculty of the Spanish Language Institute in Costa Rica. Thus developed some God-ordained relationships that were very beneficial to the work God had given us to do. The student body invited Dr. Gray Allison to visit the school and for one week be their spiritual emphasis speaker.

Dr. Allison was a missions professor at a seminary in New Orleans. When he graciously accepted the student body's invitation, two of the students asked me to drive them out to the airport to pick him up. Soon, he and I became very close friends. Often, after his morning session in the chapel, he and I would walk at a fast pace for more than a mile to reach the post office, where he would mail postcards to his friends and supporters in the United States.

On one of those walks Gray told me that he wanted to open a seminary that would be committed to teaching the inerrancy of God's word. This was an exciting idea for me and I told him that I wanted to be the first one to attend the new seminary. Gray had a friend who practiced medicine in Columbia, Louisiana—a Dr. Wren Causey—whom Gray invited to visit Costa Rica. Shortly after arriving in San Jose, Wren and his wife Edith visited our home. They soon became our good friends. "Doc" Causey later joined the boards of "Christians Sharing Christ" and Mid-America Baptist Theological Seminary, established by Gray Allison.

While Doc was in Costa Rica he gave each member of our family a physical examination. He found that our five-year-old son James needed surgery. Doc returned to the states and, unbeknownst to us, began speaking favorably of us and our work. He then invited me to bring James to his clinic in Louisiana; he said he would personally arrange for the surgery and pay for the needed care.

When James and I flew to Louisiana, we left Judy, Judy Anne, and little Cal in Costa Rica. The surgery was successful, but James needed to recuperate in a hospital bed for five days. Doc arranged for me to spend part of that time preaching in several churches. A revival broke out in one of those churches; from then on, I had standing invitations to preach anytime I was in central or northern Louisiana.

Trials and blessings

In a typical day in Costa Rica, I would leave our home at about 8 in the morning, and would not return until around 9 at night. I often felt like I had a tiger by the tail. The more we preached in the upper room, the more people accepted the Lord; and then, the more we needed to disciple them and help them grow in God's grace. Living this life placed a great deal of physical stress on our bodies. Several times Judy had to place several blankets on top of me and then lie on top of the blankets to try to stop my shaking from nervous exhaustion.

Before getting into our old VW van to drive home, I would pour rubbing alcohol all over my arms, hands, face and neck and then on the steering wheel, because during a normal day I would hug men with open running sores, with filthy clothes, and whose hands had not been washed in days.

Many of those that we ministered to daily had untreated serious diseases that were found throughout Central America in those years. Most of those diseases have now been eradicated in those countries where we minister. Arriving home, I would change into clean clothes in our washroom before I would even approach my family.

I am reminded that when I was seventeen years old I had to change my clothes in the washroom because of the filth from picking up garbage all day. God prepared me years before to do the same thing to protect my family. But this time, it was after working in His mission field all day.

I knew that I could easily take any of the prevalent diseases home to my wife and children. But none of our children, nor Judy or I, ever contracted any of the diseases that were carried by many who would know God's love through me. We knew that God loved us; He always had, and He always would.

This was an entirely different life from the life we had lived while in the business world in El Paso. At home in Costa Rica, Judy washed all of our vegetables in iodine water to help us avoid developing illnesses from amoebas or other parasites. The native Costa Ricans had long since developed an immunity to those health hazards.

Our work was continuing to be blessed, our team was receiving their monthly stipend, and everything was moving along smoothly. But on a Saturday morning, James and Cal were not looking or feeling well. I took them to the doctor and found that one already had pneumonia and the other was developing the symptoms. The doctor gave them shots of gamma globulin and wrote a prescription for a powerful antibiotic. But after paying the doctor I didn't have the money to buy the antibiotic.

At the pharmacy I learned that I would need 127 colones (about $15). While driving home with my two sick sons, I looked to my loving Lord and told Him that He would have to do something. After putting the boys to bed, Judy and I tried to figure out God's will for this situation. We bowed our heads and prayed.

My first thought was, "I can write a check on our bank account in the states and, by the time the check clears, surely there will be money to cover it." Here I was, thinking of writing a bad check to save my sons. I knew that was not God's will. Then I thought, "I will make a collect call to someone in the states and ask them to help us." Again, I knew this was not God's will. I then thought I could contact one of my Costa Rican sons in the Lord and ask for a loan. I then remembered Romans 13:8, "Owe no man anything, but to love one another."

When we raised our heads, our experience from when we rented the Upper Room came to my mind. So I said, "Judy, I guess I will go to the post office and check our mail." I started out the front door to get into our VW van. The odometer had not worked for many years. But when we had purchased the vehicle, the reading was 171,000 kilometers.

Just as I was getting into the van, Gordon Bennett, an Australian Plymouth Brethren missionary, drove up. I had not seen Gordon in several months and he had never given us any money.

He stepped out of his car and approached me with his hand held out, as if to give me something. Since Gordon had never helped us financially, I was surprised to see him giving me money. He said in his Aussie brogue, "Charles, the Lord has exercised me to give you this money." He handed me 200 colones ($28).

I said, "Gordon, you know, I just asked God to provide 127 colones for antibiotics for my two sons. Why, Gordon, did you bring this money to me?" His reply was, "I am on my way home from the Caballo Blanco leather factory, where I have just purchased a 187-colon leather footstool, and God convicted me that it was a poor stewardship of His money. I stopped at the stop sign up the street, and God reminded me of you. So I turned and came half a block and there you were, coming out your door."

Together we rejoiced in our Father's love for each of us and for my sons. Needless to say, I purchased the antibiotics; and today those two boys are 6'6" and 6'4" and are men who love the Lord. God says His love for me is greater than any earthly father's love for his son; He proved it to me that day. And He has continued over the many, many years to prove it again and again. These were some of the many ways that God blessed the formation of the ministry of Christians Sharing Christ.

Over the years, we had numerous unexpected visits from people we would later call visiting angels. One afternoon, the chaplain of the Clinica Biblica called and asked if a missionary family could stay with us. They were driving from the United States to Argentina, and somewhere in Nicaragua the father had come down with spinal meningitis. By the time they got to San Jose, he was seriously ill and in need of hospitalization.

His wife and their children stayed with us for three days until I was able to arrange with LACSA Airlines for him to be flown on a cot to Miami for medical care. Their teenage son, Steve Green, played the guitar and sang coritos (choruses) for our children. Today that boy is a grandfather and is known as one of the most accomplished Christian singers of our time.

There were not many Americans in Costa Rica in the late 1960s; so we got to know most of them who called the country their home. Among them were businessmen and land speculators, as well as American embassy personnel and of course, missionaries.

Several times I brought home American hippie types that I had picked up on the highway. Some were Christians; others we were able to lead to Christ. Some slept on our wooden bench, which served as our living room sofa.

The enemy shows his hatred

In 1970, the work was going extremely well and God was blessing everything we did. We were seeing many souls saved and many young men growing in the Lord as they learned to share the Gospel with others.

But this seemed to have got the enemy all riled up. By the end of summer, we experienced some very serious opposition from the devil. For twelve days in a row, I counted at least twelve different avenues of assault—a new one beginning each day—upon myself, my family, and our ministry. Without going into detail, I have to say that I was becoming very discouraged; I felt drained of both physical and spiritual energy, almost to the point of giving up.

Then I came across a small book in my library that was truly a Godsend. As I was reading it, I felt that it had been written especially for me and my current circumstances. God used that book and its explanation of Bible truths to pull me out of my "slough of despond" and set me on the path I needed to take at that time, a path which included a return to my roots. Looking back I can see how God is always there in providing exactly what we need when we need it. So when you go through your darkest hours and deepest anguish, know that He is just a teardrop away, willing and able to meet your every need. Later that year we would make that needed trip, leaving in place our strong Upper Room team. But we did not have the money to drive or fly. So I sold our 1961 VW van and got enough to buy airplane tickets.

A Hiatus in Texas

Judy was then "heavy with child" as our third son was due in November. We had a stopover in Mexico City where we had to change planes. We then flew on to El Paso. We spent some time with my stepmother and then rode a bus to Odessa to see Judy's folks. From there we went by bus to San Angelo and then on to Fort Worth.

Judy, Judy Anne, Charles IV,
James, Cal, Charles V

114

When our youngest child was born on November 29, we named him Charles Beatty Moore V; he recently told me he's proud to be Charles V.

While in Texas, I was invited to preach and was able to gain some monetary support from Christians for our work in Central America. We were also provided with another Volkswagen van, a blue one. When our baby boy was nine months old we all piled into that VW van. We took along adequate baby supplies for the long journey to Costa Rica. This was the trip mentioned in Chapter Four (page 40). Judy and the children were ready and eager to make that trip, and I was refreshed and ready to return to the front line of evangelism. God had "restored our souls" as David had expressed it in the 23rd Psalm.

Preaching the Blood of Christ

In 1971, the Lord gave me the opportunity of preaching a series of meetings in a church in southern Costa Rica. We had to drive over Sierra de la Muerte (Mountain of Death), the highest mountain in Costa Rica. Though often shrouded in clouds, this road afforded us that day a grand view of the Atlantic and Pacific Oceans at the same time.

Soon after preaching the first two sermons, I heard that two of the deacons were living in adultery. Although their wives were aware of the situation, and the church knew about it, in each of my meetings with these two deacons they both denied it. While I was dealing with this situation in southern Costa Rica—as I would later learn—our work in San Jose was undergoing another assault by the devil. The team member who had been left in charge of the upper room later confessed that he had been visiting houses of prostitution.

Each day in the south, I preached a message in the morning and a message in the evening. Almost from the beginning, God burdened me to preach a message on the blood of Christ. My afternoons were spent in the study of the Word; and the more I learned about the blood the more I recognized its significance. But I felt that I was incapable of doing justice to such a vital subject.

The longer I avoided preaching on the blood of Christ, the weaker I became physically. The more I counseled the two deacons, and the more I preached on other subjects, the more evident became my lack of spiritual power.

On the third day I became so physically weak I spent most of my time on the cot in the motel studying the Word and trying to understand all aspects of the blood. By Sunday afternoon, many people had been saved; but in the congregation there remained much unconfessed sin, including that of the two adulterous deacons.

While lying on the hotel cot that last afternoon, I felt that I was physically too weak to go to the evening service, much less preach a sermon. Almost all of my time with the Lord centered on the blood; but I kept making excuses to Him and to myself, claiming to be unworthy or unable to preach about such an important part of the Scriptures. That last Sunday evening I did go to the church service, and I sat on the front pew as was my custom; but I hoped that they would keep singing and not turn it over to me to preach. But soon, I was called to the pulpit.

Still in disobedience to the Lord, I began preaching a message from God's Word; and within a very short time I recognized that I had no power. So I stopped and prayed out loud. I changed my message to another verse and again almost immediately recognized that my message did not have the anointing of the Holy Spirit.

I stopped again and this time said, "I do not know what is going on in this service tonight but let's pray the blood of Jesus over it." Immediately I recognized that my disobedience to the will of God was the reason that there was no anointing.

Since I had studied for hours in both the Old and New Testaments about the value and importance and significance of the blood, I was able to preach an anointed 40-minute message on the blood of Christ. That night 38 people gave their lives to Christ. And, most significantly, each of the adulterous deacons came forward and openly confessed and repented of their sins before the whole church. Because of my physical weakness I had returned to sit on the front bench; all I could do was watch as God performed miracle after miracle in the lives of many grateful souls that night.

The invitation concluded after 11 P.M. The auditorium emptied out while I still sat alone on the front bench. Then a man came down to the front and sat down beside me. He said, "I want to talk to you." His breath, some five hours after the beginning of the service, still smelled of alcohol. I asked him, "Did you accept the Lord tonight?" He said, "No," then told me that he had been in our Upper Room in San Jose on several occasions.

So I asked him, "Did you accept the Lord in the upper room?" Again he said, "No." Then I said, "I am not going to waste my time with you. You can get on your knees right here and ask Christ to come into your life or you can leave." He knelt beside me and asked God for forgiveness, and asked to receive His son Jesus Christ. With my arm around his shoulders, we walked out the front door. There was a large crowd waiting to say goodbye, for we were leaving early the next morning. With evident happiness, I said to them, "I want to introduce you to a new brother in Christ."

One of the deacons said, "Don Carlos, did you see us put him on the very back row? And then one of us was always standing behind him during the entire service?" I said that I had not seen that. They said that he came from a Machetero family. (The Macheteros were paid assassins.) This brand-new baby in Christ said, "Yes, it is true; but all of that has changed tonight."

My reluctance to obey what God had called me to do—preach on the blood—could have had far-reaching negative results. But by God's grace I obeyed the Lord that last night, and that weeklong crusade is still known as the greatest revival in that area. For each service, overflow crowds outside were looking and listening through the back door and all the windows. From this experience I was reminded of two very important things I had learned years earlier: listen for the still quiet voice of the Holy Spirit; and obey what He leads you to do.

That Monday morning, we loaded up our Volkswagen van and headed back to San Jose. At the summit of Sierra de la Muerte my eardrum ruptured from the changing air pressure; without knowing it, I had developed an ear infection. It had to be treated with very painful injections in the glutes, which my Judy graciously administered after practicing on an orange.

That infection may have been the physical reason why my body had become weaker with each passing day.

After the final night of that revival, whenever the former Machetero was in San Jose he would come by our Upper Room. That was once or twice a month. He would excitedly share how God was blessing him and was using him to glorify Jesus. Everything he would tell me was later validated by my contacts in his church over the mountains.

Several years ago, I was blessed to preach in that church again and there was only one man alive who could remember what had happened back in 1971, when there were less than 500 believers in all of that vast area down to the border of Panama.

Yolanda

Upon returning to San Jose, I had to deal with our team member who had been visiting prostitutes near the Upper Room while we were away. One evening after that, as I began the invitation in our Upper Room evangelistic service, an 18-year-old prostitute jumped up and ran out and down the stairs. She did this several nights in a row until I had one of our team members stop her and take her into our office, where I could talk with her after the service.

Yolanda had believed that God could not forgive her for the life she was living. But that night she joyfully prayed with me to accept the Lord, and she became a new person. The next night she returned to our Upper Room and showed me the New Testament that I had given her the night before. She had read 134 pages of her New Testament and had several questions for me.

Several nights later, a young Nicaraguan came forward in our invitation to accept Christ as his Savior. Martin had fled his country to keep from being arrested after killing a man at a fiesta. During that time families with money or connections could arrange for charges to be dropped. He had come to Costa Rica to wait until his parents could make those arrangements.

Yolanda and Martin met and fell in love in my noon Bible study; they planned to marry after he came back from fixing his situation in Managua. Before leaving for that city, Martin purchased several gifts for Yolanda. One was a small portable radio, such as few in our area had.

Several weeks passed, during which time we found work for Yolanda in a small store in Heredia, a city about 30 minutes from San Jose. Every day one of our team members would catch the bus in front of the store where Yolanda worked, so we could verify her whereabouts.

Nearly a month later Martin returned and came in to the Upper Room to see me. He had been back from Nicaragua only a few hours and had heard from his past acquaintances in the market that Yolanda was again in prostitution. He would not believe me when I told him where Yolanda was living and where she was working. He chose to accept the word of others. That same afternoon he left San Jose and returned to his home in Nicaragua.

Two days later Yolanda came in to town and came up to the Upper Room. She was brokenhearted to hear that Martin had not waited to hear the truth from her. Nothing I said removed her pain and brokenness. I wanted so badly for Judy to have been there to put her arms around her and console her. Tearfully she walked out of the Upper Room leaving me with a heavy heart.

Now, more than forty-five years have passed and I have never again seen Yolanda. But this one thing I know: I will see my daughter in the Lord again, in glory.

A Man Called Toyota

The story I am about to relate spans a period of some two years. On December 23 of 1969 two young men came up the stairs to our Upper Room shortly after they had been released from prison. That night at our evangelistic meeting, one of them came forward to accept Christ. He was one of several who accepted the Lord that night and it just happened that I was to counsel him.

He said, "Two days ago, I was released from the penitentiary where I have been for the last eight years. I was sentenced when I was 16 years old for killing a man who called my mother a bad name. Tonight, my friend and I were going to break into a businessman's house to rob him and if necessary kill him to keep from being caught and returned to prison." His nickname was Toyota; I never knew his birth name. We let him sleep on our wooden benches where our newest team members slept.

Toyota's conversion was genuine and his deep love for his Savior was evident to all. He became a solid member of our team and was always there to help. I had the privilege of baptizing Toyota in a very cold river with eleven others who had recently come to know the Lord in our Upper Room.

On one occasion, a mentally handicapped boy who had always been a troublemaker made Toyota angry; they decided to settle their argument in the street in front of our Upper Room.

That afternoon when I came back up the stairs he met me and told me what he had done. He said, "I have hurt the testimony of the Upper Room and I know I must leave." In the short time I had known him I had learned to love this young man, and it was hard for me to agree with what he knew he had to do.

More than two years passed before I would see or hear from him again. Then one morning he came running up the stairs and, after giving me a big hug, he told me that he had been living in Limon, a Costa Rican port city on the Atlantic coast. He had graduated from the Four Square Gospel Bible School and was now pastoring three churches and four preaching points in northern Costa Rica, near the border of Nicaragua.

He had come to our Upper Room to invite Carlos Muñoz and myself to stand up for him as his groomsmen in his wedding to the daughter of the pastor of a large church of his denomination. Carlos and I gladly agreed. The marriage ceremony was a special blessing for those of us from the Upper Room.

The morning after the wedding, Javier (my first son in the Lord in Latin America) agreed to drive the newlyweds, with what little they owned, up to Los Chiles where Toyota had 2 horses and a mule. He and his bride would then ride horseback several hours to their home in the vicinity of the churches that he pastored.

Over the years, on all of my radio and television appearances in Costa Rica, I mentioned Toyota; I was hoping that he, or someone who knew him, would call in. But it is possible that he has used his real name all these years and no one knows his nickname. Even if I do not see Toyota again in this lifetime, I will see him in glory, and hear directly from him how God used him as a preacher of God's word.

The Bridge People

On the edge of downtown San Jose there was a "colony" of homeless people, including 87 pre-teen children. They lived under one end of a two-lane bridge that crossed a small creek. Many were children of prostitutes and did not attend school. The older children spent their days searching for food and caring for their younger siblings. I first learned of this small colony under the bridge when I took our beat-up old Volkswagen van to a mechanic whose shop was about a hundred feet from the bridge.

When I arrived at the shop, "El Ruso" (the Russian owner) told me what had happened a few minutes earlier. He said he had heard a commotion and rushed to the bridge to see what it was about. There he found that a two-year old boy had been run over by a bus. The little boy's sister was on her hands and knees banging her head on the concrete. It had been her responsibility to care for her little brother. El Ruso said, "I picked her up and tried to console her."

When I heard this I walked down under the bridge to see if there was anything I could do. That was the beginning of a long relationship with those who lived there. Their small hovels were mostly made of cardboard; by being under the bridge they avoided most of the heavy rains that began almost every day at noon.

My immediate thought was "What can I do to help these people?" I knew that their greatest need was to know Jesus Christ as their Savior. But, I knew as well that in some way I should be able to help them with their physical needs. So one thing we did was to purchase quantities of individually packaged meals of rice and black beans; I had our team distribute the packages to each family.

Our team members began a weekly ministry providing food to the "bridge people." The first week, they also distributed tracts and copies of the Gospel of John; they began witnessing first to the adults and later to the children.

That Christmas Judy and I received a check for a hundred dollars from Doc Causey of Columbia, Louisiana, who by then was on the board of Christians Sharing Christ. His gift was supposed to be used by our family to have a merry Christmas. I sent two of our team members under the bridge to write down the names and ages of all 87 children 12 years and under.

Then with the money from Doc Causey, our family went to the largest department store in Costa Rica to buy a present for each of the children on the list. What we were doing caught the attention of the department store owner and she excitedly became involved in helping us to choose the right presents.

121

When we ran out of money she discounted the total cost so we could purchase the last few toys. Then we realized that we had not taken into consideration Christmas wrapping paper. But with a happy spirit, she provided us with more than enough paper to wrap each of the presents. Realizing it would be a major job to wrap each present, we invited one team member from Bolivia and one from Chile who were living in our Upper Room to help with this enjoyable task. These two young men had to be kept on task because they would stop and play with some of the toys they had never seen before.

On Christmas morning our family loaded up all the toys and we excitedly drove to the bridge. All four of our children went down under the bridge and handed out the toys to each child whose name was on a package. To this day, our entire family believes that was our most blessed Christmas.

Through our team's effort several of the bridge people accepted the Lord and became members of the first church that we began in Costa Rica; it was just six blocks from that bridge.

Two years later one of the little girls still had her doll in the original box and it was as good as new. Even though more than 45 years have passed, I wish I could find some of those children, who are now adults, to see how they are. We will never forget the experiences we had with those people under the bridge.

Back in the city

One night I led a young black man to the Lord; he was from the Atlantic coast. His newfound joy in Christ was visible. A few weeks after returning to the Atlantic coast, he came back to San Jose. He entered the Upper Room carrying a big paper sack containing a gift for me. Lo and behold, he pulled out a 4-foot rock-boa constrictor. There was no way I could reject that gift from my son in the Lord.

I hoped that Judy would let me take it home so our children could become acquainted with one of the rare animals of the country where they lived. Judy said, "I will not have that snake in our house." So we kept it in the Upper Room for several weeks, until I found an MK (a missionary's kid) who wanted our boa.

Several times before I gave it away, I would take my rock boa with me when I went to the post office. I put the boa in my shirt, leaving only its head sticking out of the front of my shirt. Then I would walk six blocks to the post office and six blocks back, holding the snake's head out in front of me. This was great fun for me as I would watch the expressions on the faces of people I met. Many looked in surprise at a North American holding a snake that was also looking at them. It would have been worth filming if we had owned a camera.

There were many opportunities for our children to become familiar with the animals of Costa Rica; but one Saturday afternoon the experience was surreal for our three sons. They were with me as I was driving down the main street of San Pedro, a suburb of San Jose. We all were surprised to see a large anteater in the middle of this busy street. We stopped to rescue it.

Between the four of us, we managed to get this very heavy animal into our VW van. It was six feet long from the tip of its tail to the tip of its nose. It happened that day that we had removed the middle seat from the van. So we had the needed room to take the anteater home. We gave it water and tried to feed it; but it would not eat anything we offered it. I knew a North American in Costa Rica who owned an animal shelter; so I called him. He told me that it was almost impossible to keep an anteater in captivity because it eats only live insects. This friend said he would take the responsibility of releasing this large animal into the wild. How in the world did that animal get to the middle of a very busy street? And how many boys under ten years old ever helped save an anteater?

Late one Sunday night, Elizabeth Strachan, one of God's true earthly saints, called to ask a favor. She started by saying, "You are the only missionary I knew would agree to do what I'm going to ask." She then described a man who had come to her front door for help. Her description proved to be very accurate when I went over to pick up this extremely sick man. He was about fifty years old and could hardly walk. He was also having difficulty breathing. He was barefooted and was wearing only a shirt and khaki shorts, both with holes in them. I promised Elizabeth that I would make sure that he was treated properly at the public hospital.

At the hospital I located a wheelchair and wheeled him into the emergency room. The attendant said, "Leave him there," pointing to a space against the wall, "and we will take care of him when we can." I told the attendant that I was going to stay with the man until he was seen by a doctor. A short time later he was rolled in to be seen by a doctor, who also told me to leave him with them and they would take care of him. By this time, I knew they did not plan on taking care of him. So I told the doctor that I would return at daylight to check on him, and that I expected him to be placed in a bed and taken care of.

The next morning, he was still alive but passed away that afternoon. He was only semi-coherent while I was with him. I had no opportunity to lead him to Christ; but I know that he and those at the hospital knew that someone loved him, even if it was just a North American.

Many times, people would come up the stairs to our Upper Room and pretend that they were accepting the Lord, just so they could find something to steal from us. For several days one young man hung around our Upper Room for that purpose; when we recognized what he was up to, I told him to leave and not to come back until he was ready to genuinely receive Christ. Periodically I would see him around the market area and he was always up to no good.

One afternoon I was walking down a sidewalk that was about four feet wide; I could see in front of me this young man and two of his friends blocking the way. When he saw me he jumped up, and when I got close to him he said, "I am going to kill you." My reaction was to throw my arms open wide and tell him to have at it, not the reaction that he wanted his friends to see. I pushed by him and continued on my way.

Several years later I and a dear friend, Pastor Ron Dunn, went into the main penitentiary to preach. When we entered the big room, I looked across and saw this same young man. When he saw me he came towards me with a big smile on his face.

For a moment, I actually thought he was going to try to kill me. Before I could take a second thought he said, almost shouting, "Hi, Don Carlos! I have accepted the Lord." Everything about him was different and it was easy to see that it was the presence of Christ in his life.

Preaching wherever God leads

When our team had proven worthy and capable of carrying on the work at the Costa Rican Upper Room, and continuing our evangelistic ministry in the middle of that country's capital city, I began looking to another country where we could do the same thing we had done in San Jose.

Meanwhile, I received an invitation to fly to Little Rock to attend the inaugural Founders' Day ceremonies—which preceded the opening of the first classes—at Dr. Gray Allison's Mid-America Baptist Seminary. The keynote speaker that morning was Dr. R. G. Lee, who was well known for his sermon, "Pay Day Someday."

The pastor of Immanuel Baptist Church in Little Rock had been scheduled to give the afternoon keynote sermon. But health problems in his family required him to cancel. So at lunchtime, Dr. Gray Allison requested that I give the afternoon sermon. Dr. Allison, the founder and first president of the seminary, preached the evening message.

That seminary is now located in Memphis, Tennessee. Each year it graduates a large number of students who strongly believe in the inerrancy of Scripture.

One of the men I "happened" to meet at that Founders' Day service offered to drive me to Doc Causey's home in Columbia, Louisiana. Our meeting was clearly ordained of God. His name was H. E. Slaughter; his friends called him Gene. He was president of the Gideons International. We became good friends and later he became the president of "CSC" and served in that capacity until his death many years later. I took to calling him Uncle Gene. He and I had strong kindred spirits; we both were committed to winning the lost to Christ and were always looking for an opportunity to witness to someone.

A few months after the Founders' Day ceremony, I was invited to speak again at Mid-America Baptist Theological Seminary. I was scheduled to fly from San Jose, Costa Rica, to New Orleans and then on to Little Rock where I was expected to speak at the Seminary the next day. The trip to the United States should have taken only seven hours; in the Providence of God it took more than sixteen.

My late arrival kept me from preaching at the seminary that day, so I found myself sitting in a hotel lobby watching a Billy Graham Crusade on television. A bellboy was standing behind me watching the crusade. As Dr. Graham gave the invitation, he said, "You may be watching this in a hotel lobby...." I looked around and said to the bellboy, "Is he talking to you?" He responded, "Yes." I had the privilege that night of leading this young man to Christ.

My appearance at the seminary was rescheduled for the next day. As I was preaching, I told the story of the bellboy as an illustration of how God's timing is always perfect.

From the beginning, God had burdened my soul to make sure that any ministry that He began through me would continue to thrive after my death or departure. So I worked diligently to create an independently functioning board that would not wait on me to make all the important decisions. Each board member had to have a love for souls, and have a burden to reach out primarily to poor people, the down-and-out, and the people that had no hope. Drug addicts, alcoholics, people with open running sores, people who had no home or even a place to sleep—these were among the ones we had begun ministering to in Costa Rica.

Dr. Cal Guy had taught me the indigenous approach to missions. I have continued to be a firm believer in the concept that every missionary effort should be self-governing, self-supporting, and self-propagating. I found this approach to be most effective in our work in Latin America.

Tent Church

I did not feel led of God to start a church in the Upper Room; but many who received Christ kept returning each day to hear another Gospel message. For their benefit, we had to open our first church.

A group of men from a church in Fort Worth, Texas, helped us find and purchase two army surplus "mess tents" 52' long by 18' wide. These were shipped to Costa Rica. We located an empty lot and put up one tent; while it was being erected, our son James fell on a tent pin and injured his face. After he was stitched up at a hospital, I returned to the tent site and began building a floor using fresh almond wood (extremely difficult to work with, resulting in many wounds to our hands). Much of that almond wood was eventually used in the construction of the permanent building that now houses that first church.

Our first tent church was in the middle of a five square mile area that had more than 50,000 inhabitants and no evangelical church or mission. It was within easy walking distance of our Upper room; this allowed us to shepherd those who accepted the Lord each night, directly from the Upper Room down to our church. There they could hear an hour-long teaching message from God's word. Thus they were enabled to grow in knowledge and understanding.

With two team members in front of our first Tent Church

Most of these new Christians continued attending this tent church, where they could hear God's word and grow in His grace. We had services seven nights a week. This helped the preacher boys to learn how to preach and pastor a church. Each team member knew that if he did not preach a strong Biblical sermon that lasted at least an hour, he was not adequately preaching the Word of God.

I taught these young preachers to use no more than one non-Biblical illustration per sermon. This meant that they had to exegete their primary Scripture passage using other Bible verses to explain their text. We had only two commentaries in Spanish. This made their sermon preparation easier, but more difficult for them to understand the full meaning of the Scripture they would preach.

For the first two months I was the pastor of the tent church, and would preach every Sunday morning. Carlos Muñoz was my co-pastor. When I turned the pastorate over to Carlos, another dear team member named Benjamin Cabezas became his co-pastor.

Carlos was a man whom the Holy Spirit had gifted as pastor and teacher; so he did an excellent job pastoring this new church. Within a few months he was called to pastor the Cinco Esquinas Baptist Church, one of the older Baptist churches in Costa Rica. Benjamin then took over as pastor of the tent church.

You will recall that for more than a month Carlos and I had walked the marketplace streets seeking a place to rent; and that together we started the Costa Rican ministry of "Christians Sharing Christ" in the Upper Room. At that time, we had not intended to establish churches; our sole purpose was to seek lost souls and win them to Christ.

We had hoped that others would start churches in that five-square-mile area so that many of our new Christians would find a church home. When this did not happen it became necessary for us to be the ones to start the churches, beginning with the first army surplus tent.

This became the "mother church" of all nine of the CSC churches that would eventually be established in Costa Rica. It is called the Church of Christians Sharing Christ in Barrio Claret. It is still alive and well and is now housed in a permanent structure as a place for worship and for leading the lost to Christ..

There have been five pastors—including myself for the first two months, and Carlos Muñoz for less than six months. Five of the churches we started in Costa Rica were in areas that all other denominations considered to be too difficult an area in which to start a new evangelical church.

Not everything we attempted for the Lord met with complete success. We prayed about reaching people in what was known as the poorest and most dangerous area of San Jose. We rented a small vacant lot and set up the second army tent on it. This was to serve as our next CSC church.

Because it was in a dangerous neighborhood, we had to put up a high security fence to protect our benches and the lighting. We decided to forgo the arduous task of building a floor until the church membership could pay for it. During the nine rainy months of the year the inside of the tent was as muddy as the outside. We had had such a strong desire to establish a church in this dangerous but very needy area. But no matter what we did or how hard we prayed, we were never able to reach this area for Christ. I can vividly remember the day we had to close this church and take down the tent.

There have also been many success stories. From the inception of the ministry called "Christians Sharing Christ" its goal has been the evangelization of those who knew they had no hope and whose lives were so problematic that only Christ could make a difference. This is still the plan, and God has continued to bless the efforts of CSC.

Chapter IX
Expanding the Work in Latin America

> For a great door and effectual is opened unto
> me, and there are many adversaries.
> —1 Corinthians 16:9

God had burdened my heart to reach people who no one else seemed to care about. Sometime in 1972, that burden translated into two strong desires. One was to start a "jungle ministry" in an area where the only means of transportation was by boat. The other was to start the work of Christians Sharing Christ in Managua, the capital of Nicaragua, which adjoined Costa Rica to the north. So in December of 1972 Judy and I and our four children flew to Louisiana for our CSC board meeting in Ball, a suburb of Alexandria. It was decided that we should return to Costa Rica in February of 1973. After getting the jungle ministry started in that country, we would go on to Nicaragua.

From Ball, we went north to Dr. Wren Causey's home in Columbia, Louisiana. Doc Causey purchased a new Volkswagen van for us. We would use it to transport our belongings from Costa Rica to Managua, the capital of Nicaragua, to start the work of CSC in the marketplace of that city. Meanwhile, we would be able to use the van in America.

On a Friday evening, in the middle of a Louisiana thunderstorm, we left Doc Causey's home and drove farther north to the home of one of the board members of Mid-America Baptist Seminary. He had a very large furniture store in Springhill, Louisiana, near the border of Arkansas. He had invited us to come by his house, as he had some clothing he wanted to give me. He and his wife were raising two young granddaughters. When we entered their home we were ushered into a huge room with an extensive collection of dolls and toys for young girls. Considering the impact this might have on our four small children, we wanted to immediately put our hands over their eyes. They had never seen that many playthings.

This dear brother took me to a large closetful of expensive suits that reminded me of my years in El Paso. He offered to give them all to me. I thanked him for his graciousness and said, "I will take only one suit; I will not put my team members to shame. Some of them don't even have a suit."

He then opened another closet, where there were more than a dozen expensive sport coats. I again took only one. Although I thought about it, it would not have been practical or appropriate to take all those suits and sport coats to our team in Costa Rica. We thanked him profusely and we all piled into our new van.

Our children crawled onto their makeshift bed in the back of the van and almost immediately fell asleep. As I drove west toward Fort Worth, Judy and I both began weeping, thinking about how our children had very few toys. We were actually feeling sorry for them. Then the Lord very softly spoke to us both, reminding us that He had blessed all our family spiritually more than we could ever imagine. We continued down the highway with a peace that passed all human understanding.

The next morning, I planned on taking my old suit, which I had worn for at least a week, to a one-hour cleaner. That evening I was to speak at a Christmas banquet. But because I didn't get to the cleaners in time, I was forced to either wear the old, well-worn and dirty suit, or try wearing the suit I was given the night before. Every suit that I have ever purchased has had to be altered between my shoulders; otherwise there is a big puffy piece of cloth sticking up. But when I put on the new suit, it did not stick out; it fit me like it had been tailor-made for me. As I spoke at the banquet, I thanked the Lord for the blessing He had given me in the form of a perfectly fitting suit. We serve an amazing God.

A few days later, on the afternoon of December 22, we attended the funeral of a young lady who had died of Hodgkin's disease. She and her husband had supported our work for several years. At the funeral service in a large church, we heard the choir singing a song that we had not heard before: *The King is Coming*.

After the service, Judy and I rode with two other couples to the graveside service. In the car, Judy leaned over and whispered in my ear, "Charles, we need to hurry because the people in the marketplace of Managua are not ready for the Coming of the King." One of the verses of *The King is Coming* says:

'The marketplace is empty,
No more traffic in the streets,
All the builders' tools are silent,
No more time to harvest wheat.'

131

At 12:35 A.M. Managua time, just over six hours after Judy had whispered those words in my ear, a 6.2 magnitude earthquake destroyed Managua. Within minutes there were two large aftershocks. "Our marketplace" was on fire for 4½ days.

Most of the people who died in that horrible earthquake were in the marketplace; our people, the ones we had intended to witness to, the ones with whom we had hoped to share Christ. Upward of 10,000 were now dead; we were too late. We wept and agonized over not having been there soon enough to have won many of them to Jesus.

Up until then I had not read and applied to my life Ezekiel 22:30: *"I sought for a man among them that should make up the hedge, and stand in the gap before me for the land, that I should not destroy it: but I found none."*

When I found that verse, I recognized that I had been guilty of not "standing in the gap" for Managua. The word "gap" is associated with the weakest part of the wall that protects a city. I should have spent my time standing in the gap for the marketplace of Managua instead of praying for the details and logistics of our starting a ministry in that country. In early February, I put Judy and the children on an airplane to fly home to Costa Rica. I then prepared to drive there in the new van given to us by Doc Causey. I was anticipating the jungle ministry we intended to start.

I knew that the Costa Rican road to the jungle ended at Puerto Viejo de Sarapiqui; all travel from that point was usually made in huge dugout canoes, hewn from logs that were at least 8 feet in diameter. We could not afford to purchase one of those log canoes; so friends in Louisiana gave us an aluminum boat with a powerful outboard motor.

In preparation for my road trip, I strapped that boat to the top of our new Volkswagen van. I then set out with two other men to drive the 3,000 miles through five countries, with that aluminum boat for our jungle ministry tied to the rooftop. Upon arrival, I intended to launch it into the Rio Sarapiqui in Costa Rica.

After driving through Mexico, Guatemala, El Salvador, and Honduras, we entered Nicaragua. As we approached Managua, I became increasingly sad; then when I saw the destruction, and was not allowed to see the marketplace, I could no longer control my tears. I could only imagine how many thousands in "our marketplace" had died without ever having heard the simple message of salvation in Christ Jesus. Oh! If I had only stood in the gap.

We found that conditions were too difficult and too dangerous for us to begin a marketplace ministry in Managua at that time. It would have been extremely hard to find a place to live. And for as little as $7, an amateur assassin could be hired to kill someone.

We had learned the importance of standing in the gap. Then, by faith, we began standing in the gap for San Salvador and for the entire country of El Salvador. Our prayer focused on one thing only:

"Dear heavenly Father, please do not allow anything to happen to that city or that country until you give us the opportunity of sharing the message that the King is coming for those who have received Him as Lord."

Jungle Ministry

When we had brought the boat to the river, two of our team members would use it to reach the lost souls who lived along all the rivers that emptied into the large San Juan River, which divides Costa Rica from Nicaragua and empties into the Caribbean Sea.

With Uriel Hernandez beginning Jungle Ministry

133

All that we could afford as a base of operations at the end of the road was a completely-open-air shed covered with a tin roof. We made two slat beds four feet off the ground because there were several good-sized alligators in the large pond that was about 150 feet from where we slept. At night, you could hear their noises and it always sounded like they were only a few feet away. Not conducive to a peaceful night's sleep.

Our oldest team member, Uriel Hernandez oversaw what we called our jungle ministry. One afternoon Uriel came across a twelve-year-old boy and his father. The young boy had been bitten by a very poisonous snake and his father would not let Uriel transport the boy to San Jose for a shot of antivenom. Instead the father took him to the equivalent of a witch doctor. Three days later the boy died. Our hearts were broken. But our urgency for finding lost souls in the jungle, and bringing them to a saving knowledge of Christ was not diminished.

Uriel with snake-bitten boy

Uriel told about another trip into the jungle. A man, his wife and their 13-year-old daughter, having accepted Christ, wanted to be baptized. Their thatched-roof cabin was an hour from the nearest river. However, close to their cabin was a mid-sized pond. When the man went with Uriel down into the pond, he said to Uriel, "Let's do this quick because there are some big alligators in this pond." Uriel claims that he holds the record for baptizing three new Christians in the shortest period of time.

Preparing for El Salvador

In the Jungle, as well as in San Jose and other parts of Costa Rica, the ministry of Christians Sharing Christ continued. It would be about two more years before we were able to begin the same kind of ministry in El Salvador. During that time, we had faithfully been standing in the gap for El Salvador; by faith we were convinced that God would honor our prayer and not allow anything to happen to that country until we could get there to preach the gospel.

Meanwhile, in the summer of 1974, God gave us the opportunity of having a meal with the president of Costa Rica, José "Pepe" Figueres, and his wife Karen. Mrs. Figueres had visited our Upper Room and had seen what the work entailed. When she heard that we were leaving the country, she personally called and invited us to be honored guests for dinner at their home, the Costa Rican equivalent of the White House. The American ambassador and several Costa Rican dignitaries who were involved with the country's social problems had been invited, in our honor.

The first couple and their guests knew that where there had been 113 houses of prostitution when we started our ministry, there were at that time less than twenty; and there had been a significant drop in the number of prostitutes, many having left that profession when they confessed Jesus Christ as their Lord and Savior.

The President's wife, Doña Karen, asked me to share my testimony with their invited guests. I was blessed to be given this opportunity of sharing the gospel through our testimony. This was two weeks before we left our beloved Costa Rica in order to start a new ministry in El Salvador. In July of that year, I and my family made the arduous trip back to the States in our VW van. We needed to make the necessary preparations for our mission to San Salvador, which was to begin early in 1975.

From July through December, I was very busy visiting churches to raise support for our team in Costa Rica, as well as for the new work we intended to start in the marketplace of San Salvador.

During our time in the United States, we lived in an apartment in Irving, Texas. It was from there that we started out on our trip to San Salvador. When we reached McAllen, on the American side of the Rio Grande, we had to purchase new tires for our VW van. By that time, I was exhausted.

I did not think it wise to go on across the river into Reynosa, Mexico, without resting up first. So we checked into the Holiday Inn there in McAllen; and I telephoned our CSC board to make them aware of my condition.

Two hours later, our board president called me back to tell me that one dear brother had sent money for us to spend two nights on Padre Island "recharging our batteries."

After that respite, we were refreshed and ready to go. With much excitement, our family of six crossed the Rio Grande; we were on our way to a country where we could share Christ Jesus with people in a marketplace that we had not yet visited.

We made this trip from the Rio Grande all the way to San Salvador in four days, including that 537-mile stretch from Veracruz to Tapachula, Mexico, that had been so difficult when our children were much younger (see pages 40 and 115). This time we did not have to bring all the diapers and infant formula.

From Tapachula, we crossed the border into Guatemala and drove along the Pacific coast, enduring the tortuous heat with no air conditioning in our van. Despite this, we were excited because we knew that by nightfall we would be in the city and country where we were eager to serve our Lord.

El Salvador at last

That evening, in the first week of 1975, we crossed the border into El Salvador. We were greeted with a heavy rainstorm—not very common on the west coast of that country. It continued for two hours, escorting us all the way to our hotel. At 9:30 p.m. we checked in. We got our four children settled in one room; then Judy and I fell into bed, energy spent, ready to begin a good long night's sleep. But, long before sunrise, God gave us a nudge.

Twice in the wee hours of our first morning in San Salvador, our loving heavenly Father showed us that He had honored our prayers—our standing in the gap for that city and nation. What He did was perfect: He woke us up at 3 and again at 3:15, each time with a 3.5 magnitude earthquake.

No destruction, just a nudge. Today, with the same joy that I felt that night, I recognize that God was telling me that He had honored our standing in the gap for El Salvador.

God not only spared El Salvador, honoring our prayers, but He also blessed our ministry that year at least as much as He had blessed our first year in the marketplace of Costa Rica. For three months our family of six resided in the Central America Mission Home, where we slept on army cots in two little second-floor bedrooms. In San Salvador's extreme heat, we had no air conditioning or insulation, just a tin roof that seemed to absorb and concentrate all the sun's heat into our sleeping quarters.

When we found a place that we could afford to rent, we again had no beds; so we slept on the floor. That continued until Benjamin Cabezas, one of our Costa Rican team members, came to our aid. He rode the bus for twenty hours from San Jose up to San Salvador. Then he built bunk beds for our kids and made a bed for Judy and me.

We could not afford paint for the beds; so we used a mixture of turpentine and brown shoe polish to rub on with a rag. Meanwhile, I was looking for an Upper Room to rent in the marketplace area of San Salvador.

For some time Judy was teaching a correspondence course to all four of our children. I believe that our children learned more through that course than they would have learned in almost any school. Eventually, we could afford to have two of the boys enrolled in the one American school there; and Judy Anne became one of the first students at the Accelerated Christian Education (ACE) School.

One day in the center of the marketplace of San Salvador, as I was handing out tracts, a crowd began to gather. One man asked me what the little booklet contained and I used that as an opportunity to begin sharing the gospel. The crowd grew larger, requiring me to begin shouting in order to be heard. There must have been more than 200 people crowded around, anxious to hear what they needed to do to be saved. Looking around I found an open 55-gallon drum filled with garbage; I asked several men to help me stand on it. Balancing myself with one foot on either side of the rim, and leaning against a pole, I continued preaching.

Those many Salvadorans just stood there in the heat of the day to hear the simple message of salvation. They must have been amazed to see this tall North American balancing on the garbage barrel and telling them about Jesus. This was in the early days of upheaval that in a few short years would lead to the civil war that brought death to thousands in that country. Some look to God only when faced with danger or despair.

One night as I left to go preach I saw a dead body lying on the side of the street; two hours later when I returned it was still there. One day at lunchtime while a man who worked in a bank was waiting at a bus stop, thieves assaulted and killed him just to steal his watch.

Man does not see the importance of seeking the Creator God until he has no other recourse. But there comes a time when each one must consider the shed blood of God's own son Jesus Christ, which provides the only means of eternal salvation.

My hope is that many who heard the simple plan of salvation preached to them from the top of an open garbage can were subsequently saved, and that I will see them in heaven someday in the not-too-distant future.

When we found our new Upper Room and started the work as we had done in Costa Rica, it seemed that it was all much more difficult in El Salvador. Still, we found that God greatly blessed everything we did.

**Team member Felix preaching in our Upper Room
in San Salvador**

Our children were now old enough to go with me to the Upper Room and to the crowded market to buy vegetables. Using some of my army experience I taught them certain signs that I would make with my hands and my arms signifying that they could be in danger, or that they should come to me quickly. If there had been an American soldier watching, he would have been greatly surprised to see an American civilian giving the sign to form up followed by a sign to do it quickly.

God opened the door for me to preach weekly in numerous churches. This was in addition to my preaching many sermons in our

Salvadoran Upper Room as I discipled our four-man team. Today, two of these men are pastors of churches in the Los Angeles area. Despite all of the hardship that our family endured, we were tremendously blessed to see hundreds of people saved. I couldn't preach a service without seeing at least a dozen people saved.

Beyond Our Upper Room

Besides preaching in churches and our Upper Room, I taught a weekly Bible study in our home, which was open to the saved and unsaved alike. This was attended by members of some of the country's wealthiest families, some of whom became our good friends. There were several decisions for Christ right there in our home. One of the men who accepted the Lord in our home later became the president of the largest telephone system in Latin America.

Each week, I taught a three-hour course on ecclesiology (church history) at the Salvadoran Baptist Seminary. From our home, I recorded a daily teaching and sharing program that was broadcast on a Dallas, Texas, radio station.

During that year in El Salvador more than 15 people from the U.S. (one, two, or three at a time) came to see our new work. They each stayed in our home long enough to see and appreciate all that God was doing through our ministry. Judy had the responsibility of being the host to these visitors, and to the many Salvadoran visitors who graced our door each week.

Also during that time, Judy had a helper living in our home, a teen-age high school girl named Paula, who attended evening classes. She was a great help to Judy with household chores as well as in caring for our young children. My Judy was home-schooling three of our children; they could not go outside alone for fear of being kidnapped. Living in El Salvador was much more dangerous than it had been in Costa Rica.

One afternoon in San Salvador, James and a friend of his were in a car being driven by the friend's father. At a stoplight the man in another car held out a gun and pointed it at the father, who immediately pulled out a gun and pointed it at the man in the other car. Neither one fired but when James got home he told us how scared he was because he was sitting in the front seat and felt like both guns were pointed directly at him.

We had bars on the windows and double locks on our door; still at night I would walk through the house checking that everything was safe. In the marketplace going to or from our Upper Room I always had to keep an eye on what might be happening behind my back.

Every other month I would travel back to the U.S. for seven to ten days in order to visit supporting churches and encourage others to support our ever-increasing ministry. Whenever I had to fly to the States without my family I would keep in touch with Judy by short wave radio. On one such occasion when I contacted Judy, she was crying as she told me that right on our own front steps Paula had been stabbed. My heart ached for Judy; I could not be there to put my arms around her and comfort her. By God's grace, Paula survived, and several years later became the bride of a young pastor in El Salvador.

In Costa Rica, we had felt safer. Throughout the red-light district and marketplace of San Jose, even the toughest men and women lovingly referred to me as the "Gringo." As late as 10 at night, my Judy could safely walk through the roughest area on her way to meet me at the Upper Room. She was known as the wife of the Gringo who loved them, and no one would allow her to be harmed.

One afternoon in San Salvador, I was surprised by our oldest son James. When I came home, he came running to me and said, "Daddy you will never believe what Mommy did today." He said that his mother had a shoe repairman on his knees in front of our house praying to receive Christ. That put a warm smile in my heart.

A dear Salvadoran pastor invited me to the wedding of his cousin. It was to be held in the northwestern mountains of El Salvador. He requested that I preach the evangelistic message that would precede his performing of the marriage ceremony. The service was followed by a delicious meal. As was typical for a special occasion, the main course consisted of rice with chicken.

Afterwards, as I stood outside under the only streetlight in this small Native American village, several men gathered around me. While we were talking, the crowd grew larger. One man worked his way up to stand directly in front of me; he asked, "What do I need to do to be saved?" I inferred he had not been inside when I preached the evangelistic message.

His question gave me the opportunity to present a very simple plan of salvation. By then there were at least 200 men standing around me. I suggested that all those who wanted to be saved and receive Christ, repeat after me the prayer of salvation. With me were my older son and a visiting seminary student from Tennessee. Late that night in a torrential rain, we cautiously made our way down the mountain to our home.

Two mornings later while I was reading that day's newspaper, a picture from an ID card caught my eye. The government of El Salvador required every citizen to carry an identification card; a copy was kept in government records. The picture I saw on one of the back pages was of a familiar face. Surprised to see that picture, I quickly asked my son if he recognized the man in the picture. His reply was, "Yes, that is the man that asked you the question." The visiting seminary student agreed that it was the same man, the one who had asked me the question two nights before, about how to be saved.

Under the picture, the news story said that this young man had been killed with a machete the same evening that I had answered his question. Did he ask that specific question because he had a premonition that he might be killed that night? How many others prayed to receive Christ that night because of this young man's question?

A Special Baptism

Among the wealthy unsaved that attended our weekly home Bible study was a young married couple. One night I received a call from the husband. He started the conversation by saying he wanted to receive Christ. He and I prayed together and then rejoiced in his salvation. He hung up and in less than 5 minutes my phone rang again. The same man said that his wife wanted to receive Christ. I said, "You know what to tell her; so I don't need to talk to her." I then told him to call me back within 15 minutes to share the result.

Minutes later, his wife called; she had prayed with her husband to receive Christ. We rejoiced together and then she said, "When my husband said that you didn't want to talk to me, I couldn't understand why you did not want to lead me to Christ." We both laughed; but I knew he needed to begin leading people to Christ starting with his own wife. I had the privilege of baptizing this young Christian couple, as well as the man's mother. They have remained faithful to Christ ever since.

For their special baptism at a Sunday morning service, I did not want to get my pants and socks wet. So the pastor lent me his "waders" like what fishermen wear to walk out into the river. Little did I know that there was a hole in one leg of the waders. In spite of my best effort at keeping my clothes dry, one sock and pant leg got soaking wet. Native American "Indians" might have named me "One wet leg man" as I stood up before the church to preach. Amazingly, despite this distraction, God blessed the sermon and several came forward at the invitation.

Once every two months I visited our team in Costa Rica, as well as our missionary in Guatemala who was starting God's work in that country's marketplace. We were continuing the work that had already been established; and we were actively seeking to find more missionaries to open CSC ministries in the marketplaces of other countries.

God did a tremendous work in El Salvador. As I look back, I can see that the Lord had us there at one of the most important times in the history of the country. In July of that year (1975) 22 students were killed within a kilometer of our home. We heard the machine-gun fire and found a bullet hole in our roof. This occurrence was part of the very beginning of the civil war that would cause the deaths of thousands of the people of that beautiful country, many of whom had accepted Christ and had been saved through the simple preaching of a message of hope by Christians Sharing Christ. I thank and praise God for sending us to start that work.

Just before leaving El Salvador

Leaving El Salvador

After a little less than a full year in the country for which we had stood in the gap for two years, both of us were worn out. With the stress of dealing with the physical danger in that area, and all our activity in the nearly unbearable dry tropical heat, I was down to what I had weighed as a freshman in high school; and Judy's health was deteriorating. We needed to return to the States at least for a while. So, with much relief and some sadness, we prepared to leave San Salvador. But we did not abandon those precious people.

We left a dedicated four-man team there, who continued preaching twice each day the message of salvation in the middle of the market area of San Salvador. And I planned to continue visiting both our Costa Rican team and our Salvadoran team once every two months for as long as I could.

Salvadoran team members jailed

Before I made it back for a visit to our team in El Salvador, there was an increase in the violence in that country. Within four blocks of our San Salvador Upper Room, numerous people were shot to death and hundreds wounded. The country was declared to be in a "state of siege."

Our team was not permitted to have services in our Upper Room; so they had an all-night prayer meeting asking the Lord to give them opportunities to preach. The next night, they projected the film on an outside wall of a bar across the street. Several people were saved.

The next day, an invitation came from a pharmacist to do the same thing on the wall of his building. Two evenings later, as they were showing the films on this man's wall, over 200 soldiers with machine guns surrounded them. After questioning our team, the officer in charge said, "If you are evangelicals, quote some Bible verses." Felix, who was our team leader, quoted them Romans 3:23 and 6:23 then continued on with the Romans road to salvation.

The officer then said, "let us see the film you have just shown." So the film was projected again. At the end, the officer said, "Explain it." Felix then preached the message of Christ to over 200 soldiers and a few civilians, after which two of our team members were put in jail. They told the same officer that this was of God, for they had prayed for an opportunity to preach to the people; and both the pharmacist and the officer had given them that opportunity. These two witnesses for Christ had joined the ranks of 100 generations of Peters, Johns and Pauls who had been incarcerated for proclaiming the Gospel of Christ to a lost world. Score one for the Salvadoran team, all for the glory of God. These two were released early the next morning.

I was greatly blessed by the fervor and continuing spiritual depth of our team in El Salvador. At that time we had marketplace teams in Costa Rica, El Salvador, and Guatemala. My responsibility continued to be the oversight of our teams and assuring that they received support, both spiritually and financially. This required me to travel to each country at least once every two months, while my family remained in Texas.

Ministering to Judy

It was our hope that after a little rest Judy and I would be able to take our family to Tegucigalpa, Honduras, and start a marketplace ministry there. But less than a month after our return to the United States, Judy collapsed from nervous exhaustion and was rushed to the hospital; she was diagnosed with Desert Lung Disease. Her recuperation would require three months of total bed rest.

Several years earlier one of my three beloved mentors, Dr. L. Nelson Bell, told me how at 85 he had driven his wife—whom I endearingly called Mama Bell—from Asheville, North Carolina, to Los Angeles for a visit with one of their children. At that time she was an invalid; Dr. Bell had to lift her in and out of the car, help her in and out of restaurants, help her to the bathroom, and help her with all her needs.

Dr. Bell then said something to me that I would never forget, but would not understand until years later. He said, "I am blessed to have to take care of her." When he told me that, I thought I could never say what he had just said. However, in a few short years, I could easily repeat his words, when I would be blessed to take care of my precious and beloved bride for three months.

It was at that time, beginning in 1976, that God blessed me with the privilege of taking care of all Judy's needs, and assuming all of her responsibilities. I took care of our children, did the cleaning and washing, cooked all of our meals and served Judy her meals in bed.

Subsequent to her diagnosis, she was treated at the Scott and White clinic in Temple, Texas. This required me to drive her 135 miles each way every two weeks for three months, so she could have chest x-rays; later this was reduced to an x-ray every month. For several months her health needed to be monitored, after which the doctors were reasonably sure that the nodules were benign. We had not wanted Judy to have surgery unless there was conclusive evidence that they were malignant.

While I was caring for Judy during her time of recovery God began doing things in my life here in the United States. For several years, our home church had been MacArthur Boulevard Baptist Church in Irving, Texas. Whenever we returned from Central America, that was where we worshiped and fellowshipped. The members of our church in Irving took us under their wing and tried to help us through what they felt was a difficult period in our life and ministry as we were unable to return to the mission field of our beloved Latin America.

We became very active during this time in the ministry of that Church. I taught a Sunday school class for men who had a heart for God, some of whom were wealthy businessmen or politicians. I believe my life and teaching influenced them to put Christ first in their daily walk.

One of those men was Ken McGovern; this was the beginning of a long and blessed friendship with him. He would later become the president of CSC (Christians Sharing Christ) and faithfully serve God in that position up until 2016 when because of his open heart surgery and failing health he had to step down.

A venture into politics

Through politically active Christians in Texas who were trying to effect changes in public school textbooks, I met John Conlan, a former U.S. Congressman from Arizona. I felt that his burden was real, and was something that I needed to become part of to bring about solutions to problems in our government. John began teaching me how to organize the Christian community to have an impact on state and federal legislative bodies.

John invited some of the influential Christian leaders in our country to gather in Washington to lobby for the tuition tax credit bill. By that time, Judy's health was improving and she was able to go with me to our nation's Capital. John and I trained these men on how to lobby their Congressmen. One of the men we trained was John Whitehead who became the founder and president of the Rutherford Institute, an organization that fights legal battles for Christians.

Others I trained were some of the most politically astute Christians in positions of leadership. I would take them in the morning, two or three at a time, to visit a Congressman's office; and they would sit or stand watching as I dealt with either the Chief of Staff or with the Congressman himself. Then in the afternoon they could do what I had taught them that morning.

One night after many of us had eaten at the famous Blackie's House of Beef in downtown Washington, I took John Whitehead to the Lincoln Memorial and the Jefferson Memorial, which he had never visited before. As we stood at the Lincoln Memorial John read the Gettysburg address out loud; then I read Abraham Lincoln's second inaugural address, which very clearly calls upon the name of the Lord. These readings brought tears to our eyes.

During that time in Washington I met Don Shea, a Catholic priest who was my counterpart lobbying for the tuition tax credit bill. Don and I became good friends. God in his omnipotent grace had brought Don and me together, and He would bring us together again in a few short years to accomplish an even more important goal. Oh! How I can see God's hand in all this, and how he was leading me. What an amazing God we serve!

Back to Latin America

For several years it had been my desire to start a marketplace ministry in West Africa. However, The President of Christians Sharing Christ insisted that I was needed to oversee the work in Latin America. So in 1977, after Judy's recovery, we moved back to Costa Rica and lived in a hotel apartment for five months. Our children went to their old school and I spent my time traveling between the countries where we had teams, as well as visiting our supporting churches in the United States.

When we had left El Salvador, it was our hope that after a little rest Judy and I would take our family and move to Tegucigalpa, Honduras, where we would start a marketplace ministry in that country. That apparently was not God's plan, as evidenced by Judy's illness.

But now that we were again in Costa Rica, I made several trips to Honduras where I still hoped that God would open the door for us to start another marketplace ministry. However, while visiting that country, I realized that He was not at that time opening the door to Honduras for Christians Sharing Christ. The only way we could start the marketplace ministry in Honduras would be to send our children to a boarding school in Siguatepeque, far from our loving care. To see them on weekends, we would have to drive two and a half hours each way. God was showing us clearly that this was not His will.

So it seemed wiser and more practical not to return our four children to the Central American mission field, even if we could have. Those five months in Costa Rica turned out to be the last time we would live for any length of time in the Central America whose land and peoples we had come to love so well.

By that time, it was becoming increasingly evident that for me to stay with the ministry that God had used me to begin in the marketplace of San Jose, Costa Rica, I would have to become an administrator of a ministry whose direction was changing. The President of the board of Christians Sharing Christ, a man whom I had chosen, had a vision for the ministry that was different from the one God had begun through me.

Under the direction of President Gene Slaughter, God was changing the direction but not the purpose of our ministry. Christians Sharing Christ became a ministry dedicated to showing Christian evangelistic films throughout each country in Latin America.

Eventually, the ministries of the Upper Rooms, CSC churches, and "Christians Sharing Christ Film Ministry" (CSCFM) were winning the lost on three continents. That which God had used me to begin was being used to accomplish even greater things than when I was actively involved. If I had thought that the work was mine, I would have been humiliated; but because I knew it was of God, I was humbled and filled with awe at seeing how He had expanded and multiplied the results "without my help."

Christians Sharing Christ Film Ministry has reduced its effort in Central America in order to use more resources in areas where few have heard the message of Jesus.

I am truly grateful for the soul-saving vision God gave to my friend Gene Slaughter as President of Christians Sharing Christ. Someday soon I will see "Uncle Gene" in glory where together we will praise the Lord for all the souls that He gave us the opportunity of winning to Jesus.

For many years now the president of Christians Sharing Christ Film Ministry has been Patrick Calhoun, a man whose heart for the Lord and for the lost is as my own. He has my deep respect and admiration. It has been due in no small part to this dear brother's leadership that hundreds of thousands throughout the world have come to know and follow our Lord Jesus Christ.

CSCFM has Christian men showing evangelistic films about Jesus in seven South American countries, fourteen African countries, and seven countries in Asia, including India, Pakistan, Nepal, and Burma (Myanmar).

Patrick Calhoun with his team in Nepal

In each of these areas Christian men are now using lightweight portable video players to show films to the lost in some of the most remote places on this earth.

God has blessed this ministry with more than 3,000,000 people coming to know the Lord Jesus Christ throughout Latin America, Africa, and Asia.

Our God continued closing doors to us in Latin America until Judy and I knew for a certainty that, even though our hearts remained in the marketplaces among the poorest of the poor, it was God's will for us to abide in the United States for the time being. But that did not mean that our ministry was over. There was much more ahead, both in Latin America and right here in North America.

Chapter X
Wherever The Lord Leads

> *Now when they had gone throughout Phrygia
> and the region of Galatia, and were forbidden of the
> Holy Ghost to preach the word in Asia, after they were
> come to Mysia, they assayed to go into Bithynia: but
> the Spirit suffered them not.* —Acts 16:6-7 KJV

Upon returning to the States, we settled in Irving, Texas, where we knew we would be among friends. All of our children had started their formal education in Latin America. They had been taught by correspondence course and had been able to attend a good school in Costa Rica. But we were now going to be away from there for an unknown length of time. Judy and I knew our children needed continued good education. So that was something that we factored in as we began looking for a place of ministry.

We learned that there were very good schools in Irving, a community known for its conservative position. The majority of school board members were born again Bible believing Christians. So we enrolled our children in good public schools in that city. And we trusted and prayed that God would give us a ministry here in the United States.

Our pastor at MacArthur Boulevard Baptist Church was Ron Dunn, a man who could rightly divide the word of God. He was a dedicated student of God's word. A verse that I might have known and preached many times would be preached by Ron and I would recognize a profound truth that I had not seen despite having researched the commentaries.

While we lived in Irving, Ron would often call me in the morning and say, "Charles let's get together for lunch. I have something to share." We would usually eat at a little Mexican restaurant and he would share what he had just learned during the wee hours of the morning about a portion of God's word. In a real sense I felt like I was talking to a man who was as close to being like the Apostle Paul as any man I have ever known. Let me say that the most important thing Ron taught me was the importance of properly exegeting God's word. He also reinforced my belief in the importance of prayer.

One of the men that I had trained to lobby in Washington was Bill Kelly, the superintendent of schools for the Christian Unified School District in El Cajon, California. When he returned to the West Coast, he started tooting my horn. Another man I had met in Washington was Paul Kienel, Executive Director of the Association of Christian Schools International. These two men who lived in southern California wanted me to lobby on their behalf in Washington, representing them on issues such as the rights of Christian students and parents, which were little-by-little being jeopardized by secular humanists. I flew to Los Angeles to discuss with them the logistics of opening an office in D.C.

Bill Kelly had driven up from San Diego to meet me at L. A. International Airport. We drove directly to Whittier where we met with Paul Kienel. After we discussed the D.C. project, Bill called Tim LaHaye, Senior Pastor of the church in El Cajon of which Bill's schools were a ministry. It was suggested that I ride down to El Cajon with Bill to meet with Tim that afternoon. We arrived at about 4 P.M. While we waited for Tim to return to his office, we took a short tour of Scott Memorial Baptist Church. It was occupying the campus of a former Catholic girls' school.

After the introductions, Tim suggested that he and I speak in private. Within fifteen minutes he said, "God wants you to come out here and head up my ministry." Smiling I said, "God hasn't told me that, Tim."

I flew back to Texas with absolutely no interest in becoming the Executive Director of Tim LaHaye's ministries. I was happy serving as the men's Sunday school teacher at our church in Irving. And I was blessed being Pastor Ron Dunn's confidant while he was my mentor. We were together many times during the week. Ron taught me so much about the importance of prayer, and he blessed me in so many ways. From the time I left the business world until the present I have always been a man on a mission, looking for something that I can do to glorify my Savior and be used in His service. That has been my lifestyle and that is how it was during our time in Texas.

We were content with our lives in Irving. But Tim LaHaye was not accustomed to taking no for an answer. He and Beverly were having their Family Life Seminars on Saturdays in many parts of the United States. Not by accident they would arrive at the Dallas-Fort Worth International Airport with a two-to-four-hour layover between flights. En route from one coast to the other they would call us to pick them up and take them to lunch or bring them out to our house; it was only a 15-minute drive from the airport to our front door.

Tim never let up on his campaign to convince me to come and work with him. He had a vision of organizing the pastors in California into becoming an influence for God in the State Government. He and I would talk during those layovers in Texas; I began to get caught up in the excitement about what we could see happening to stem the tide of immorality that seemed often to start on the West Coast. So much was spewing out of California that was hurting our country.

Tim and Bev invited Judy and me to be their houseguests for a weekend in San Diego County. We found ourselves sitting out in their hot Jacuzzi discussing all aspects of what together we could do. Always in my mind was what could be done to impact America for Christ.

By now, it was late 1978. Judy Anne was fifteen years old, and our youngest, Charles B. Moore V, was going on eight. We knew that a ministry of Tim LaHaye's church was a good Christian school system in El Cajon. With the understanding that our children would be enrolled there, Judy and I decided that I should accept Tim's offer.

I told Tim that we would come for one year, during which time he and I would organize what would become known as Californians for Biblical Morality. I agreed to be the first Executive Director of this ministry that would be formed with a membership of 1,100 pastors in California. The board would be made up of Christian leaders of the highest caliber, including John MacArthur, Chuck Swindoll, Jack Hayford, Chuck Smith and Royal Blue.

On the 17th of December in 1978 our family of six arrived in El Cajon. Judy and I checked into a motel and began our search for a home. In just a few days, we celebrated Christmas with our four children, opening our presents from under a small Christmas tree on top of a table in one of our two adjoining motel rooms.

We probably experienced more culture shock moving to California than when we had arrived in Costa Rica. But, God soon provided a home for us to move into, and a new ministry in which I could serve my Lord Jesus Christ.

Family Life Seminars

Tim LaHaye, whose offer had brought us to California, was Senior Pastor of Scott Memorial Baptist Church in San Diego County. Before organizing and launching CBM (Californians for Biblical

Morality), Tim wanted me to begin working for him as Executive Director of Family Life Seminars, a ministry that he and his wife had felt led of the Lord to begin. I had been somewhat hesitant to take on this responsibility, since it was not evangelistic in nature. But once I was convinced that it was God's will for me to accept this paid position, I felt led of the Lord to sign a contract with Tim for a one-year period. He told me he had never signed an employment contract, but I was insistent; the only man I had ever worked for, the only "boss" I had ever had, was my father. The contract was signed and was to be valid only during the year of 1979.

Ready for the work

On January 2, I assumed my position as the executive director of Family Life Seminars (FLS). At that time there were about 30 employees. The organizational structure included five different departments. I soon found that there was a tremendous amount of dissension among the five directors of the different departments; in fact, two had gotten into a fight before I arrived. So I could see what my priorities needed to be.

In the Upper Room on the day of Pentecost, all of the disciples were in one accord and one spirit. This was also true of our Upper Rooms in Costa Rica and El Salvador. I believed it was essential that the directors and staff be in one accord and one spirit if we were to see God bless Tim and Bev LaHaye's ministry as we hoped. So I immediately scheduled a luncheon at our home for the five directors. From 10 in the morning until 2:30 we all talked about how the Lord would have us to be at one in the Spirit.

God blessed that time of prayer and discussion, as well as subsequent times; the directors became a harmonious team, exhibiting a sweet spirit. Each director and department soon became much more effective.

Things immediately began to improve and the whole atmosphere at FLS changed. During that year, our staff expanded to 47 and the overall ministry thrived. We significantly increased the number of cassettes that were mailed out each month, and counseling by mail grew beyond our expectations. Attendance at the actual in-auditorium Family Life Seminars as well as the film seminars began flourishing.

Also in that year, we started the FLS radio ministry, and laid the foundation for the FLS television ministry.

Another thing that I considered important in a Christian ministry was that each staff member be considered as a brother or sister in the Lord with individual spiritual gifts and personal needs. I had been accustomed to working with a team. Therefore I tried to develop this very large staff into a team, one that would rejoice with the successes achieved; one that would also feel the pain of those who were hurting, while being willing and eager to help those within the team who were in need of help. To this end, I set aside time every Tuesday morning to teach a one-hour Bible study with our entire staff present.

At the close of each Tuesday Bible study, we prayed for Tim and Bev's ministry and the individual needs of each staff member. Several of the staff later said that the Tuesday morning time was a high point in their week. I do know that this brought about a real oneness of spirit among the vast majority of staff.

Meanwhile, about two months after arriving in El Cajon, California, I began serving as the Executive Director of the newly formed CBM (Californians for Biblical Morality). I held that position until November when we hired another man to succeed me.

Two or three times each week Tim and Bev would ask Judy and me to go out to dinner with them. Bev did not especially enjoy cooking at home after a busy day with CWA (Concerned Women for America); but they both enjoyed spending hours brainstorming ideas with us. So, Judy would prepare dinner for our children, and then we would meet the LaHayes, or they would pick us up, and we would have a good meal at a nice restaurant.

There we would talk for several hours about different ideas that we could incorporate into the ministry or develop in the political world. Tim and I thought that it was important that Christians assert their positive influence into the political fabric of our country.

The decisions made over dinner needed to be conveyed to those who would be carrying them out. So at home, after the kids had gone to bed, I would often use a small recorder to dictate letters until midnight or later.

The next morning I would be at the office by 8 o'clock. Sometimes on weekends our family would go to one of San Diego's beautiful beaches, and I would lie in the sun dictating letters while Judy and the children enjoyed the sand and the sea. Once when the stress caught up with me, Judy and I took a couple of days off to relax in Palm Springs. It was during this stressful time of working at FLS that I visited a cardiologist for the first time; it would not be the last.

In late October, I told Tim that as of the first of January I would have fulfilled my one-year contract and would be leaving Family Life Seminars. I felt strongly that this was what the Lord would have me to do. So when Tim made it very clear that he thought that I should stay on, I told him, "For Judy and me, God is the one who provides and leads. I will follow His leadership."

When January 1, 1980 came, I was without a job or ministry. But that was not the end of my relationship with my dear brother Tim. I would again be working on projects of his after some involvement in politics. For now, I will skip over the political arena, where to some extent Tim was also present. That will be covered in the next chapter.

In the rest of this chapter I want to focus on the work that the Lord gave me to do in association with Tim LaHaye. In late 1980 Tim and I became business partners; we formed a film distribution company called Family Life Distributors.

154

Initially, we were distributing only a four-film series on "Love and Marriage" that featured Tim and Bev expounding on practicing Christian principles within the family. But realizing that we needed other top quality films to distribute, I partnered with my dear friend Jack Dabner of Seven-Star Productions. He and I found Christian investors who financed our production of seven Christian films to be distributed by Family Life Distributors.

With director Jack Dabner at film opening

These films were directed by Jack Dabner. One was titled *A Sure Foundation*. We used Hollywood actors to present the message of the inerrancy of the Holy Scriptures. Jack and I received an award for this film from <u>Christian Film Distributors of America</u>. Through viewing this film thousands came to understand and appreciate the inerrancy and trustworthiness of the Bible.

For the next three years, I continued as president of Family Life Distributors. I was also involved in ministries of Tim LaHaye's church as the chaplain of Christian Heritage College as well as the teacher of the largest Sunday school class in the state of California.

But I believe the most important and challenging job I had during those three years was being the father of our teens and pre-teens.

Our growing children

While our four children were attending Christian schools in El Cajon, I wanted to make sure they had a solid foundation of Bible knowledge that would shape and undergird their actions, attitudes, and character for the rest of their lives. I knew that Scripture memorization is one of the most effective ways of accomplishing this. The young Jews in the time of Christ were required to commit to memory lengthy passages from the Torah (the books from Genesis to Deuteronomy) as well as from the Psalms and the Prophets.

The Apostle Paul alluded to this fact in his second letter to his protégé Timothy, when he said in 3:15, "And that from a child thou hast known the holy scriptures, which are able to make thee wise unto salvation through faith which is in Christ Jesus." During each summer vacation from school, our children were required to memorize, and be able to recite word perfect, a significant part of the New Testament. First was the book of Ephesians.

Cal,   Judy Anne, James, Charles V

Each one fulfilled our expectations. Next they all memorized the book of Philippians; then the first six chapters of the book of Romans. For good measure they also then memorized the book of Colossians. In these four books of the New Testament, they learned the basic doctrines of Christianity and how to apply them to their daily walk with the Lord. What they learned back then, they have never forgotten; and they are still committed to putting Jesus Christ first in their lives.

All four or our children excelled in academic and social life at school. Judy Anne was a cheerleader and was voted Homecoming Princess; James was elected student body President in his senior year; as a sophomore, Cal was chosen class president.

All of our sons were athletic in football, soccer, baseball, or lacrosse. In his senior year young Charles was named to the San Diego County Lacrosse All-Stars. He also played in the lacrosse state North/South game. I thank and praise God for His love for my family.

Chapter XI
Political Involvement

> *But the Lord said unto him, Go thy way: for he is a chosen vessel unto me, to bear my name before the Gentiles, and kings, and the children of Israel. For I will show him how great things he must suffer for my name's sake.* —Acts 9:15-16 KJV

Even though for several years, Judy and I were physically far from our beloved Latin American mission field, our work there was not over; nor was the ministry of Christians Sharing Christ. It continued while we remained in the States; but our hearts and prayers were continually there, and one day we would be there again in the flesh as well as in spirit. But meanwhile, I received a call that led me in a somewhat different direction, one for which the Lord had begun preparing me many years earlier.

In 1979 Ronald Reagan announced his candidacy for the office of President of the United States; in 1980 he ran a successful campaign as a Republican. He of course was the well-liked Hollywood actor who had served two consecutive terms as Governor of California. He had also sought the Republican nomination for President in 1976, winning in California as a "Favorite Son" but losing nationally to incumbent President Gerald Ford, who then lost the general election to Jimmy Carter.

Early in January, 1980, John Conlan, the former U.S. Congressman from Arizona (1973-1977) with whom I was acquainted, told me that one of the four key men in Ronald Reagan's presidential campaign was a man from New Mexico named Andy Carter. Andy and I had known of each other since my early years in El Paso. A meeting was arranged with him almost immediately. We met at the Reagan campaign's main office in one of the high-rise office buildings next to Los Angeles International Airport. Andy and I had lunch and talked about the Christian community. As a result of that meeting I was asked to be the liaison between the Reagan campaign and the evangelical community.

Meanwhile, Reverend Jerry Falwell, a prominent leader among Evangelicals, had been having discussions with Tim LaHaye about forming a new movement called the Moral Majority, through which Christians could be motivated to influence the outcome of political elections. Since I had previously worked with Tim on a similar movement—CBM (Californians for Biblical Morality)—of which in 1979 I was the first Executive Director, he knew this new movement could benefit from my experience.

On Tim's recommendation, Jerry invited me to fly to Washington for a meeting with the two of them. This meeting turned out to be one of the first planning sessions of the newly formed Moral Majority. Jerry asked me to become the first National Field Director for that organization, essentially doing what I had done with CBM. This position seemed like a natural in light of what I was doing for the Reagan campaign. I felt that it was God who was enabling me to fulfill both roles successfully.

During the months after that first meeting with Jerry Falwell, I became well acquainted with him. You could not know Jerry very well without recognizing that his heart was for the Lord and that he truly wanted to make a difference in our country.

He strongly believed that if America did not obey God's word, He would remove his hand of blessing and we would experience the decline and fall that every previous civilization had experienced over the centuries. I never believed that vanity or pride played a part in Jerry's life and ministry.

For the Reagan campaign, Andy Carter asked me to put together a meeting of wealthy and/or well-known Christian leaders and businessmen. He and I both agreed that John Conlan knew more of the wealthy businessmen while I knew more of the Christian leaders; so John and I worked the project together; we invited 22 men to attend a fund raising dinner at the home of Ronald and Nancy Reagan. As it turned out, the day of that meeting was the same day that the American hostages were taken in Iran, which event would later deprive Jimmy Carter of many votes he would otherwise have garnered.

We met with these men first at the Beverly Wilshire Hotel in Beverly Hills. We then boarded a bus and rode up to the Reagan home in Pacific Palisades where we were greeted by Ronald and Nancy at their front door. Their home was nicely decorated and seemed like a home filled with love. On their baby grand piano they had pictures of their family and close friends.

I was seated at a roundtable. Eight others were at the same table, including Sam Moore of Thomas Nelson publishing and Jim

Mathers, the owner of Mr. Steak, a chain of steakhouse restaurants. I had met Jim previously at a Washington, D.C. meeting that we both attended.

After dinner we stood up and chatted for a while before sitting down for dessert. During this time staff member Mike Deaver, a long-time friend of the Reagans, told a few of us that every morning before Governor Reagan came into his office, a few members of his staff would place their hands on his chair and ask God to bless the governor that day. He also mentioned that there was a young secretary who would anoint his chair with oil.

For dessert, I sat at a card table directly across from Governor Reagan. On my left were Pat and Shirley Boone; they had come in after dinner. In response to a question I asked him, Ronald Reagan told us a story that brought tears to his eyes, and ours. He started by explaining why he was opposed to abortion. He said, "Several people took the time to teach me about abortion and what it does to a woman and they showed me that an abortion is nothing less than murdering a living child, and that a fetus is actually a live human."

He then went on to say that he had received a beautiful painting in the mail. In the letter that accompanied the painting he had read, "Dear Governor Reagan, I painted this picture for you holding a paint brush in my teeth. You see, I was a thalidomide baby and I was born without arms or legs. If abortion had been legal, I and many other babies would have been killed." Then he said of that artistic young lady, "Abortion would have robbed society of the value in her life." We all knew right then that he was the man we needed in the Oval Office.

For the next several months, I was extremely busy in my position with the Moral Majority and in organizing meetings and directing efforts for getting Ronald Reagan elected to the Presidency. Ultimately, I believe with God's blessing, we were able to achieve our goals.

After the election and before the inauguration, Andy Carter called and we talked at length about the things that we had done to help get Reagan elected. This was an enjoyable time without all the pressure of the campaign. Andy then said, "Charles, would you like to become Reagan's Director of Urban Affairs?"

This was a second level position in the White House. The person holding it would be the liaison between the administration and all religious groups of all denominations. I said, "No, Andy, I know that it's not God's will for me to move my family to Washington."

Soon thereafter Charles Cade of the Moral Majority called to let me know that the Presidential transition team was asking him to persuade me to accept that position in the White House. I was not persuaded.

I later found out from Andy that it was President-elect Reagan who had personally asked for me to become a member of his staff. I believe he wanted people on his staff that he knew loved Jesus.

During my time with the Moral Majority I spoke to hundreds of pastors about getting involved in politics, but only to a God-honoring level. Never did I aspire to become involved in the non-Christian political arena. Nor did I suggest that any pastor quit the ministry God had given him to do, in order to spend time promoting himself and campaigning for a position of power in government. Rather, I encouraged pastors to keep their congregations aware of the issues as well as the voting records and moral integrity of men and women who were seeking their votes.

With all of my heart I believe my time with the Moral Majority as well as my time helping to elect godly men and women to positions of public trust has had redemptive value. My motives were honorable, and my efforts under the leadership of the Lord have borne much good fruit. I am grateful to God that during a time of being stuck as it were in the United States, I was still able to bear fruit; not the same as thousands of souls being won to Christ, but I believe it was fruit pleasing unto God.

Pro-Life Plank

In 1973, the Supreme Court had struck down every state law restricting abortion; unborn babies were now being slaughtered all over the country. Beginning in 1980, God gave this nation a legal avenue for repentance. As He often does, He used two men to start the process.

I believe it was not by coincidence, but by divine appointment, that in 1977, I had become friends with the Catholic priest named Don Shea, the lobbyist in Washington D.C. (see page 146). At that time, Don and I had worked together on trying to get the Tuition Tax Credit Bill passed in Congress. This bill was intended to reduce the financial burden of parents who were paying taxes for public schools while their children attended private schools. Don Shea, a Catholic priest and I, a Baptist preacher, became lasting friends. For three years, we had stayed in touch. In 1980 God brought us together again.

As you read the next thirteen paragraphs, I would ask you to consider that everything that was done or said—by myself or anyone else mentioned here—was planned and motivated by God. I believe that every verb, whether negative or positive, whether denoting action or inaction, describes the carrying out of God's will, whether the participants knew it or not. And the resulting plank was His way of giving America a concrete means of turning back to Him in repentance and obedience, for which He was ready, willing and able to forgive and wonderfully bless this nation again. Otherwise, His blessings would be gradually removed.

1)   Shortly after the dinner at the Reagan home, I flew to D.C. for a meeting; while there I called Don Shea. By then, he had become the Director of Urban Affairs for the Republican National Committee (RNC). Don and I agreed to have lunch at the Capitol Hill Club, a restaurant that adjoins the RNC building. Over lunch Don and I discussed the need for the Republican Party to take a stand on moral issues if they were to receive widespread support from evangelicals.

2)   In the following week Don and I had several telephone conversations. Among other issues, we talked about how Evangelicals and Catholics would both support a pro-life plank in the Republican Party Platform. We also arranged a meeting where Moral Majority leaders and other influential Christians could discuss the most important issues that the Republican Party needed to emphasize. This meeting would be held in the RNC "War Room," where we expected these Christian men to clearly state these moral issues to Bill Brock, the Republican National Committee (RNC) chairman.

3)   Among the twelve men of stature in Christian leadership who accepted the invitation were: Jerry Falwell; Tim LaHaye; Bob Jones of Bob Jones University; Charles Stanley, senior pastor of First Baptist Church in Atlanta, Georgia; D. James Kennedy, founder and senior pastor of Coral Ridge Presbyterian Church in Fort Lauderdale, Florida; Bob Dugan, executive director of the National Evangelical Association; and Jack Wyrtzen, founder and director of Word of Life ministries.

4)   When one of the twelve cancelled at the last minute, I felt led to occupy the vacant seat. When RNC Chairman Bill Brock asked these men for their input, none of them said anything about the moral issues facing our nation; they mentioned the economy, military preparedness, etc. Then Don said, "Bill, you need to hear from Charles." I briefly reiterated the moral issues Don and I had talked

about. But before these could be discussed any further, the meeting was adjourned for dinner.

5) A short time later at dinner in a private room of the Capitol Hill club, the RNC chief counsel Ben Cotton asked me to elaborate on what I had said at the meeting. It was then that others from the meeting began to indicate agreement with what I was saying.

6) Over two more weeks, Don and I continued our conversation by telephone regarding the Pro-life plank we would be promoting. One day he called me and said, "Charles, I'm sending you by special delivery a final draft of what we decided on." Ben Cotton, Chief Counsel for the Republican Party, had reviewed the final draft and made a few changes that did not in any way reduce its impact. I sent a copy to the executive director of the Moral Majority; I asked him to copy and distribute it as he saw fit. After reading it, the entire leadership of the Moral Majority expressed wholehearted agreement with it. Harry Covert, as the editor, even published it in the Moral Majority newspaper.

7) Ben Cotton helped to assure that the Republican Party Platform Committee would keep the exact wording of what Don Shea and I had put together. We knew that the social moderates of the Republican Party would fight to keep a Pro-life plank out of that year's platform. So I began taking steps to overcome that opposition.

8) In September, 1980, I helped Tim LaHaye put together a meeting in the Long Beach Arena that was to represent the families of America, including the majority of all women. In that meeting, which was attended by several thousand people, we heard messages by many Pro-life advocates. Among these were: Jerry Falwell; U.S. Surgeon General Dr. C. Everett Koop; Tim and Beverly LaHaye; Dr. Mildred Jefferson, who was a well-known Pro-life obstetrician from Boston; Paul Weyrich, the founder of the Committee for the Survival of a Free Congress; Senator Jesse Helms of North Carolina (1973-2003); and Phyllis Schlafly, founder and CEO of Eagle Forum.

9) After the meeting, I offered to drive Senator Jesse Helms back to the Queen Mary, the cruise ship/hotel where he was to spend the night. He was the chairman of the Republican Party Platform Committee; he would be at the Republican convention in Detroit the next day. I spoke with him about the platform and the Pro-life plank. I also informed him that three state chairmen of the Moral Majority had been named to his platform committee, and that I was certain they would be willing to help him in any way they could.

10)   That afternoon in my car, Jesse Helms told me emphatically that he would see to it that the wording in the Pro-life plank would not be altered. The next afternoon, Sunday, I saw Jesse Helms interviewed in Detroit and heard him say on national television, "This year's Republican platform will contain a Pro-life plank."

11)   Jerry Falwell and I discussed how we could best educate and mobilize key pastors throughout the United States. We decided on arranging a meeting to which we would invite a large number of pastors. There it would be explained what needed to be done in order to get Pro-life candidates elected across the country.

12)   Jerry and I decided that I should organize the meeting to be held in Indianapolis, and to be attended by 2,900 pastors from more than 30 states. We discussed having Don Shea speak at the meeting, about how the Republican Party was now supporting the fight for morality and decency in the United States. When we asked Don to speak, he, being a Catholic priest, said, "Charles, should I wear my collar?" Jerry and I talked it over and then said, "Why not?"

13)   Many of the pastors at this meeting, being strongly Protestant, were not accustomed to fellowshipping with Catholic priests or having them speak at their gatherings. But when Don finished speaking, all 2,900 pastors gave him a standing ovation, whereupon I took the podium as the final speaker.

After the meeting adjourned, I was approached by a young man who wanted to express his agreement with our cause. He had started, and was currently pastoring, a Christ-honoring church in Fort Wayne, Indiana. This was my first meeting and conversation with David Jeremiah; it would not be my last. A few years later, by God's Grace and Providence, David succeeded Tim LaHaye as Senior Pastor of Scott Memorial Baptist Church, now called Shadow Mountain Community Church. This is our home church in San Diego County; and David Jeremiah is our Pastor as well as a very good friend.

Because God ordained it, that Pro-life plank has remained in the Republican Party Platform ever since 1980. It has been up to the elected executives and legislators as to how they would uphold it and build upon it. But, with God's heart for the innocent human babies in mind, I had done what I could to bring glory and honor to Jesus Christ. And to this day, I have continued to support the pro-life movement.

The Reagan-Bush Era

In 1985 I became a political consultant, helping godly Christians get elected to offices where they could faithfully present the message of morality and decency through our government. As a political consultant I chose to advise only men and women who were known for their honesty and integrity, and had a history of being right on the moral issues that face our country. The overwhelming majority of these were born-again Christians who truly loved the Lord.

In 1989 I became the executive director of a Christian lobbying organization, which was involved in educating both politicians and the public on issues of importance to Christians. I had several staff members including some very good attorneys. We focused especially on the rights of Christian parents and students with regard to public schools.

Meanwhile, in 1988, George H.W. Bush, with whom I had campaigned in El Paso back in 1964—when we both lost—won the Presidential election. He then succeeded Ronald Reagan in January, 1989. President Bush offered me the same governmental position that I had declined when it was offered by the Reagan administration; again, I did not rush to accept it. Rather, I continued my work as a lobbyist and educator for four more years.

Twice a month, members of all nationally-known Social Conservative Organizations in Washington, D.C., met to keep all these organizations on the same page and keep each aware of what the others were doing, as well as to discuss pending legislation and ways that they could impact government policy. Usually I did not attend these meetings—which were called the "Library Court"—but designated someone from our legal staff to represent our organization.

A Constitutional Jurist

One morning when I happened to attend the Library Court—I believe, by God's design—one of the guest speakers was a young black man who had been nominated several months earlier for the U. S. Court of Appeals for the District of Columbia Circuit. His nomination had been submitted to the Senate by President Bush.

This man told his audience that the Democrat who chaired the Senate Judiciary Committee was stalling the confirmation process by not allowing it to proceed to the Senate floor for hearings and a vote. As I listened to the testimony of this conservative Christian lawyer,

165

the reason for the delay became very evident to me. The liberals on the committee knew that this young man, if confirmed, could easily become a future Supreme Court Justice nominee.

On Capitol Hill as a Christian Lobbyist and educator

After the meeting, I sat down with this eloquent young man and asked, "Who is handling your nomination process?" He responded, "I have been doing it myself." I offered my organization's assistance to begin moving his nomination through this very difficult process. He readily accepted.

I assigned one of my legal staffers to obtain all of the pertinent information. We then proceeded to design and publish a very thorough and attractive news release package.

One of our interns hand delivered the release to every Senator's office, as well as to every major news outlet in Washington. And just for good measure, it was also delivered to the Congressmen, even though they could not vote on judiciary nominations.

Within one month, the Senate Judiciary Committee started hearings on the nomination of this remarkable man of great integrity and compassion. The Senate confirmed his nomination by a significant majority, and he became an appellate Judge.

The liberals who had stalled his nomination would later fight even more vehemently his nomination to the Supreme Court. But that nomination was also confirmed, and he became one of the jurists most committed to the Judeo-Christian ethic as one of our nation's nine Supreme Court Justices. He is Judge Clarence Thomas, defender of a strict interpretation of the Constitution.

I still have a few copies of the press release packet that helped move his confirmation forward. And he is still serving as a voice for clear-thinking, God honoring citizens as he expresses his opinions from the bench of the highest human court in our land, fully aware of the One in whose Court we must all someday appear (Rom. 14:10-12).

Until the Clinton Presidency

I had begun helping candidates get elected when I was seven years old and joined my father's campaign, singing songs in Spanish. I also was involved in his second and third campaigns, as well as my own. Not until many years later was I working to get Ronald Reagan elected. Thereafter, until the election of 1992, I had been a consultant to 32 candidates; at least 25 of these were elected with my help.

During my time as a political consultant, I would never consider taking a campaign for a man or woman who had not lived the decent, reputable life that they professed to know.

God continued using me by giving me the spiritual insight into who were the candidates worthy of the time and effort I would need to expend in order to get them elected. But, most of my clients were not able to pay for my labor; still, I considered them worthy of my effort. This meant that my income was seriously diminished.

Judy and Charles circa 1990

By 1992, I was 53 years old. All our children were then adults and had "flown the nest." Judy and I could no longer afford to rent a house or apartment, or even a room. Again God provided. While we had almost no income and did not qualify for public assistance, Judy and I were invited to move into the home of a very gracious single lady, a retired Wycliffe missionary. For fifteen months, we lived in one of the two bedrooms of her house and I did what I could as a handyman keeping her house in good repair. We are extremely grateful to her and to our God for generously providing for us during that very lean time. Recently, Judy and I had a delightful luncheon visit with her. Since 1990 she has been Judy's best friend.

Chapter XII
Broken Body

> *Yet it pleased the LORD to bruise him; he hath put him to grief.* —Isaiah 53:10a KJV

I did not know that with the ending of the Reagan-Bush era, my work and my ministry would be rudely and painfully interrupted. On January 20, 1993, William Jefferson Clinton was inaugurated 42nd President of the United States. Three days later, as I slid out of a restaurant booth and stood up, I caught my shoulder on a decorative wooden overhang. Instantly, my body was racked with unbearable pain.

At a hospital about three months later, an orthopedic surgeon fused two vertebrae in my neck, expecting that this would alleviate my inordinate and excruciating pain. It didn't.

Eleven months later, I was diagnosed with Reflex Sympathetic Dystrophy (RSD); and the prognosis was not good. I was given 31 very painful ganglion blocks, which involved injecting a needle into my neck until they found the C7 vertebra and then pulling the needle out 1/8 of an inch and injecting Lidocaine.

During a period of six months I was in the emergency room 38 times, just to survive the pain. And for several years I was on heavy doses of time-release morphine.

Two different doctors told me outright that because of the pain I would eventually commit suicide.

For more than ten years, it seemed that my life was consumed with pain. I felt that I could not do the things I had grown accustomed to doing.

I could not involve myself in trying to make America better through getting good men and women elected. I could not throw myself into missionary work, or teaching Sunday school or leading any ministry.

Ministries that I had been involved in were now in the hands of others or were no longer even functioning. I was barely functioning myself. I began to think maybe those two doctors whose prognosis was suicide had known whereof they spoke.

The pain remained. My joy in serving the Lord was gone. My body was not all that was broken.

Chapter XIII
Broken Spirit

> *Hear my prayer, O LORD, and give ear unto my cry: hold not thy peace at my tears...O spare me, that I may recover strength, before I go hence, and be no more. —Psalm 39:12-13 KJV*

In 1997, in the midst of my anguish of heart and spirit, I wrote this letter to God.

Dear Heavenly Father,

Why? Why, God? Yes Lord, I know I have no right to ask you "Why?" But I am beyond that. For years I would say that one should only ask you "What" you were going to do as a result of something bad, and never ask you, the Omnipotent God, "Why" you caused it or allowed it.

You tell me that you are a loving God, and you have even told me that you <u>are</u> Love. I have remembered, many times, that you have said that you love me greater than an earthly father loves his own son. I know how much I love my children; and I would not allow two doctors to tell them that their prognosis was suicide; nor would I let them suffer nights on end when I knew that their screams of pain were muffled in a pillow! Why should I only find some relief in over

240 milligrams of time-release morphine each day? How could I live if I thought for a minute that I could make a difference in my child's peace of mind or help him in his pain, and yet didn't do it? You, a loving God, have turned your back on me. I do have a right to ask "Why."

You know I have confessed every sin that I have even thought about committing. And how many times have I claimed nearly every one of your promises? Godly people have anointed me with oil many, many times. I also know well the story of your deep love for Mary, Martha, and Lazarus, and how you turned your back on them for at least four days. Of course, I know it was for a greater good, that of raising Lazarus from the dead.

But my Father, that no longer helps me. Father, I know you turned your back on your own son and allowed Him to cry out to you, "My God, My God, Why have you forsaken me?" I understand that this was done for a greater good, that of providing all of mankind the opportunity of salvation. For me to even mention my Savior's experience in the same letter is presumptuous; however Father, I am trying to understand "Why."

You have taught me that my reward will be in heaven and not here on earth. God I truly do not expect a reward on earth. I have asked for one thing and one thing only, to again know your "Peace that passeth all human understanding."

To me, that encompasses the essence of the Christian life. Why is that too much to ask of a loving God?

Lord, it has been astonishing to hear so many godly people say, "You must feel like Job." Your Bible has told me that all of my righteousness is as filthy rags, yet Job was a righteous man in his own right. My righteousness is solely because of my position in Christ and because of his shed Blood. So what consoling value is there for me in the book of Job?

Paul said he would rather glory in his infirmities because he was made strong in so doing. I am not Paul; however, for years you allowed me to see the truth in this statement. I, like Paul, believed that "I can do all things through Christ Jesus who strengthens me." For more than four years, rarely have I seen the reality of this promise.

This same man of God also tells me to "always give thanks for all things." I know that this verse means exactly what it says. The word "all" means nothing less. So of course, God, I have thanked you for things that have destroyed me, hurt the ones I love and in my finite mind seem to be harmful to the on-going of your kingdom.

Do I have a right to look for logic? Or do I have the right to ask you "Why?"

God, do I have any right to ask for you to show me your love? Why have you not honored your Word? There are so many of your promises that I have claimed after fulfilling the accompanying condi-tions. Father, is it really true that, "everything works together for good to those who are loving God and are called according to His purposes?" Why should you not keep all of your promises if I am obedient?

I have stored up my treasure in heaven instead of here on earth. God, when you saved me you placed in me a love for you that transformed my life. You gave me all the things the world says a person needs to have for happiness.

You gave me a lovely Christian wife, eleven cor-porations from Maine to Florida to California, and over 500 employees, a 15,656 acre ranch, private air-planes, and a corporation that became the largest of its type in the United States. That you blessed me financially is an understatement.

Then you led me to give it all away.

God, when you caused me to be voted Layman of the Year for 41 churches, you made it very clear to me that I was not being recognized for my love for you or for my godliness, but because I knew how to get things accomplished.

You gave me fame and fortune and then showed me that there was something missing; that there was more to the Christian life than the "do's" and "don'ts."

You humbled me as you revealed how much I loved the things of the world. My heart was broken as I was made to realize how much you loved me and how little love I had for you. Why did you teach me so great a lesson about your love, only to remove it in my later years?

After you taught me this lesson, it became very evident that I could no longer serve two masters. You had given me a wife with a kindred spirit, who willingly followed me as I literally was led by you to walk away from a life of luxury and a future of even greater wealth.

You placed us in Costa Rica to sleep on the floor for two months, to do without a stove or a refrigerator for weeks and all of this with small children.

You taught us to never feel like we had sacrificed or given up anything because our lives were in the center of your will. You caused me to be arrested and thrown in jail for preaching on the street. You let us endure all kinds of hardships, and to experience the all-out attack of Satan and his demonic host. Never once did we look back, for you were a loving, caring God; and being in the center of your will was the most blessed place on this earth.

We experienced over and over again the reality of your promise that if we asked for bread, You would not give us a stone. You were the God of the Old and the New Testament and you were intimately involved in our lives. From a spiritually poor little rich boy you changed me into a spiritually rich, materially poor young man. You performed miracle after miracle. One of these miracles was providing us an "upper room" in the middle of the red light district and main market of the country where over 18,000 people walked in

front of our building every day. You burdened our
hearts to begin reaching out to these thousands, many
of whom had open running sores; others were prostitutes, alcoholics, drug addicts; and all were people
with absolutely no hope.

You put us where there were 113 houses of
prostitution within a block-and-a-half radius of our
building. You allowed our hearts to be broken by seeing
more than a hundred girls between the age of 8 and
12 living a life of no hope. Yet to us you were a great
and loving God because you had sent us to reveal your
love to the unlovable. We counted it a privilege to be
used by you to reach literally thousands with your love.

As I look back I can see how great a work you
did in the ministry you gave us. There were less than
14,000 evangelicals in the country when we arrived;
yet in our first two years you used us to see 5,000 lost
souls cry out to be saved. You were truly a great God
to serve.

Do you owe me anything? Do I have the right to
say yes? Monetarily, you owe me nothing even though
you have allowed us to become almost destitute and on
food stamps. Physically, you owe me nothing because I

know my life was purchased at Calvary. God, do you owe me anything?

I believe you do. What do you owe me? You owe me the continual knowledge of your presence and your love that I once knew.

Return unto me the joy of my salvation and the sweetness of the relationship that I have known. I only desire to know you, which is not something unreasonable. My heartbeat is only to know you.

God, I no longer ask you to heal me, remove my pain, or make our lives easier. Just keep your word. You have promised you would never leave me or forsake me. What have you done? You have said that we have not because we ask not. God, if you love me more than I love my children, why do I have to beg to know your love and your peace. WHY, OH MY GREAT GOD, WHY?

Your Son Because of CHRIST,

Charles.

It was more than seven years later that my loving Heavenly Father answered this prayer, this letter. He has allowed me to again know His sweet presence and His peace. How did this happen?

No, He did not take away the pain. In fact, even now, in 2019, my left arm feels like it is continually on fire. It is as if my arm were lying on an extremely hot griddle. In addition to this RSD pain, I live with the constant pain of both peripheral and autonomic neuropathy.

But in 2004, God allowed me to clearly see what He was doing in my life, and what He wanted me to be doing in Christ.

Chapter XIV
I Can See Clearly Now

> But I would ye should understand, brethren, that the
> things which happened *unto me have fallen out rather
> unto the furtherance of the gospel.*
>
> —Philippians 1:12 KJV

In March of 2004, doctors at the University of California San Diego (UCSD) Medical Center diagnosed me as having peripheral neuropathy. This meant that the nerves in my feet and legs were degenerating and eventually this would also affect my hands and arms, which condition is now one of the sources of my constant pain.

Later, another doctor from UCSD diagnosed me with autonomic neuropathy which is the degeneration of nerves from my waist to my neck. Their prognosis was very bleak. My pain became so bad that the 240 mg of time-release morphine that I was taking each day became ineffective.

Our children became very concerned about their father, and wanted to do something to somehow help. Under God's sovereignty they decided that I needed to go to Costa Rica for "one last visit." They knew that I would be blessed by seeing many of my children in the Lord, and that I would be especially blessed to see many of "my preacher boys."

James and Cal, our two older sons, said that they would go as well, and I agreed to make the effort in spite of my pain. We anticipated that this trip would turn out to be very special for all three of us, and especially for Cal, who would be returning to the country of his birth.

Charles V was unable to go because of his work, but he provided needed funding for the trip. The children made the airline reservations for the following Saturday.

However, on Friday night I was admitted to the hospital with internal bleeding. Our tickets were nonrefundable; so the next morning, James at 38 and Cal at 35, boarded the plane for Costa Rica, with the assurance that I would join them as soon as possible.

My three days in the hospital were not without contrary incident. I was given an injection of a wrong medicine; this resulted in

180

a violent adverse reaction that made me believe I was going to die. But I had to survive; I had promised my sons. So, by God's grace, two days after leaving the hospital I boarded an airplane for Costa Rica.

The previous 43 years had seen me leave Judy and our home—wherever it was—and take to the skies in excess of two hundred times. But this was the very first time Judy and I both wept as I was leaving for the airport. We both knew there was the very real possibility that this would be my last, and that I would meet my Maker without returning from Costa Rica, the land of the people we loved.

As I was rolled onto the plane in a wheelchair, the stress and pain I was suffering caused me tremendous agony. I did not know that the Lord had already begun to work a miracle in my life. When by God's grace I arrived in Costa Rica without any delays, I was met by James and Cal. Also there to meet me were Ken and Kevin McGovern, dear longtime friends from Texas, and four of my dearest Costa Rican children and grandchildren in the Lord.

I felt that if this was to be my last trip, I wanted to hit the ground running, in spite of my physical condition. I had a deep desire to show my sons and dear friends where our ministry began, and to share the details of what had happened at each location.

I was greatly blessed to be able to stand where the parking lot had been, and to recall those memories of long ago. That was the same parking lot that I had rented for two hours every Tuesday. That was where I had stood and preached in front of a house of prostitution. From the windows of that brothel, for the first three weeks the women shouted vulgarities at me; but then, by the fourth week, enough of them had come to know the Lord that they would applaud after the invitation was given and people had come forward to give their life to Christ. I was even blessed to be able to show my sons and the McGoverns where the jail had been, the one I was locked up in for several hours after being arrested for preaching on the street.

We then went to the two-lane bridge under one end of which there had been 87 children and 12 adults living. There I recalled how God had used us and blessed us in a truly remarkable way. All five of us wept as we recalled the story of the two-year-old boy who had been run over on the bridge. Then we rejoiced in how James and Cal, along with Judy Anne and Little Charlie (Charles V), had agreed to take the $100 that Dr. Wren Causey had sent from Columbia, Louisiana, for their Christmas, and use it to buy presents for each of those 87 children (pages 120-122). To this day our children still remember that morning of taking the presents to the children under the bridge as their most blessed Christmas.

We all stood in front of where our "Upper Room" had been for 31 years. It would have continued as a place for winning souls to Christ had it not been torn down to make way for a three-story concrete building. I shared with my sons and the McGoverns how God had led us to rent it and how He had greatly blessed the simple plan that He had given us for the salvation of souls.

The work of *Cristianos Compartiendo a Cristo* in Costa Rica never depended on me or any other human being. We were only tools in God's hands. He started it, He blessed it, and He continues to bless it. Today there are more than 75 churches—in several countries—that began as a result of men being called to preach in the Upper Room.

James and Cal experienced the blessing of seeing some of our old team members who had babysat them when they were small children. They also heard dozens of Christians testify to the goodness of our Lord in using the members of our different teams from Chile, Peru, Ecuador, Bolivia, Venezuela, Nicaragua and Costa Rica, who led them to Christ. I do not believe that my two older sons had cried as much since they were in diapers. The tears were both for joy over the salvation of so many and for sadness because of the thousands in the market place of San Jose who were still not ready for the coming of the King.

Easter came while we were there. And on that Sunday I sat in a chair and preached a one-hour message in the largest of our "Christians Sharing Christ" churches. After the service, a gray-haired man who had been taking a video of me came up and said, "I accepted the Lord in the Upper Room nearly 30 years ago while you were preaching." This man, who had kept an appointment with his Savior in the red light district way back then, was now an oncologist in Costa Rica and was still living for the Lord. After I spoke with that man, Pastor Rafael Porras, my dear son in the Lord, invited all of my "preacher boys" and other men that I had discipled, to come up on the platform. God had given me the opportunity to win to Christ and to disciple many young men who would later become pastors.

A very large number of these men came up and filled the platform behind me. A Christian Mariachi band then walked in; they sang about how God had blessed people through missionaries. That Easter morning was a great time of rejoicing for all of us as we recalled the marvels of what God had done in and through the Upper Room.

One of our pastors and his wife had left their home in northern Costa Rica at 3 a.m. and rode a bus five hours to attend this special service. They then caught a bus for home; he preached the Easter service at their church that night.

Even though I was in tremendous pain, I accepted an invitation to preach in one more of our churches. This required me to travel over a rough and winding mountainous road. The service that afternoon was a blessing for me as well as for the church. However, the return trip down the mountain caused me even more pain.

Late that Sunday night, James, Cal and I crawled into our beds, all in the same small bedroom. Their snoring let me know they were asleep; but sleep would not come for me even though I had taken my prescribed dosage of morphine. Around 3 a.m. in the midst of my pain, I thought with fond memories of each of the "preacher boys" that I had discipled and mentored. I prayed for each one of them as I thought of their names. At some point God reminded me of one of the things that I had made sure to teach each one of them: "When you get to heaven God will ask you, 'What did you do with the gift that I gave you?'"

It was at that moment that I received from God the clear answer to the anguished question I had asked in that letter seven years earlier: "Why, God?"

Numerous times during the 10 years of horrible pain and suffering I had pondered the question: "What sin or sins have I committed that could be the cause for the loss of the sweet relationship that I had with the Lord." I had confessed every known sin that I had committed, and had asked the Holy Spirit to reveal to me any sin that I could not remember.

After making two "sin lists" and confessing everything to God and to the individuals that I had sinned against, I still did not know the "joy of my salvation." Had I become a castaway or was there something else that had caused such a great loss in my life?

I knew that it was not my salvation that was lost; only the joy was gone. And like the Psalmist, I yearned for that joy of salvation to be restored unto me (Psalm 51:12).

It was that night in Costa Rica, after recalling the question, "What did you do with the gift that I gave you?" that I recognized the answer to my question of "Why?"

I knew now that I had "quenched" the Holy Spirit. God showed me that I had received from Him the gift of faith, and for years I had used that gift to glorify Him by taking each step of faith in obedience to His will.

I now saw clearly that during those 10 years of pain I had been paralyzed by the belief that He could not use me because of my pain and disability. How wrong was my thinking! Oh, how dreadfully wrong I had been in yielding to—and thus adding to—my physical pain; adding the spiritual pain of losing the joy of my salvation.

I realized that I needed to again live by faith—not by sight, and not by feeling. The old gospel song says, "Trust and obey, for there's no other way to be happy in Jesus but to trust and obey."

Trust and faith go hand in hand. I knew that henceforth I needed to trust Him, not my senses; and to obey Him, not my pain.

I needed to day by day exercise the faith that He had given me; to go where He leads and do what He says.

And I resolved to do exactly that for as long as there is breath in my body.

Chapter XV
Five More Years

Take heed to thyself, and unto the doctrine; continue in them: for in doing this thou shalt both save thyself, and them that hear thee. —1 Timothy 4:16 KJV

Recognizing my disobedience to God, and my quenching of the Holy Spirit, I asked for forgiveness. I then asked my Heavenly Father to give me five years in which by faith I could glorify His name by following the leading of the Holy Spirit daily. Instantly I knew that God had answered my prayer and in essence I had made a pact with Him for five years.

It was then about 3 a.m. on Monday, the day after Easter Sunday in 2004. Not knowing how long it would take for my body to be able to begin those five years of Spirit-led preaching, teaching, and evangelizing, I initially calculated as of that day.

But those five years of ministry, which I intended to carry out in spite of the pain, did not begin immediately. There were more surgeries scheduled and many months of recuperation. The first of those surgeries actually resulted in a partial mitigating of my extreme pain. The second brought a little more relief. On a scale of one to ten—ten being unbearable pain, accompanied by thoughts of suicide—I had been hovering between 8 and 10. After those two surgeries, my pain leveled off at 5, which is what I have experienced as normal ever since. There are still times when it goes back up to 7 or even 8, and on rare occasions, may spike at 9.

Before undergoing those surgeries, I was allowed, by God's grace, to make one more trip to Costa Rica. Despite my extremely high levels of pain, God used me to preach 13 times in 12 days and to see revival break out in several churches. This turned out to be a preview of what God would do through me in the years ahead. Each time I preached, the pain would not allow me to stand; I was forced to address the listeners while seated in a chair. For many years I had been a fiery, animated preacher and would become excited as I preached God's word. Having to preach sitting in a chair was difficult for me. But I knew "I can do all things through my Christ Jesus who strengthens me."

Nearly three years passed before I was physically able to begin those five years of full-time ministry, which I understood God would grant me before my life on earth was over. Since I did not actually start the new ministry until January of 2007, the ending date of the five-year pact would be in the first month of 2012.

Between 2004 and 2007, during my down times of recuperating after each surgical operation, I was able to prepare for the coming years of ministry. During the period of recuperation after my first surgery, Judy and I had the privilege of hearing Dr. Ron Cline preach a powerful sermon at a local church. Afterwards we had a blessed time talking with him about Latin America. For 25 years he had been the president of worldwide HCJB radio network located in Quito, Ecuador.

In our conversation, Dr. Cline gave me some exciting information. He said that for every child born in Latin America four people are born again. He further explained that this was making it necessary to train more pastors. Upon hearing of this need I began praying that God would use me to solve this "good problem."

Beginning shortly after our time in Glorieta, New Mexico, in 1965, God had been giving me messages to preach from His Word that were worthy of being heard by every Christian layman. When I heard of the need for more pastors to care for new Christians, I thought of how many laymen had been called to preach because of the ministry that God had given us in the Upper Room.

I wondered, "Could it be that God would use me in Latin America to train Christian men to fill the need for more pastors? Would God allow me to train these men to start churches that would accommodate all those new Christians, wherever they might be?"

Ron Cline arranged for me to attend a meeting in Juarez, Mexico, that was supposed to put together a strategy for reaching Latin America for Christ. At this meeting God showed me what was the greatest need for not only the pastors in Latin America but for pastors throughout the world.

When I returned to our apartment in southern California, I began developing a Pastors' Seminar that I could teach in either Spanish or English. I believed that when implemented under the power of the Holy Spirit, it would have a positive impact on pastors.

Some years earlier, I had heard that a seminary had sent a number of their students throughout the United States on a research project. Through this research it was discovered that the average amount of time a pastor dedicates specifically to prayer was 20 minutes a week. This was alarming information, and it clearly exposed the reason why so many pastors and their churches were powerless in their attempts at reaching the lost for Christ.

Our experience at Glorieta in 1965, where we learned the importance of prayer in the lives of the missionaries to China; our study of God's Word, and of various books on revival; the testimony of many godly pastors; all these made us realize that we needed to establish prayer as the foundation of our ministry of Christians Sharing Christ. And God has honored that.

In the 1970's our home church in the U.S. was MacArthur Boulevard Baptist Church in Irving, Texas. The pastor of that church was our close friend, Ron Dunn, the last of my three mentors. He was also a member of the board of Christians Sharing Christ. He had led his church to establish a non-stop, 24-hour-a-day intercessory prayer ministry in a small room of the church building. God blessed my life and ministry through what I learned from Ron's expository preaching, especially his messages on prayer. In essence, prayer is simply talking to God and listening for His answer. After having met Dr. Ron Cline, the more I prayed the more I knew that God wanted me to teach pastors the importance of prayer, and how to pray. If it had not been for the Lord's leading I would never have had the audacity to presume that I knew more about prayer than the average pastor.

During my rehabilitation after the second surgery, I began reviewing my sermon notes, reading the books that I had on prayer, and most importantly, revisiting passages about prayer in the Bible.

Over the course of five days I read the entire New Testament, underlining every verse that referred to prayer. Examining and categorizing those verses, I found that 95% of them were about intercession, 2% were about petition, and the remaining 3% were divided almost equally between thanksgiving, praise, and confession. Discovering this pattern allowed me to see what Christ and the apostles considered most important in talking with their heavenly Father.

Our new ministry begins

By January of 2007, I felt that I was ready to begin fulfilling my part of the five-year pact I had made with God. I trusted that He would fulfill His part by keeping me alive and blessing the ministry that He gave me to carry out each day, pain notwithstanding. Our first pastors' seminar was held in Arizona on January 17, 2007, for a group of 12 Hispanic pastors whose churches were in the greater Phoenix area. From the beginning, each time I have taught the seminar I have been blessed, as God continues to reveal new truths from His Word.

After the Phoenix seminar, I began making arrangements to travel to Costa Rica, the land that Judy and I loved and where we were best known. Right at the beginning of that Latin American Seminar and Evangelistic tour, I sent a newsletter to churches and individual Christians in several parts of America.

These were the ones I believed would be supporting us with prayer. In that newsletter dated April 21, 2007, I reminded them that when we had started our missionary work in Costa Rica back in 1968, there were seventeen widows and single ladies in western North Carolina who were praying for our ministry each and every day. I said the success of our ministry was due totally to God's response to the intercessory prayer of these ladies.

I then said:

"Now I want to ask you a very personal question: Will you make a promise to God that for the next 8 months and 9 days (until the end of this year) you will pray for our ministry by name each and every day? This is a commitment to Him, for you to be part of a ministry that can be used of God in ways that will be truly astounding. Your intercessory prayer in this ministry is more important than anything I will say in any and all of the seminars.

"Remember your promise is to God not to me. My hope is that He will lead at least 17 people to do what those 17 ladies did so many years ago."

In answer to the prayers of those dear Christian men and women, God blessed our new ministry in Latin America in magnificent ways. More than 85 Pastors gathered at our "kick-off" Seminar in Costa Rica. There was no public advertising ahead of time. The only way pastors heard about the seminar was by word of mouth; but they still came.

What God did was so amazing that there are tears in my eyes as I write this. It is just like what He did in our lives in the early years, when Judy and I were continually overwhelmed by His greatness and His goodness as He used us in His ministry.

The leadership had me go forward after the Seminar; and they all prayed for me and for the cities that lay ahead for us. The president of the Costa Rica Ministerial Alliance came up afterwards and said, "Don Carlos, I give you my word that I will pray for you and your ministry every day." And he then repeated, "*Te doy mi palabra*, I give you my word." Right after that first seminar, I wrote to our prayer partners:

> "You are the reason God blessed today and you are the reason that my pain left me before the seminar, and did not return until after I finished. Please continue to pray!!!!"

Then I was invited to speak to more than 3,000 Christians who had come for an annual meeting from all over Costa Rica. These were those that met on every Wednesday in local churches to pray for revival in Costa Rica. I was greatly blessed to see that many of them had traveled from the most remote areas just to attend this annual meeting. And I was doubly blessed when so many of them told me that they were my children or grandchildren in the Lord, and were still faithful to Him. Providentially, at this gathering I met Rigoberto Vega Alvarado (Rigo).

With Rigoberto Vega Alvarado

Rigo had worked for the Billy Graham Association organizing pastors in many Latin American countries. This meant that he knew the evangelical leadership in those countries. Rigo and I became close friends; he treated me like his own father and his young adult children called me grandfather. For the years thereafter, Rigoberto and I traveled together to the pastor's seminars that he organized in Bolivia, Peru, Venezuela, Panama, Costa Rica, Nicaragua, Honduras, El Salvador, and Guatemala.

For the other seminars, I was usually accompanied by either Judy or my son James. I rarely traveled alone. Interwoven with the seminars were evangelistic services that I held in churches throughout Latin America.

God greatly blessed me—as well as thousands of others— through the intensive and extensive ministry he gave me to do in that part of the world. In fact, during the next ten years I spoke to more than 250,000 pastors and leaders throughout Central and South America. And it continued to be true that THE ONLY TIME I did not feel pain was when I was proclaiming the Word of God before an audience.

Much of the emphasis was on effectual prayer. I shared with the pastors what God had taught me through His Word, His Spirit, and the gifted teachers He had put in my life. In my years of study, I have seen four essentials to effectual prayer, with none being less important than the other three. These are: Faith: Perseverance; Praying in the name of Jesus; and Praying according to God's will.

FAITH - When we talk to God we need the faith to believe that He hears us, and (like so many loving parents of grown children) He wants to hear us and answer our prayers, more than we want to talk to him.

PERSEVERANCE: Many examples in the Bible are given to show us the importance of continuing to pray until we receive God's answer. The best example of this is the widow with the unjust judge. See Luke 18:1-8.

PRAY IN THE NAME OF JESUS: In John, chapters 14 through 16, Jesus tells us four times that we are to pray in His name. He made it very clear that no one can come to the Father except through, or in the name of, the Son, Jesus Christ himself.

PRAY ACCORDING TO GOD'S WILL: One of the best examples of praying according to His will is the prayer of Jesus in Gethsemane. He knew beforehand what he would suffer at his crucifixion, and he asked his Father to "remove this cup." But he added, "Thy will be done."

I also spent a good deal of time in each seminar exhorting pastors and leaders to live according to the admonition that Paul gives in Romans 12:1-2:

> I BESEECH you therefore, brethren, by the mercies of God, that ye present your bodies a living sacrifice, holy, acceptable unto God...And be not conformed to this world: but be ye transformed by the renewing of your mind, that ye may prove what is that good, and acceptable, and perfect, will of God.— KJV

I spoke to them about refraining from secret sins, such as being involved in pornography. I referred to a report that as many as 40% of American pastors have repeatedly viewed pornography. I told them that they ought to be reflecting the presence of Jesus Christ through their living lives that are holy, acceptable unto the Lord.

I emphasized that God would not honor them if they lived a lie. I told them, "You always tell the truth even if it hurts." I said that if they could not live a life holy, acceptable unto the Lord then they should go back to selling insurance or real estate or anything other than standing up in the pulpit preaching a message with no power.

I challenged them to spend a minimum of eight hours in prayer before they preached a sermon to their church. I explained that if they did, it would not be just a sermon they preached, but a true message from God.

I have been told on many occasions that I preach and speak with more authority than most pastors. My response has always been, "God allows me to do that because he is the Lord of my life. To live a life of hypocrisy would rob me of the blessing of His using me for HIS glory."

Completing the first year

While traveling from one city to another on our first Costa Rican tour that year, God blessed by using me to lead two cab drivers to Christ. The one who drove me to the airport prayed to receive Christ on the way. After a rough flight to northern Costa Rica (CR) in a small airplane, we landed in Liberia, CR. Then the cab driver who picked up a pastor and me received Christ as he was driving us to the church for my second seminar. I am always blessed to see the light turned on in someone's life. To have a cab driver pray the sinner's prayer with you as he is driving you to your destination is a joyful experience. That night from 6:00 until 9:30 I taught the second seminar to a hundred pastors and church members.

The flight from Liberia back to San Jose was delayed for two hours, causing me to wait in the heat for nearly three hours. Arriving in cool San Jose was a great blessing. God then gave me an hour trip with a brother who wanted to learn how to pray and how to teach his family to pray.

Next was Panama: a 4-hour seminar and 7 hour service. God used me to speak to more than 200 pastors and leaders of several denominations in Panama. He brought many of these pastors to their knees as they confessed their unworthiness to be in His ministry. And with His blessing, I participated in one TV/Radio interview.

Television interview in Panama

On this trip God blessed pastors and lay people in ways that seem almost like New Testament times. To see dozens of pastors crying to the Lord for forgiveness, and pleading to be used to win their country to Christ, brought me to tears many times. What a blessing to see the front of large churches filled with people broken before our Lord. My gracious and loving Lord Jesus Christ has blessed me and this ministry in unbelievable ways!!

By His grace and Spirit, we held three seminars in six days—two in Costa Rica and one in Panama—where 1,500 heard the messages; He enabled me to spend 14 hours preaching (in two church services and one pastors' luncheon, plus the seminars); and in His strength, I endured 39 hours in airports and airplanes.

With a heart full of love for my Costa Rican and Panamanian brothers and sisters I left for home for a short rest before returning to Guatemala and Nicaragua and then Peru, Bolivia, and Venezuela.

This trip was the start of a new journey of ministry that will last until God brings it to an end. My heartbeat is to see pastors learn that sin robs them of usefulness and absence of prayer robs them of power. We teach the Word, exhort Christians to die to self, and share testimonies of things that God has done in our lives through prayer.

Much of what I communicate comes from what I learned from Dr. Cal Guy, Dr. L. Nelson Bell, and Pastor Ron Dunn, the three men who have had the greatest impact on my life, till now.

My dear brother Rigoberto, who had organized these seminars, provided me the support and spiritual warmth to do what I had thought for years would have been impossible. He and I are at one in spirit; we both want to see revival come to all of Latin America.

Rigo had traveled with the Billy Graham crusades to almost every country in Latin America. He knows the pastors that have a hunger to reach their country for Christ. Rigo and I work as a team; and with all honesty, I physically could not have continued this ministry without his walking beside me. Rigo's knowledge of all the ins and outs of each country and its pastors, plus his ability to organize the seminars, has been essential. Rigo was used powerfully when I physically could not preach in churches where I had been scheduled to preach. He and I have the same heartbeat.

The tours of Latin America continued. I taught seminars, spoke in churches, and did evangelistic work. God blessed it all. At the end of 2007, I wrote the following letter as the first annual report to Ken McGovern—then president of the board of Christians Sharing Christ (CSC).

Ken,

This report tells the story of what HE has done and is doing in and through our ministry. Your making the trip to meet me in late January and early February will be a great blessing for both of us and to our ministry. I like the idea of taking people with us on future trips. But if we do, as busy as I am, Judy will have to act as tour guide and translator.

First seminar to Hispanic pastors in Arizona was in January, 2007.

Seminars held from April through December:

2nd seminar in San Jose, Costa Rica
3rd in the North of Costa Rica (Guanacaste)
4th Panama City
5th Chimaltenango, Guatemala
6th Guatemala City
7th Santa Cruz, Bolivia
8th Lima, Peru
9th & 10th Northern Guatemala (State of Petén)
11th Panama City
12th Caracas, Venezuela
13th Barquisimeto, Venezuela
14th Maracaibo, Venezuela
15th Lima, Peru (mini 2 hours)

During the last 6 months, 10 Cab drivers were won to the Lord; 2 shoe shine men were won to the Lord in a Guatemalan airport (one of their wives has now also come to the Lord); several thousand have come forward in services and seminars for salvation or commitment (7 accepted Christ in one small church); more than 25,000 have heard the message of revival and of living the victorious life, as well as the importance of prayer.

Below is a picture of a Mayan woman who asked me to pray with her at a pastors' seminar in Chimaltenango, Guatemala. She was the wife of a pastor.

I preached for at least an hour in each of thirty churches in seven countries and held 14 five-hour pastors' seminars. I gave a strong challenge to a meeting of more than 3,000 intercessors in Costa Rica.

In July and November, I gave strong messages in Peru to several hundred leaders in government positions; these included a former Vice President of Peru, the Speaker of their congress, three Army Generals, more than 35 Federal Judges, a Lima City Councilman, and other high officials of the Peruvian government, as seen in the photo above.

I did ten radio interviews and four television interviews on the need for prayer and repentance and revival. I also preached over nationwide TV several times.

It seems with each successive seminar, attendance increases along with more conviction and repentance. I have seen some of God's greatest Christians, ones who love God with all their hearts and live lives that truly honor HIM. Some of those who have blessed me the most cannot read; but they preach messages that would set many of our affluent churches on fire for the Lord.

A dear Christian friend named Rosa, and her ten-year-old son Cristofer—I love him like a grandson—walk along a muddy snake-infested path for more than an hour to reach a paved road; there they always hope to get a ride, and if they can't, they walk another hour to church. These dear friends never miss the two weekly church services; and their return to their small hovel of a home is always in the dark. Cristofer is a straight-A student and walks more than an hour each way to his school. My God has blessed me by allowing me to know the poorest of poor, who are the richest of the rich in the Lord.

I have flown over the Amazon region, crossed the Equator, seen man-made islands on the highest lake in the world, seen some of the world's poorest people and have seen a small portion of a 1,700,000 acre ranch owned by one man. I have seen families living in small houses, level upon level, one upon the other, from a valley to the top of a 3,000-foot mountain.

My heart was broken when I saw, for the second time in Latin America, a boy who is permanently bent at the waist; he has to walk on his forearms and his feet. Both times I have seen this I have been unable to control my emotions.

How my loving Lord has blessed me. My years of pain were His way of making me see and understand the deep pain of others. Tears have flowed as I have remembered some of these momentous opportunities that my loving Lord has given me in the last six months. He has already given me a full life, and every day that He continues to use me and bless me is like honey on my lips. We truly serve a great, wonderful, and loving Lord.

2008

This ministry that began with the seminar for Hispanic pastors in Arizona is different from the missionary work Judy and I had begun in Costa Rica in 1968. Since 2007, I have been focusing primarily on Pastors and other Christian leaders, teaching them to love Jesus Christ above all, to spend time with God in prayer, to live a holy life, acceptable unto the Lord, and to evangelize the communities around their churches, seeking the lost souls and bringing them to salvation.

In January of 2008, Judy and I made a trip to Guatemala and El Salvador. In one seminar, with more than 2,400 in attendance, I spoke for three and a half hours without stopping; no one left or fell asleep.

Some of the 2400 pastors at 3½ hour seminar

Besides those in the main room, a large number of the pastors were in overflow rooms viewing and listening via closed circuit television.

On this trip, we were in Guatemala for two weeks and El Salvador for four days; we were mightily used of our gracious Lord in ways we had never experienced before.

A doctor and a certified translator accidentally found themselves in our seminar, and days later told Ken McGovern that they had not stopped talking about it and were in the process of arranging for us to speak in their 13,000-member church.

I preached in five churches; two were Mayan Quiché. I held a prayer meeting for the staff of a computer company; the owner was involved in a ministry to the gangs in Guatemala City.

We held three Pastors' Seminars in the two countries with a total attendance of 3,100. Two of the pastors rode a bus 12 hours each way to attend one seminar. It was amazing that in each seminar all were eager to hear God's word about prayer and revival. These are special Christians who want to see revival come to their country. I am sure there are many such Christians in my own country; I wish I knew more of them.

We were truly blessed by the Lord in leading two cab drivers to Christ, and almost persuading our helicopter pilot to receive Christ. In a church in San Salvador we saw 11 people come forward to accept Christ.

In just the seminars and the churches, I spoke to more than 12,000; there were many more viewing and listening by way of television. We recorded one of our most powerful seminars; it was edited and distributed to thousands of pastors throughout Latin America. The five television messages were duplicated and shipped to Spanish-speaking TV Stations throughout the world.

In San Salvador, El Salvador, we had a one-hour TV interview on prayer and revival; it was seen in more than 17 countries throughout Latin-America on an international Christian television network. We are still hoping and praying that, for the first time in recorded history God is going to send true revival throughout the Spanish speaking world, starting in one or more countries in Latin-America.

Two pastors from the largest church in Honduras attended our largest seminar in Guatemala, and were quoted as saying, "We have never been more blessed in a seminar." The president of our small, non-profit organization, Ken McGovern, who spent 12 days with us on this trip, said, "To win Latin America to Christ we must see revival in individuals, in churches, and in entire countries." Ken heard our team member, Rigoberto, preach a powerful message in San Salvador. We continue to be extremely grateful to God for Ken and Rigo; these two men have meant so much to us personally and to our ministry.

God blessed Judy and me with many lasting Christian friendships, not only in the churches, but also in our hotels, in restaurants, and in taxicabs. There were so many who blessed us beyond anything we could expect. Let me relate some of the ways they blessed us.

One dear Christian friend took off her beautiful Ruana and gave it to Judy to keep and wear because Judy was cold. The five days we were "live" on television were days when everyone treated us like we were their parents. Their love was contagious. Thirty professionals saw to our every need; on the last day there were many good-bye tears.

In order to hold a three-hour seminar in northern Guatemala, we had to endure five hours of shear agony and pain riding over a rough road to Quezaltenango. Our dear brother Benjamin Orozco recognized my severe pain (level 8). After the seminar (which by God's grace I was able to complete) he called another of our dear brothers in Guatemala and asked him to find an alternate means of transporting us back to Guatemala City so we would not have to endure the painful return trip by car. That night my crying out from pain woke me up.

The next morning we were told that a helicopter would pick us up and fly us back to the city. You may find it hard to believe that I was able to continue my ministry in my physical condition. But remember, I had a pact with God; I had to go on with or without pain. And it was almost always with.

Almost beyond comprehension was the amount of relief and love we received straight from the Lord as we gently flew down the mountain. God has given us many Christian friends in many places. On this trip, He brought Pastor Luis Fernando Solares and his wife Marta into our lives. We now have a oneness in the Lord with these two Guatemalans; we will always love them.

After we returned home from this trip, Judy wrote a letter to our children. I want to share that letter with you.

February 22, 2008

My dear children,

      As I sit listening to the most recent disc that Judy Anne shared with Dad & me (while Dad is at a lunch with our pastor) I am awe-struck once again at the boundless love of our Lord for Dad and me as it is so very often expressed through each one of you whom we love so dearly.

      From the first, when you all put your heads together and acted on James's idea of sending (No, taking) Dad to Costa Rica—what an act of love and self-sacrifice! Beginning even with Cal's heart's cry, which saved Daddy from the unutterable—from that beginning, then James being healed of his pancreatitis, and his heart-born idea to take Dad to Costa Rica, to the acting out of that idea in the first trip—Charlie's credit card, Judy Anne & Rick picking Dad up and getting him on the plane, the hearts of cooperation of each spouse involved—how it drives me to my knees to realize that when we were on OUR LAST LEGS, you ALL gave us legs to stand on again, and the results—each of the things you read in our newsletters—are every bit as much YOUR ministry, Each One of you, as it ever has been of Dad or me.

      I can say that with my whole heart, knowing full well that this ministry is something the Lord Himself wanted to do and IS DOING—through ALL of us!!!

I just don't know how to praise and thank HIM enough for using us as a family as never before—the answer to every prayer I have ever prayed for all of us, from the time you were just born, and "being ready" to be born, and for sure, including each one of our precious daughters-in-law, and our dear son-in-law, who, knowing it or not, were interceded for from the time of those births. as God put each one of you in my arms, including our grandchildren, the prayers rose up, prayers that I, myself, cannot even take credit for, because the Lord in His great love for each of us put those very prayers in our hearts for love of each one of us, and all of the people who are even now benefiting from this ministry.

I cannot even begin to understand that kind of love and forward thinking, even through all of the suffering that some of us have experienced, each and every thing was known by HIM ahead of time, and the answers were waiting for us to "scoop up" in His own time and way.

Matchless is His Name, His love, His covering—I cannot ever be grateful enough for that care and attention from His own hand, from before the foundation of the earth!

Each time Dad has traveled, or when I have gone with him, and all of the "before and in-between" times, you all have "been there with your gifts of money, groceries, meals, fellowship, credit cards, the car, the microwave, the garage sale, the love and care for, and visits with, Gran, the willingness to cooperate and provide whatever the need has been, and Dad and I KNOW your heart-prayers for his healing and well-being.

We could never, never be grateful enough for the people you each are—your great love, your great gifts, your concern and love so far surpasses anything we have ever known of anyone else on this earth, that we just have to pause to bless God for HIS gift of each one of you to us, and we watch in awe and expectation as He places you in the lives of others whom He wants to bless!

Just know that every heart touched, every taxi-driver won, every interchange of encouragement that cannot be numbered or mentioned for the next opportunity being in front of us, is etched, marked, WRITTEN in the Lamb's book of life, with YOUR individual investments of love marked down by our Lord, Himself, and duly noted by us. THANK YOU!

THANK YOU for who you are, for your great love for the Lord, and for us. THANK YOU for each and every act of love that you do every day toward us, and toward the many that we never get a *chance to hear about who are blessed because GOD so long ago deemed us blessed to be able to call you Son, Son-in-law, Daughter, Daughter-in-law, Grandchild, friend.*

We love you all so much,

Mom, Grammi, Mimi, Mother-in-law

In March of 2008, Judy and I made a very fruitful week-long trip to Western North Carolina. Not only did Judy and I gain needed rest, but we spoke to nearly 40 Hispanic pastors at Fruitland Bible Institute, preached in a Hispanic Church, and had the blessing of renewing friendship with old friends. One dear friend from years past, Kaye Dunn Robinson, gave us permission to translate some of Ron Dunn's sermons into Spanish and to distribute them throughout Latin America. Ron was one of three men who had the greatest influence on my spiritual life.

For a while, we were members of Ron's church in Irving, Texas, and he was a member of our CSC Board. He made an unforgettable trip to Costa Rica with me in the seventies. Although he is in the presence of the Lord, his preaching ministry continues to impact lives through his recorded messages from Lifestyle Ministries Inc.

On a very hot day in 2008 (Monday, April 7), Judy and I were able to spend some pleasant time on the island of Flores. After sitting for more than an hour on the edge of a beautiful lake in Guatemala, we were picked up for a meeting with a select group of godly pastors of several denominations. Our time with them was spent discussing essential aspects of revival for Guatemala.

We were in the State of Petén, several hundred miles north of Guatemala City. The previous Saturday night we had our first Pastors' Seminar in the city of San Benito. Twelve hours later on Sunday morning we rode two hours south to Poptun, where we held our second three-hour-long seminar. The combined attendance at these seminars was around 1,000. In each meeting, as in all our seminars in Guatemala, we saw a hunger for the Lord and for His word.

We have learned to love the people of Guatemala. We made another trip to that country in June of 2008, arriving there by way of Honduras. First we flew from San Diego to Houston where we boarded a flight to San Pedro Sula, Honduras. Actual flying time was just a little over six hours; but total time from San Diego to the airport in Honduras was ten hours. We were met in San Pedro Sula by a pastor who had heard about us from another Honduran pastor, one whom we had met three months earlier at Fruitland Bible Institute near Asheville, North Carolina.

We always wanted to reach the most people for Christ with the finances available, and were willing to go through numerous hardships to accomplish that goal, ministering in as many venues as we could in the shortest time possible. Because of our limited resources we had asked the pastor who had arranged for the seminars in Honduras to put us in a hotel that we could afford. He made a reservation for us at a hotel that fit that one criterion. We checked into that hotel at 4:30 p.m. We had to be ready at 6 o'clock that evening to go to where we would hold a three-hour pastor's seminar. Entering our room, we saw that the floors were so dirty that we could not take off our shoes; we cautiously washed our hands in a not-so-clean bathroom sink. Only the sheets were clean.

The seminar that night was poorly attended; still, I taught it like there were a thousand present. After having had a not-too-wholesome meal, we returned to the hotel around 10 p.m. We recognized that we were not going to be able to take off our shoes except to crawl into bed.

Exhausted after our long day of travel from San Diego, and our ministering to the pastors, we fell into bed, only to be awakened several times in the night by noises in the hall. Then to go to the bathroom at night we chose to put our shoes back on. The next morning, we were packed and ready to leave early because we had to be at the airport at 8:15. When we opened the door of our room we realized that the couch in the hallway was used by prostitutes, which explained some of the noises we had heard during the night.

That morning, we flew from San Pedro Sula to Tegucigalpa, the capital of Honduras. From there we were driven by a pastor and his wife to Talanga, a small town just two hours away in which there were no paved streets. There, we checked into a clean six-room hotel.

That afternoon, I taught the second seminar to a larger group of pastors than the night before. Then I was interviewed in a local broadcast television studio whose programming could be heard and viewed on only 60 TV sets. That evening we had a typical Honduran meal; then I preached in a church. After showers and a good night's rest we drove four hours to a city near the Nicaraguan border. There in Cholutecahen that day, I taught a seminar to a good number of pastors.

A street in Talanga, Honduras

The next morning Judy and I sat at the front of the auditorium and held hands as we prayed that God would use us for his glory in this our time of weakness. As a welcome respite from the heat, this church was air-conditioned. God blessed the service, and we were very grateful for the pastor and his wife; they were loving and sensitive to our needs. Lunch was arroz con pollo.

We then took a nap before being transported with our luggage to a church that was not air-conditioned. There I preached and taught for nearly an hour and a half. At 9 o'clock we began our nearly three-hour trip to a two-star hotel in Tegucigalpa. We checked in at 12:30 in the morning. We had to be ready and waiting at 5:30 a.m. to be taken to the airport for an early-morning flight to Guatemala.

The propeller-driven airplane had mechanical problems and we didn't take off until 12:30. We landed in Guatemala City at 2 p.m. Two dear men had driven 5½ hours to Guatemala City from Huehuetenango, expecting to pick us up at 9 a.m. My pain level was extremely high as we drove the 5½ hours to Huehuetenango over a road with more than its share of potholes. More than 13 hours after leaving our hotel in Honduras, we arrived in Huehuetenango. When we reached our destination at 8pm there were 22 men waiting to greet us. Seven of these men had traveled five hours to Guatemala City to attend our seminar in January.

This time, they told us how their lives had been changed in that seminar. Now they had put together two seminars and a lunch meeting with us. And they had rented the presidential suite for us, a brand new area of the hotel that was not to be opened until June 28.

The only problem: it was on the third floor and the elevator was not yet working. This meant that we had to climb up those three flights of stairs, which for me was sheer agony. The five or six men that carried our suitcases and helped me up the stairs said good night and we closed the door, a door that was made of mahogany. These accommodations were a far cry from what we had experienced at the "cheap" hotel in San Pedro Sula a few nights earlier.

We went into the suite and Judy fell into my arms crying. She cried tears of joy and gratefulness for a long time after they all said goodnight and left us in our room. We both were overwhelmed by their love and their joy at seeing us in their city. The next morning at 8 o'clock in a special banquet room of the hotel I taught about 50 men.

That afternoon in a church I taught about 200 for three hours. That evening after returning to the hotel and having a quick bite, Judy and I were picked up; she was taken to speak to many women, and I taught about 30 men of a group called "men in action." We were within 30 miles of Totonicapán where in 1932 the only true revival in Latin America had begun.

The next day I preached for 6½ hours to a packed auditorium filled with pastors from many churches, and a multitude of church members of many different denominations. As the final service concluded, the response was scary. No one wanted to leave the church and everyone stood there in complete silence even though the service was over. Then they all left the auditorium in silence.

In the next venue, in the middle of the seminar my eyes fluttered from side to side and I felt like I was about to black out. Several brothers came up and I drank some water and sat down to finish the seminar. We had an hour break and these dear brothers literally held my arms and helped us get back to our hotel. When it was time to return, Judy was with me waiting to be picked up for the last two hours of the seminar; then as the car drove up, she said she was not physically able to go with me and went back to our room.

The next day we were driven the 5½ hours down the mountain to Guatemala City. There we collapsed into bed. The next morning we had to catch a plane at 11:30 for San Diego. Judy suggested that I include here the following message, which we sent to our children while we were preparing to leave Guatemala:

We are in Guatemala City after painful 5-hour trip down mountain from Huehuetenango. The last two days have seemed to us to be the most blessed time of all of our travels. Ten hours of preaching in two days to fantastic people who would not let us go. When we weren't preaching we were answering questions and sharing with Huehuetecos.

Your mother was used of God like never before, and we had people at our hotel until late at night and then early in the morning saying goodbye to us. We left part of our hearts in Huehuetenango.

Last night the church was packed after the two previous services and no one wanted to leave their seats when I finished. It's the most awesome feeling to see people fall in love with Jesus, and cry because of wanting to know Him more.

In one week in Honduras and Guatemala, we had taught our three-hour seminar five times, and preached five sermons, and driven 23 hours by car. Until then, this was by far our most physically demanding trip and the trip that was most blessed; twenty-three hours of teaching and preaching in a seven-day period. There were two several-hour services where no one wanted to leave when we finished. God blessed so many and so much. In the preceding 13 months we had traveled over 180,000 miles by airplane and had taught seminars and preached in ten countries to nearly 70,000 pastors, leaders, and church members.

Back to Guatemala

The western part of Guatemala is populated by hundreds of small Mayan villages. On our next trip to this country, in July, 2008, we held a three hour seminar on prayer, holiness, and true revival for more than 500 pastors who had gathered from all over this region.

While in Guatemala this time, we were privileged to meet the Ekstroms. Getting to know David and Helen was a great honor for Judy and me. Both of these dear Christians are MK's (missionary kids) who had by then lived in Huehuetenango for more than 50 years, translating the New Testament into several Mayan dialects. They were a real inspiration to me and a true example of faithful endurance.

With Helen and David Ekstrom

We are often asked, "Why do you push yourselves?" And some wonder why our seminars and other ministries are important in Latin America. God has called us to redeem the days we have left on this earth by teaching others that true love for Christ requires us to present our lives as a sacrifice, holy, acceptable unto Him, and to develop a genuine prayer life.

If the churches, and especially the pastors, are going to see all of Latin America won to Christ they must first love the Lord with all their hearts, minds, and souls. This is His message that we are preaching to all of Latin America.

Much of what I know and teach and practice I owe to those who have gone before. Three very special men greatly blessed my Christian life. Each of these men helped develop my ministry so I could be used of the Lord. Dr. Cal Guy, Dr. L. Nelson Bell, and Pastor Ron Dunn; they were all men of God. These three friends and mentors have faithfully finished their earthly course. One day soon I will be with them at our Savior's feet where together we will sing, "Glory! Glory! Glory..."

Before we began our current ministry, I called Dr. Guy, who in his 80's had made numerous trips half way around the world to minister to the pastors of Bangladesh. When I had finished describing what God was leading me to do, he said, "Charles, your vision is too small." I had just told him about trying to reach all of Latin America and, chiding me a little, he urged me to lift my eyes to other continents that need the same message.

We do have invitations to hold seminars in several countries in Africa, Europe, and Asia; but for now HE has us only in Latin America. However, I will not forget Dr. Guy's exhortation should the Lord see fit to keep me on this earth.

Pastors who asked me to hold seminars in Malawi

Dr. Guy—on the field, in his missions classroom, and in the pulpit—always challenged me to preach only Jesus and to keep the message straight from the Word. He was my mentor, our pastor, our seminary professor, and our dear friend.

Dr. Guy and his wife had two children, a girl and a boy. While Judy and I were at Seminary, they were teenagers attending the little country church that their father pastored, and we knew them well. Years later, these two were used of God to bless our lives.

On September 6, 2008, we received a letter from Lynette and Ray, saying they knew that if their father were here he would have tried to assist us in our ministry's time of need. For that reason they decided to send, from his estate, support for our ministry. We are grateful for their honoring our ministry, and their father, in this way.

Back to El Paso again

I was invited to be the speaker at the 80th anniversary of the El Paso International Airport, which was to be held on the 10th of September in 2008. From 1949 to 1954, my father was the manager of this airport. Because I was one of the "still living" from that era, I was asked to tell the story of the airport during that period of time. The airport paid for our trip to El Paso.

While in that area, I of course took advantage of opportunities to do the work of the Lord. Our 8-day stay was very busy; and we were blessed to be used by God.

This trip was personal for us in many ways. As you know, it was in El Paso 50 years earlier, on August 30, 1958, that I confessed my faith in Jesus; and on October 31, 1958, I fell in love with my Judy. That same year we both began teaching a Sunday school class across the river in Juarez. So 2008 was our "year of jubilee."

On this trip to El Paso, God blessed me with the opportunity of:

• Teaching a seminar in Spanish to pastors from West Texas and New Mexico;

• Teaching at a seminary south of Juarez, Mexico;

• Teaching a seminar to pastors of the Juarez Ministerial Alliance;

• Preaching in churches I had preached in 45 years ago;

• Speaking at the 80th Anniversary celebration of El Paso International Airport;

• And teaching two classes at El Paso High School.

We received much kindness and love; one example involved Judy's teeth. After 34 years of dental practice in El Paso, our dear friend, Dr. Rene Rosas, retired to become a "dentist for the people." In his 70's, Rene for 12 years had been working 40 hours a week providing dental care for those who were living below the poverty level.

Rene was not only an excellent dentist and a great humanitarian, but he was the first Hispanic elected President of the Texas Dental Association, and the first Hispanic elected to the board of the American Dental Association. God used this prince among men to bless my Judy. Because we are on Medi-Cal (the California version of Medicaid), which does not provide adequate dental coverage, many of her dental needs had gone untreated. Rene spent hours over four days fixing Judy's teeth. We will always be grateful for the love we received from him and his sweet wife Irma. In El Paso and Juarez we renewed acquaintances with many friends, including one we had not seen in 50 years.

Back to Central America

In October of 2008, Judy and I experienced a very busy and fruitful trip to Costa Rica and Guatemala. Rigo did an excellent job of organizing our seminars.

Forty years earlier, when we arrived in San Jose, Costa Rica, en route to Lima, Peru, little did we know that God would keep us in Costa Rica and allow us to see more than 5,000 souls accept Christ in our first two years of ministry there.

Preaching on Costa Rican television

211

On this more recent trip, everywhere we went, we found people whose lives Christ had changed through our "Upper Room" ministry. You cannot imagine the joy we felt at seeing men and women still faithful to Jesus Christ after those many years.

We paid a heavy price physically to teach a seminar on the Island of Chira in the Gulf of Nicoya; but our loving heavenly Father blessed us beyond measure for this effort. Our trip by small boat through alligator-infested channels was truly memorable. Few travel to this remote area to minister to the needs of the people living there. But God led us there, and He blessed us and the lives of many others.

**Praying with my Judy during a break in
the pastors' seminar; in 98° heat
and 98% relative humidity**

At each of our seminars, I teach that "the most powerful weapon for good on earth is a man who presents his life holy, acceptable unto the Lord." The world needs to see not only pastors, but every Christian, live a life of holiness and repentance.

212

We found an example of such commitment on that October trip to Costa Rica: for 22 years after accepting Christ in our Upper Room, Leonides had traveled as a missionary throughout Costa Rica, showing films for Christians Sharing Christ. Through that ministry he led more than 25,000 to Jesus. This dear brother then pastored one of our churches in northern Costa Rica. That church doubled in size in the first 14 months of his pastorate.

We spent 11 days in Costa Rica. During a period of 2½ days we traveled 800 kilometers (500 miles) by car, much of it over very difficult roads, to reach areas where we held three pastors' seminars and preached in a church less than 10 miles from the Nicaraguan border. We also held a seminar for pastors in San Jose and preached in three other churches.

We were scheduled to be in Huehuetenango and Guatemala City for 8 days, but for health reasons we had to cut our time in Guatemala down to 4 days. Three brothers drove 6 hours from Huehue for a lengthy meeting with us in our hotel. We also were able to meet with several other Guatemalan leaders while we stayed close to our hotel. On our last morning in Guatemala City, God gave me the opportunity to share His love with 80 Catholic businessmen and professionals at a breakfast. During that trip three individuals prayed with us to receive Christ, and many more accepted His gift through the preaching of His word.

For the rest of the year, we continued to make trips to Latin America. By the end of 2008, we had challenged more than 70,000 Latin American pastors and leaders to live lives of holiness and prayer.

2009

In March of 2009, Rigo and I preached 6 times in 6 cities in 6 days in the northwest region of Costa Rica during their hottest season, with temperatures over 98 degrees. God blessed increasingly, as we progressed on our trip. Our message was, and continues to be: Love Christ with all your heart; live in obedience and holiness before Him; and allow God to use you to win many to Christ. God richly blessed on this trip.

The invitation in one large church lasted more than an hour; the pastor and his wife were among those who, in brokenness, openly expressed their desire for passion to love Christ more, and their desire to win their city to Christ. Sunday afternoon, this large church went out knocking on every door in a small nearby town where there was no church, witnessing and telling everyone about Christ's love.

Preaching in Latin America

God had begun something great in a Costa Rican businessman who was in his early thirties. We had known him all his life and loved him dearly. He had always been very active in his church and lived an exemplary Christian life. Then, in his quiet time in God's Word, the Lord convicted him of his lack of true love for Christ. But while we were there, Javier Esteban seemed to become a different man.

His love for Christ became very evident and God began using him mightily. Much of his time is now spent in prayer and fasting. His three employees have become more effective in his business, and God continues to bless him financially.

On a Monday morning after a pastor's conference in San Jose, two men came up to me to tell me how God had blessed them through the ministry of our Upper Room. One pastor told me his wife accepted the Lord with me when she was 15-years old. Another pastor, who was blind, told me that 38 years earlier, he also accepted the Lord with me and had been a pastor for the past 30 years.

New tires

Let me tell you about one of the blessings God bestowed upon Judy and me in 2009, right here in southern California. For years, for financial reasons, we had always bought used tires for our car. When we again needed tires for the front wheels, we went into the Discount Tire Store in Santee. The Manager looked at all four tires and said, "It is dangerous for you to drive on the freeway. They all need to be replaced."

To purchase four of their cheapest tires would have cost us $360. He did not know that we had only $87, but he said he would make us a special deal, and give us the tires for $280, which was below their employee price. I went out to the car to call one of our sons to see if we could use his credit card, but he was not available.

While we sat in the car looking to the Lord for his leadership, the Manager walked out and said "Give me your keys; we are going to give you the tires free." He did not know anything about us, but God did!

Judy and I both wept in front of this dear man. On the sales invoice we read: "A needy couple...just trying to do the right thing." HOW GREAT IS OUR LORD, to direct our path straight to that good-hearted manager!

Back to Costa Rica again

Shortly after this, during the wee hours of Tuesday morning, April 14, God spoke to my heart and led me to take several steps of faith. God had recently blessed in a significant way the service at a very large church in Miramar on the side of a mountain in rural Costa Rica.

Then that morning, God led me to call Martin Ramirez, the dear Pastor of that church and explain to him all that God had burdened my soul to do.

The Pastor readily recognized that this was of the Lord, and that we should follow the plan that God had laid before us. On Friday, April 24th, we would begin a series of meetings in his church on repentance, love for Jesus, and revival. Pastor Ramirez agreed to my request not to publicize or advertise these meetings. The results would be in God's hands and there would be no effort to try to share in His glory.

**Pastor Martin Ramirez and his wife Sonya
in Miramar, Costa Rica**

I asked the Pastor to have the church pray for only three things:

• That their own lives would become totally obedient and surrendered to the Lord.
• That their church would be in "one accord and in one spirit" (as on the day of Pentecost).
• And that the Pastor and I would be totally hidden behind the Cross of Calvary.

By God's grace, I was able to make that anticipated trip to Costa Rica. And God abundantly blessed all those involved. The results are best expressed in a newsletter I sent out after returning home safe and somewhat sound to my wife and children.

From newsletter of
May 1, 2009

For more than Two years, we have traveled thousands of miles and have spoken to thousands of pastors and leaders about the importance of prayer—talking to God—and about the price to be paid to see true revival come to their country.

We have known that if God is going to visit Latin America for the second time in history, it will be because His people have cried out to Him, not for more blessings, but to in reality know His presence in a way that their lives, churches, and country will be changed forever.

One week ago, my Loving Heavenly Father allowed me to preach four messages in three days to a church that desires to see revival come to their country and to Latin America. No way can I begin to tell you how God "moved" over this large number of genuinely broken people. Every service lasted a minimum of three hours; many would prostrate themselves on the concrete crying out to the Lord for forgiveness and expressing love for Him.

The last night there in Miramar, there was a large number of dear Christians who stood in line for a long period of time, just to hug my neck and share with me how God had blessed them and what they believe He is doing and will continue to do in and through their lives.

That same weekend, about a hundred miles away, several hundred pastors of both large and small churches of all denominations met for 8 ½ hours; God's Holy Spirit moved on them, bringing forth confession of sins, repentance, and reconciliation, both with God and their fellow pastors.

One hundred miles in another direction, in a church where I have preached many messages on revival, God has begun something marvelous among a group of young high school students. A 16-year-old, during recess, fell to his knees and began weeping, asking God for forgiveness and praying that his fellow students would come to know Christ Jesus. A

217

Christian teacher, a member of the same church, persuaded the Principal of the school that it was important to "not interfere" as many were on the ground praying. She said, "This is of the Holy Spirit."

Later, students asked teachers for their forgiveness, and others threw away their drugs and have forgiven each other. Felipe, the 16-year-old, was one who had been baptized only three days before this occurred.

Last week, at this same church, the members tore down a back wall and rapidly enlarged their sanctuary because the lost are flocking to their church and many are being saved.

Moving forward

Between 2009 and 2012, I was asked many times if I would ask for another five years when my pact with God was completed. My answer was very simple, "No, for the life that I will live from that time forward will be an act of obedience to His will, and He can take me home at any time that he desires."

Charles and Judy Moore circa 2012

By God's grace, I have now survived more than another five years beyond that 2012 date. And He has continued to use me. But He has often let me know that my time here on earth could be over in the twinkling of an eye.

218

I am no stranger to hospitals and doctors' offices. In my lifetime I have had sixteen surgeries, including a quadruple (or quintuple) heart bypass. Each and every day that I live, I will live with the faith to believe that He will use me for His glory until I am called home or He returns for all His own.

Until now (more than twelve years since the beginning of the pastors' seminars), He has given me the opportunity to teach more than 250,000 pastors and leaders throughout Central and South America, as well as a smaller number here in North America. Primarily I have been teaching them the importance of having a continual conversation with their heavenly Father, and living their lives for His glory.

In the next chapter I want to relate some of the ways and places God has blessed me, protected me, and led me during the last eleven years. I will include a few newsletters as well as some events that I will relate as I think of them, in no particular order as to time and place.

Chapter XVI
For the Rest of My Life

> *I am crucified with Christ: nevertheless I live;*
> *yet not I, but Christ liveth in me: and the life which I*
> *now live in the flesh I live by the faith of the Son of*
> *God, who loved me, and gave himself for me.*
> —Galatians 2:20 KJV

In early September, 2009, I was planning a tour of Guatemala where I expected to be holding seminars and conducting evangelistic services. I also had plans for preaching in the very same church where the revival had begun in 1932. And I anticipated speaking at a seminary, appearing on a television program, and speaking on radio.

The sermons would have been preached in Spanish and translated into Mayan dialects. Imagine an English-speaking North American preaching in Spanish and the message being translated simultaneously into several Mayan dialects. But in God's sovereignty, when the time came to go, the needed funds had not come in and the trip had to be cancelled.

Announcing the trip cancellation in a newsletter at that time, not knowing what was about to occur, I wrote:

> Our heavenly Father knows why additional funds did not arrive; but we don't, though we have tried to understand. Rigo and I know there is no better place on earth than the center of God's will. Even though our hearts ache for not being in the mountains of Guatemala we are at peace being in His will.

Although God foresaw my looming heart attack and emergency open-heart surgery, I did not. So, as I was eagerly making my plans for that trip to Latin America, I could not understand why I was being restrained.

Open heart surgery

Then, that very week in September, 2009, I had to undergo emergency open-heart surgery in San Diego. As soon as they received word, several pastors in Costa Rica—friends of both Rigoberto Vega and myself—paid Rigo's airplane fare so he could come and be close at hand to pray for my recovery. After that surgery, the doctor told me that he had operated on the other patient scheduled for that day first because he thought my heart was the stronger and could wait for the afternoon. He also said that my heart had required a quintuple bypass (I had thought quadruple was the maximum).

There was one other thing the doctor told me that made me very grateful that Judy and many others were there praying for me. He said that while they were opening up my chest, and before they could attach the heart-lung machine, my heart stopped! But for the grace of God, that would have ended my ministry and my life on Earth. One of the doctors on his team quickly put his hand into my chest and massaged my heart for 10 minutes and 22 seconds until they were able to attach the mechanical pump.

The surgeon told Judy that there was a possibility that the temporary loss of oxygen to my brain might cause problems with my memory. In fact, I have experienced some memory lapses, even briefly forgetting my own son's name. Rigoberto recently reminded me that the doctor had said that could happen. Let me share the first newsletter I sent out after that near-death experience had occurred.

From newsletter of
October 24, 2009

Dear Prayer Partners,
Friends, and Loved Ones,
Most of you know that 4 weeks ago I underwent quadruple (or was it quintuple?) by-pass open-heart surgery. My heart actually stopped beating; my survival depended upon a doctor massaging it for more than ten minutes, until a heart pump could be connected. How great is our God to give us those doctors! Here is the rest of the story:
The Sunday night that Judy rushed me to the emergency room was the night I was to have had the honor of preaching in the church in Totonicapán, Guatemala, where in 1932, the only widespread revival in Latin American history began.

With Heberto Garcia

Our beloved brother, Heberto Garcia, Superintendent of several thousand Guatemalan churches, had arranged this blessing for me and was to drive me 3½ hours up the mountain to preach that night. If I had been in Guatemala that night and not in our hospital in California, it is conceivable that I would have died preaching the message of revival in the church where revival began 77 years ago. I have always hoped that when God calls me home, it will be while I'm preaching the message of revival.

For two and a half years and more than 200,000 miles, we have physically taxed our bodies in order to preach the message of revival to 100,000 pastors and leaders throughout Latin America. Why? Because we know that once revival begins, literally millions will come to love our Lord.

For many months, on each trip, I had endured severe sternum and shoulder blade pain. We thought this pain was from my RSD, or was associated with lifting our heavy suitcases or traveling rough roads. Little did we imagine that this was associated with my heart. It was; but thanks to God and His perfect timing, I have lived to preach another day.

222

Judy continues to be an excellent nurse and together we are redeeming this time of rest. Doctors will not allow me to travel to Latin America until February.

Personal thanks: throughout the Americas our friends received word of my emergency surgery. Prayer requests were aired on radio and TV stations in several countries. A concert of intercessory prayer went up to Heaven. While Rigo was here, we estimated that at least 20,000 known prayer warriors had been praying for the doctors and the surgery.

To those of you who prayed, we are humbled and grateful for your love. We are grateful to the Christian leaders in Costa Rica who paid Rigo's airfare so he could be here with us. One large church sent a large banner signed by all their members wishing me a quick recovery; other Churches helped us by sending many cards, love offerings, and special healing milk. Members of our home church came to sing at my bedside but were restricted to singing outside, where many more were blessed.

Three dear Christian brothers of our church who have had open-heart surgery were a source of encouragement as they daily visited me. Thank you for all the prayer, hospital visits, phone calls, and cards. But most of all, we are deeply grateful for your expressions of love for Judy and me.

Detached memories

The many newsletters sent out since 2007 could fill a small book, and maybe someday they will. For the rest of this chapter, I want to share some of my random memories.

1.   During these last 11 years Judy and I have experienced many different circumstances and situations; but one blessing stands out above most of the others. As I have spoken in different countries, the word has spread resulting in more opportunities to hold seminars than I can accept. But there was one unusual opportunity that both Judy and I wanted to accept, because it seemed that no one else had ever thought to minister to these pastors.

It involved riding over water through a long channel where we watched alligators that were visible on both sides; then across a large distance of open water of the Gulf of Nicoya, to an island where I would teach eight pastors my seminar on prayer and living the Romans 12:1-2 life.

We had no problem getting out of the boat but walking 100 yards in the mud to get to dry land was something we had not expected. The pastors who greeted us were very kind as they provided us with buckets of water to remove the smelly mud from our legs and feet.

While we were doing that I saw the chariot that was waiting to take us to the small church where I would hold the seminar. Judy sat in the front seat and I sat in the back of the truck on a bucket as we bounced along a muddy road.

In all of our travels we have tried to avoid eating food that might not sit well with our North American stomachs but we had to eat the food that was offered to us at the lunch. It was different but by God's grace we did not get sick. One thing that I did not mention is that the temperature was well into the 90s and the humidity seemed like it was higher than the temperature. The only time we were somewhat cool during those seven hours was while we were bouncing over the waves in that speeding boat.

2.   Tegucigalpa, Honduras, was the ideal place for me to take three dear Christian friends to show them how most Latin Americans were hungry to hear the simple plan of salvation. These men—Ken McGovern, Ed Human, and Leo Humphries—could not speak Spanish; so they each took a marked dual-language New Testament with verses in English on one side of the page and verses in Spanish on the other side.

We went out on the busy streets of this capital city to witness. It was easy to find people who would stop to find out what these American men were trying to say. Each of my friends pointed at verses such as John 3:16; then, pointing to their heart and using sign language, they would tell the lost about Jesus.

When someone understood them well enough they would say, "Charles, he wants to accept the Lord." I then was blessed to explain in Spanish what they needed to do to accept Christ. Many gave their hearts to the Lord during those two days of our witnessing on the street.

At 11 o'clock one night I took these three men to a place they least expected to go. We spent three hours witnessing to the lost in the red light district of that city. They were amazed as they saw more than fifteen men and women accept the Lord.

225

Around 2:00 in the morning we piled into a taxi and headed back to our hotel. The three of them were packed into the backseat of this small taxi while I sat in the front seat and witnessed to the cab driver. The driver was very interested as I shared Christ with him. He said he wanted his sins to be forgiven and wanted to ask Christ into his life so I said, "Repeat after me this simple prayer." After the driver began to pray, those three men in the back suddenly shouted, "Charles, tell him to open his eyes!" He did, just in time to avoid crashing into a bus. After that, I made sure that cab drivers accepted Christ with their eyes open.

3. After my open-heart surgery I made an appointment with Dr. Richard Katz, the cardiologist I had known as a friend for thirty years (see page 154). I told him that the following week I was flying to Guatemala, and that while there, I would travel up to a town called Huehuetenango which was 6,900 feet above sea level. I said I would be making this trip in order to teach a special pastors' seminar to 450 pastors from throughout Central America. Exasperated, he said, "Why do you have to go up to the mountain to preach?" My reply was, "It is God's will for my life that I make this trip."

He then told me that before speaking at the seminar, I should take three days of rest in Huehuetenango so that I would become acclimated and there wouldn't be as much stress on my heart. Dr. Katz is one of the best cardiologists in all of San Diego County and I consider him a good friend. So I listened to him and thought I would do my best to heed his advice.

I arrived in Guatemala City late at night. The next morning I began the seven-hour drive to Huehuetenango. Because of the altitude, while in that city, I was connected to an oxygen tank on wheels, which I had to pull behind me. The following morning, I taught the 450 pastors for three hours; the next day, another three hours. The conference concluded on Saturday. But Sunday I preached in the morning and in the evening.

The next morning at 5:45, I awoke with a bad pain in my chest. I took one nitroglycerin pill, which made my head feel like it would explode. After putting on my suit I went down stairs to the car that was to take me to a Monday morning church service, where I was to speak at 7 o'clock. By the time I got in the car I needed to place another nitroglycerin pill under my tongue, severely exacerbating my headache.

About quarter to eight, as I was speaking, my chest pain had increased and I needed another nitroglycerin pill under my tongue. I concluded that I needed to go to the hospital.

Preaching to the thousands in Huehuetenango

We got to the hospital (actually, a clinic) a few minutes before eight; the doctors had not yet arrived. I sat on a bench with my back against the wall waiting for someone, or for something to happen. Standing directly in front of me and only about 15 feet away, was the security officer with a shotgun hanging over his shoulder. My first thought was, "Lord, you don't really want me to witness to him, do you?" Well, God gave me the tremendous blessing of leading Gustavo to Christ. As he prayed with me, large tears came out of his eyes. A few minutes later, two nurses came down the stairs and, one on each side, walked me up to the second floor, where I was helped onto the table and given an EKG.

One nurse in her mid-20s prayed with me to accept Christ; again I saw large tears. A short time later a doctor friend of mine and the doctor in charge of the clinic came in and told me that I needed to get off of the mountain as soon as possible, and then rest for one day in Guatemala City before catching a plane for home. They gave me strict orders to see my cardiologist as soon as I got home.

Both the security guard Gustavo and the nurse Miriam had tears in their eyes as they were saying goodbye to me. Upon arriving in Guatemala City after that seven-hour drive down the mountain, I was greatly relieved to be freed from that oxygen tank and its tube in my nose. I never told my cardiologist about my Huehuetenango "adventure" in Guatemala; but I'm sure he will find out by reading this book.

Several times I have heard my pastor, David Jeremiah, say that God will take us only when we have finished what he has called us to do. I believe one of the evidences of this is my preaching in Huehuetenango after having taken those nitroglycerin pills.

4.   In 2008 I was invited to teach one of my seminars on live television in Guatemala. This was to be presented in five one-hour segments. These programs were aired from 11am till noon every day; it was projected that the audience would be two million people. Each segment would also be recorded for future re-broadcast.

Teaching on Canal (Channel) 27 in Guatemala

Now here's where it had to be God who was enabling me to get through this very difficult ordeal. Each of the five mornings at 10:30, I went into the green room to be prepared for the studio lights and cameras. Then, at exactly 11 o'clock, I was introduced, and for one hour I taught the seminar without so much as a cough or scratching my head or doing anything else except talking into the two cameras. I was able to turn my head and body slightly from one camera to the other.

If I were giving a seminar to a group of pastors, I could get up and walk around, stretch my arms, even take a drink out of the bottle of water. But I could do none of this on live television. I so looked forward to the floor manager giving me the countdown of five minutes with his hand; then when the red light went off, I just sort of collapsed. After one or two of those programs I actually fell across the pulpit weeping at what God had done through me in that hour.

At the end of each broadcast, Judy and I were immediately taken back to our hotel where I had two very important things to do: eat meals with sufficient protein and then spend hours preparing for the next day. The hardest part was making sure that I was mentally capable of getting a message across that would bear fruit in the life of whoever was watching, or whoever would watch it on future television programs.

Several months later, Judy and I were in the state of Petén in Guatemala; our hotel was on the tiny island of Flores, which is connected to the city of San Benito, about a 12-hour drive from Guatemala City.

Girl holding baby saw me on television

One morning we walked around this island enjoying the curio shops. Entering one very small shop, we found a mother and her

229

daughters, all more than willing to help us choose something to buy. One of the girls, about eight or nine years old, kept looking at me in a strange way; finally she blurted out, "I saw you on television."

5.   When we held our first pastors' seminar in Caracas, the capital city of Venezuela, we did not have access to a car. In order to get from that city to the next, we had to ride a bus. The ride from Caracas to Barquisimeto took five hours.

Upon arrival we checked into a hotel. The hotel staff told us not to go out on the street even though we were directly in front of the police station; it would be too dangerous. The next morning, we gave our seminar to a very reserved group of pastors.

The following morning, we rode a bus seven hours to Maracaibo. That night we checked into a hotel. Returning from dinner, I opened the door to our room. Suddenly, a foot-long lizard scampered in causing Judy to literally run in and close our suitcases. That night we tucked in the covers and Judy snuggled up closer than usual. When we returned to Caracas, we saw a massive demonstration that nearly blocked our progress as we were trying to reach the airport.

We already had seat selection; but when we boarded the airplane we found that the ticket agent had changed our seating assignment to the very back row, immediately across from the bathroom. Being North Americans does not always mean you will receive preferential treatment.

6.   On one of my trips to San Pedro Sula, Honduras, I was given the opportunity to accept the invitation of the prisoners in one of the most dangerous prisons in the world. They had heard about my schools of evangelism, and in particular the one that I taught at Choloma, an adjoining town to San Pedro Sula. Choloma at that time had a very high murder rate. I learned that it is the prisoners that control the prisons. A few months earlier, the prisoners had hung their warden and then cut off his head, which they then fed to the dogs that were in the prison. I found out that the new warden was named Chepe. I made an appointment for fifteen minutes with him on the same night that I was to teach more than 400 prisoners how to lead someone to Christ.

When I arrived at the prison I was interrogated and frisked by the federal warden and his guards. Then I was allowed to knock on the door of the prison and identify myself and the appointment I had.

230

Once I was inside the prison itself, prisoners did the same thing that had been done to me by the federal guards.

Chepe, the resident warden, cancelled his appointment with me; so I went straight to an open area where a large number of prisoners were singing praises to the Lord. I was given an hour to teach them and I took every minute of it. When I finished, many of the prisoners begged me to come back and teach them more from God's word. When I was led through the pathways of the prison and was finally at that door to the outside world, I again went through a brusque search; first by the prisoners and then by the federal guards.

I never felt unsafe, but I recognized how their culture was different from the culture of the others living in San Pedro Sula. I was never able to go back into that prison to teach this large number of prisoners what it means to love Jesus. And just recently I heard that there was a massive riot in that prison, resulting in many deaths. It has now been closed and the remaining prisoners have been dispersed to other prisons in the country. I had hoped that I would be able to teach these prisoners again in December of 2017 in conjunction with our school of evangelism in San Pedro Sula, Honduras. I am saddened and disappointed that I could never try again to win Chepe to the Lord.

7.   Several years ago, I began teaching the school of evangelism that I had designed. I tried to limit these schools to 300 people; but this was not always possible. On one of my trips I held three schools of evangelism in three different cities in a period of 31 hours.

For one school that was to take place on a Saturday, we had 300 registered. However, on the preceding day, I took the opportunity of teaching my school of evangelism for one hour on a radio station that reaches all of the country. Because of that program, the next day at our school of evangelism we had 450 students and barely enough chairs.

That radio program had a tremendous impact on many people in that country. For example, a very famous Christian leader that I had known since the 1960s was in the radio station when I presented our school. Afterwards he told me that three days earlier, his doctor asked him what he needed to do to be saved and my friend didn't have an answer for him. He expressed with much joy that he could now lead his doctor friend to Jesus.

The next day at the school, a lady said that for 13 years she had wanted to witness to her family and friends but didn't know how to do it. With great emotion, she expressed the joy and anticipation of sharing Christ for the first time with the lost members of her family. One of the ways that I could tell that God had done a marvelous work in the lives of many, was that close to 100 people came to me after the school, wanting to shake my hand, have their pictures taken beside me, have me sign their Bible; and some, with tears, shared what God had done in their lives, as they listened with their hearts during our school of evangelism.

8.   We have been able to hold only one Pastors' Seminar in the country of El Salvador, where we had lived for almost a year back in 1975. Judy and I enjoyed revisiting San Salvador; but we saw very few of the people we had known more than thirty years earlier. Among them were two very special people from our time of living there.

God gave us the joy of seeing Paula, the young lady who was stabbed in front of our house (see page 139-140). She is now the wife of a dynamic pastor with a very strong church.

With Paula and her husband, Pastor Silas Calderon

I was given the opportunity to preach in his church where I saw more than a dozen people come forward to accept Christ.

We were also able to see the dear pastor friend that invited me to preach an evangelistic message at his cousin's wedding in the mountains of northern El Salvador (see page 140). This dear brother came close to being killed during his country's Civil War.

Because of the Civil War in the 1980s most of our friends were either dead or had moved to other countries including the United States.

While in El Salvador I had a television interview about prayer and revival. This hour-long program was seen live in 27 Spanish-speaking countries.

9.   I was invited to be one of the speakers at the 28th annual Peruvian National Congress on Prayer. I had spoken at a previous annual Congress, but this year's meeting will always be remembered because of what one elderly woman did to impact our lives. Because there is always such a large crowd, they have the ushers rush the speakers off the platform and then to a room where they will not be mobbed by the enthusiastic attendees. I do not like that practice.

Invariably, people give me cards or notes asking for special prayer. Because of the press of people, I put these little epistles of love and need in my coat pocket where, upon my return to the hotel, I will read them. After I spoke in one session, the men had a hard time getting me out of the press of people. One very poor elderly woman pushed her arm between the men and said, "I am sorry this is all that I can give you." Saying thank you, I took the wad of paper and put it in my coat pocket.

That night when we finally got to our room I began taking out the notes and cards. From one coat pocket I pulled out what the elderly woman had given me. As I opened it I began to realize that it was just three pieces of toilet paper and there was nothing written on any part of it. I showed Judy, and she immediately got tears in her eyes as she explained to me that there is no toilet paper in the public toilets of Lima; people have to bring their own. We both stood there humbled by what this poor woman gave me as an expression of her love and gratitude. That expression of love is in a picture box in my office where I can see it and remember receiving something like the widow's mite (Luke 21:1-4).

10.   As a student of revival, I have researched conditions and circumstances that were common in each great revival. The only great revival in Latin America occurred in 1932 in a small village called Totonicapán. After talking to grandchildren of those who were present during that revival, and reading all the information on it that was

available, I wrote a small book titled *Revival in Guatemala*. My very dear friend David Ekstrom did the translating into Spanish; only a few months after he did this labor of love, he went to be with his Lord.

David and Helen Ekstrom had been missionaries in Guatemala for 60 years. The booklet is dedicated to David and 40,000 copies were distributed to churches throughout the country that he loved and gave his life for. Christian friends have shared with me how that book was used to bring church growth in certain areas of Guatemala; but the great revival that David and I so much looked forward to seeing, still has not come.

11.   We had a well-attended pastors' seminar in Tipitapa, Nicaragua. This is a suburb of Managua. There we stood in the Managua square viewing the Cathedral clock that stopped at 12:35 a.m. on December 23, 1973. This was when the earthquake struck and God changed the direction of our lives from starting a ministry in the marketplace of Managua to starting a marketplace ministry in San Salvador, El Salvador. You will recall from page 132 that God taught us that we could stand in the gap for a country, a place, or a people; something that we had not done for the people in the marketplace of Managua.

With My Judy at Cathedral in Managua

12.   I was in Venezuela when, through the internet, I received an invitation to speak to a group of government leaders in Lima, Peru, during the time that I would be in that city holding a pastors' seminar.

I didn't know anything about Jorge Marquez, the man who was extending the invitation. But this turned out to be an invitation that was ordained of God. Jorge Marquez was a Regidor (City Councilman) for Lima, one of the most populous cities in the world.

Jorge became a dear friend. The meeting he wanted me to speak to was of Christians who were in various positions within the Peruvian government. He specifically wanted me to talk about my experience with the Moral Majority, and how that organization made a difference in the government of the United States in 1980.

In this meeting, attended by 250 government officials, there were 65 federal judges, several congressmen, the police chief of Lima, and a former Vice President of the country. My message was that you cannot separate your walk with Christ from your office or political position.

Jorge Marquez in the City Council chambers

13.   Jorge Marquez was the one who first opened the door for me to see Pamplona Alta. Jorge took me to have lunch with the mayor of San Juan de Miraflores, who then took me on a tour of a part of his

city. Pamplona Alta is an area where 150,000 people live on five hills at about 1,500 feet above sea level.

With my Judy in Pamplona Alta,
Lima, Peru, in March, 2015

These people do not have running water or a sewer system. Water is delivered in large trucks and each family has to come down to the road to collect the water that is left in large barrels. It was Jorge

236

who, at my request, took me back to that city to meet the new mayor. From those meetings, Christians Sharing Christ Crusades has been working to not only lead many of these people to Christ, but also to try to help them in their difficult lives.

At this point, I want to share one more newsletter, followed by a letter Judy and I received from our son James while we were in Peru.

From newsletter of
March 13, 2015

Wednesday night I preached a message to a church in Pamplona Alta from Chapters 6 and 7 in the book of Judges, about how God used 300 men to defeat an army whose camels alone were innumerable.

There are 150,000 people who live in Pamplona Alta and less than 1,500 people attend church on any Sunday. If ever we need to see a miracle of the magnitude found in the book of Judges, it is here.

After the service, while we were on the street trying to get into our taxi to return to our apartment, we were mobbed by excited Christians who had been turned into believers in the possibility that they could win Pamplona Alta for Jesus.

One lady had gone across the street from the church and brought a lost next-door neighbor for me to lead to Christ. A few minutes later, another lady walked up to me, bringing her neighbor. Each of these two women prayed with me to receive Christ and the joy in their eyes and faces was very visible, even though we were illuminated by only a street light.

Our cab driver that night was a member of that same church. He had attended a Baptist seminary for two years. I was blessed of my Lord to be used to encourage this young man in his calling.

When we arrived home at our apartment here in Miraflores, I sat on my walker on the street and continued the conversation with this dear taxi driver.

When I said goodnight to him and walked into our apartment building, I found that Judy had led Pedro, the young man at the desk, to Jesus. Yesterday we bought him a New Testament and were blessed to see his smile of gratitude. In weeks past he had always been very quiet, with a little sadness in his eyes. The difference now in his countenance is visible.

I feel so incapable of telling you all of the things that God is doing here. Everything that we purpose to do has one thing in mind, winning all of Pamplona Alta to Jesus. Every night is dedicated to preaching a message of exhortation and encouragement in a different church in Pamplona Alta. The expectation is that each Christian in these churches become "on fire" to testify about Jesus in their own lives. What fun it is to see their faces change from serious in working for their Lord, to the visible excitement of winning others to Christ.

Tuesday afternoon I will speak to more than 1,000 intercessors from throughout Lima. My speaking at this gathering has already been advertised on radio for several days, and my challenge will be for each intercessor to stand in the gap for Pamplona Alta, and to pray that God will do that which only He can do, use every Christian in the area to win hundreds to Jesus.

I have at least three more four-hour Pastors' Seminars during the day, in different parts of this city of 10 million people. Our son James continues to recover from his heart surgery. Three weeks ago, his aortic valve was replaced with a bovine valve.

He and our oldest grandson Thomas are praying together and preparing biblical messages to teach to churches and pastors here in Lima. I have added here a letter that we received from James this week.

Dear Mom and Dad,

I am feeling an extremely powerful call to come to Peru as soon as possible. Time is short

238

and the laborers are few. I walked over a mile and a half yesterday and still got up this morning, made it to church on time, went furniture shopping and walked another half mile this afternoon.

Please prayerfully consider whether the Lord might be able to use me for His Glory in some capacity there; perhaps to energize or revitalize the work that He has already started with you all. I am an almost 100% healthy, semi-young, man. I have a new servant's heart and a sense of urgency to reach as many people for Christ as possible before his imminent return.

I love you both, and am praying for guidance in this as well. May our Lord use you both mightily and protect you.

James

14.   At the end of the seventh chapter of this book, I quoted from the very first newsletter sent out by the newly formed board of Christians Sharing Christ, Inc. It was signed by six men. Each of these men lived in Asheville, North Carolina.

None of those original board members is still alive, but their love for souls is still bearing fruit today. Christians Sharing Christ has been used of God to bring more than three million souls to salvation in Jesus. Our beloved board members of old can rejoice in heaven over what God has done and is still doing through the ministry of CSC, CSCFM, and CSCC.

How I wish today I could go up to the third floor of the S&W cafeteria in Asheville and find those first six board members, and together on our knees again spend time praying to our heavenly Father.

Only in glory will I be able to express my gratitude to those first board members for who they were and what they did to glorify my Savior. Today I can, and do, express my gratitude to our present board members for what they mean to the continuing ministry that God began so long ago. One of them is my dear friend Carlos Muñoz, who helped me establish the Upper Room in Costa Rica. He continued to work with me for years in Latin America; today he pastors a solid Bible believing church in Burbank, California, which Judy and I have visited more than once. I am grateful to God that Carlos is also a wise counselor as a present board member of Christians Sharing Christ Crusades.

15.   In His omnipotent grace, God allowed my last flight as the pilot of an airplane to provide me with a perfect example of a Biblical truth. Sitting beside me in the front of the airplane was my 5-year-old daughter watching me fly while her mother and younger brother were strapped in, in the back of the airplane.

She looked over at me and said, "Daddy can I fly the airplane?" "Of course," I said as I allowed her to take the yoke to control the airplane.

The first thing she did was push the yoke forward which caused her stomach to seem to hit the ceiling, she then quickly pulled the yoke back and her stomach seemed to hit the floor. She shouted, "Daddy, Daddy, take it!" As her hands released the yoke, she did not cry out, "Daddy, Daddy, help me." I did not have to fight her for control of the airplane. She had quickly learned that she was incapable of flying the plane.

Over the years I have heard thousands of people, including pastors and missionaries, praying and asking God to help them. But, nowhere in the New Testament do you find anyone asking God to help them.

New Testament Christians understood that either you do it yourself, or God does it Himself through you. He is not there to assist us in doing our will, or for us to ask Him to help us on our projects.

In Philippians 1:1, the Apostle Paul refers to himself as a servant of Jesus Christ. But the Greek word translated "servant" is *doulos*, which properly translated means "slave" or even "bond slave." Paul, by an act of his will, became a slave to his Savior. A slave would never ask his master for help doing his own thing.

Anything that we do on our own is subject more times than not to failure; however that which the Lord does in and through us is always successful and filled with blessing. God is not our copilot; He is the Pilot, the Commander of the ship, or of the airplane, and of our souls. We are the passengers who obey His commands.

The story of Judy Anne's inability to fly the airplane has been used by me hundreds of times to explain how allowing God to be "in command" of our lives is the only way our lives are to be lived.

16.   Our oldest son has for some time now been the Field Director of Christians Sharing Christ Crusades (CSCC). He travels often to the countries of Latin America teaching thousands of Christians how to accomplish the vital work of evangelism. He has the Spirit, the heart, and the sense of urgency that his parents have for winning souls to Christ. He has been able to go and spearhead the work that needs to be done, even when neither Judy nor I could do so for health concerns. He spent his formative years in Latin America and speaks Spanish as well as his dad, perhaps better.

I do not know another bilingual soul more qualified and willing to carry on the ministry God gave to Judy and me for His glory. And James's wife Maribeth is solidly behind her husband in his love for Jesus and his desire to glorify Him above all.

In August of 2017, there was a church service in San Jose, Costa Rica, during which the mantle was passed from myself to my oldest son James Wilson Moore. This took place forty-nine years and four months after Judy and I first arrived in San Jose with our two small children, Judy Anne and James Wilson. The church where this symbolic passing of the mantle occurred was the only church that I ever pastored.

In 1972, two army surplus tents were sent to us from Texas, to be used in starting churches. When we were putting up one of those tents, a seven-year-old boy fell over a rope and his face hit one of the steel rods driven into the ground to support the tent. I rushed him to the hospital where the doctor stitched up his face; the scar from that accident has remained all these years on the left cheek of my oldest son, James Wilson Moore.

That tent was replaced many years ago by a more permanent structure, wherein that same church that I founded and pastored for two months in 1972 now holds its services. Rafael Porras, who is my son in the Lord, has pastored this church for the last 27 years.

Let me describe the service of symbolically passing the mantle. James and I were seated at the front of that sanctuary, which was filled to capacity by the congregation. Pastor Porras and Fabian

Gutierrez, one of the former pastors of this church, placed a large blue cloth around my shoulders and read from the book of Second Kings, Chapter Two, the story of the passing of the mantle from Elijah to Elisha.

Pastor Porras behind James and Charles Moore

Rafael and Fabian then extended the mantle over the shoulders of both myself and my son James as they told of Elijah's influence on Elisha.

They then took that same blue mantle and removed it from my back and placed it solely on the shoulders and back of James. This was an emotional time for both father and son.

The ministry of Christians Sharing Christ Crusades is now in the hands of a man who is named for his great, great, great Grandfather James Wilson Moore, who was the first Presbyterian missionary and preacher west of the Mississippi River.

Since that ceremony, Judy and I have made only a few more trips to Latin America; the last sermon I preached there was by invitation, in a church pastored by our friend Solomon McFarland of Antigua, Guatemala.

Charles and Judy Moore with Pastor and Mrs. Solomon McFarland of Antigua, Guatemala

My great, great grandfather's legacy did not end with a plaque in Arkansas; it continues in the hearts and lives of millions of souls the world around, to the glory of God the Father and of His dear Son, Jesus Christ my Lord.

Although our hearts are in Latin America and we continue to love and pray for the dear souls there, Judy and I are well aware that we may have made our final trip to that part of God's mission field. Our health is failing; our bodies are tired. But we would not have changed a day of our lives for any other. Our greatest joy has been in knowing that we have been in the center of God's perfect will.

The mantle is on our son James now, and he is carrying on the work and expanding the ministry under the power of the Holy Spirit and the blessings of Jesus Christ.

Epilogue

In these final pages of my life story, I want to step aside and let you hear from my wife Judy and our four grown children. In their own words you will read some of their thoughts and feelings. First a few words from my Judy, followed by those of Judy Anne (Sis), James, Cal, and Chuck (Charles Beatty Moore V); and finally, my Judy's closing thoughts.

Judy

My life as the bride of a dynamic young businessman was moving forward at a happy clip. My greatest joy was wrapped around three things: our home, our precious two-year-old daughter, and our church. These were the major parts of my love for Charles, and of the life we were living on our fourth anniversary in June of 1965.

It was a good time to be alive. People were still more or less riding on the coattails of prosperity. Vietnam was not the full-blown issue it would later become. Good friends at our church and a busy life with them, as well as good friends accumulated through my husband's business and former-school connections, made for me an even, readily anticipated and accommodated, schedule of things to do each day and each week. But by the latter part of August, both Charles and I had become conscious of an undercurrent of discontent with our lives as a whole. We were not truly talking about it; but each of us was aware that with all the prosperity and easy access to the best of everything in this world, "something" was still missing.

Then our church began publicizing the upcoming conference that was to be held the last week of summer at the Glorieta conference center in New Mexico. At this much-celebrated week-long missions conference, with its emphasis on spiritual renewal, missionaries from all parts of the world, who found themselves on furlough from the lands where they served, would gather and relate their stories, telling about their lives in foreign outposts of the Christian faith.

By the prompting of the Holy Spirit, there grew in me a longing to be at "Glorieta" for that special week. I wanted Charles and Judy Anne to be there as well. When I shared this longing with Charles, something sparked in him, and he quickly made arrangements for the three of us to attend that missions conference.

245

I soon began to seriously doubt that we could even begin to make it; Charles had to spend long hours at work and then engage in long phone conversations at home, just to keep the various businesses on track. There seemed to be little time left for us to spend with each other, let alone taking a trip that did not have to do with business. However, our excitement grew in the week before we were to leave, as bags were packed, and the actual plan to travel began to fall into place.

We flew in our plane to Santa Fe, and rode the conference shuttle to the conference center. There we began a week—from Thursday afternoon through the following Thursday morning—that would convict, convince, and astonish us with the fast-track God would put us on toward a life we had never dreamed of.

The effort of travel had been exhausting. Then the daily trek to the nursery for Judy Anne and the meetings for us throughout the days put a huge demand on our energy. After two days we moved from our private cabin to a dormitory, which provided its own excitement and social opportunities, with little time for rest.

The last message on Wednesday night was from a white-haired man with a glow on his face like few you meet in life. It was a message about his own mission field in China where he, his wife and his co-workers were challenged by their lack of visible gains in winning that part of the world to Christ.

By the time we heard his testimony, Charles and I were in tears with a longing to be in that place, or some other, with our whole world caught up in winning souls to Christ; and that suddenly became our life's goal, our mission.

Our lives had been lived happily, full of ourselves—*our* desires, *our* dreams, *our* notions of what 'we' wanted for 'us'—and of our own personal goals. But that night at Glorieta, we prayed in utter brokenness over our new convictions with a missionary we met there. He had served in Colombia with his dear wife and three sweet children.

God Himself put into our hands an article to confirm the powerful impact in our lives of that missionary message. In our room that same night, our little girl fast asleep, we fell across our bed to look at a home-missions magazine, with an irresistible article about "being in love with Jesus, and loving Him more than our own life."

We began to appreciate the importance of prayer time; we heard His 'wake-up' call from a life of "serving me, mine and ours" to one of "Jesus paid it all; all to Him I owe." Now, sharing that message

246

was all we longed for, without even a glimpse of where that future might lead. There was no turning back.

Flying home to El Paso that Thursday, seven months pregnant with our son James, I felt my heart abound with this new sense of purpose, with its hope and excitement over what lay ahead, whatever that might come to be, because the confidence in our renewed love for Him who died for me was all that I needed to know.

With absolutely no apprehension for changes that might come, we flew home that early afternoon anticipating only the coming birth of our son, our sweet girl in her preschool, and Charles working in the corporations he had received from his Dad (which he now ran alone). We knew that whatever was ahead of us, we wanted only to honor and serve the Lord, whom we now loved more than life itself. And we knew that He would show us day by day, minute by minute, how that was to be.

Shortly after the birth of our first baby boy on October 25th, while America looked forward to Thanksgiving with a heightened awareness of the war raging in Vietnam, we received a visit from Home Mission friends in charge of the Baptist Goodwill Center in El Paso. They came to see our new baby; but they also had a question for us: "Have you considered, at all, the possibility of going to Seminary?"

That question and subsequent discussion led to our investigation of, and enrollment in, Southwestern Baptist Theological Seminary. By mid-January, we were headed to Fort Worth, with Judy Anne comfortably installed on top of clothing and bedding in the back seat, and three-month-old baby James in my arms.

Our furniture and other belongings were to follow in the back of a (clean) garbage truck driven by an employee. Our very small home at Seminary was previously unknown to us; it had been chosen by our new friends from Glorieta. When we moved into it, Judy Anne expressed her wholehearted approval for "our new little house."

Thus began what would become a lifelong 'quest' to know God and to live a life dedicated to whatever would become apparent to us as His will for our lives, day by day (hopefully) and (for certain) event by event and year by year. I wrote this poem to reflect some of my impressions and feelings minus all the details of the unrolling years in the center of God's will for our lives.

An Overview

Messages and pleasures.
Phrases in measure,
Unfolding untold Treasures.

A Message.
A Prayer.
A Heart, to care.

The Scripture.
The Goal.
A lost man,
A Soul.

Dances in Honor.
A song,
A wonderful creation.
Music of Joy,
A Celebration.

Hills and waysides.
HiWays and Valleys.
Fields and flowers.
A fence.
A ruin.

A color of paint.
A flower.
A child.
Doors and walls
Cubicles
And stalls.

A store
A door.
A street
A seat.
People to meet.

Epilogue

Folks and faces.
Beauty in places.
A 'spread'
Some bread.
Trying 'not' to "run ahead."

A fever.
A doctor.
A friend.
A companion,
Up and through the very end.

—Judy Moore

Charles V   **James**   **Cal**

Judy   **Judy Anne**

In the prime of life

Judy Anne

Isaiah 38:19 *It is the living who give thanks to You, as I do today; A father tells his sons about Your faithfulness.*

My parents' life of ministry always paralleled their ministry to us, their children. Far from neglected, we enjoyed many rich experiences and loved the people that we encountered alongside them as part of our fast-paced well-traveled lives.

We witnessed both Mom and Dad share the gospel with others out of a vibrant and loving relationship with God. In the home, you could often find Mom worshiping the Lord with hymns, while scrubbing a sinkful of dirty dishes, or Dad sharing with us a nugget he had just learned from the Word. While an eyewitness would find our family life as imperfect as any other, they often noticed the strong bond of love between us.

When I was 5, I went down the aisle in response to my Dad's altar call in a tiny church outside of San Jose, Costa Rica. I could easily answer all the questions asked of me after the service, which led those in charge to believe my conversion.

However, at the age of 7, I began restlessly questioning my own heart. "Did I really know what I was doing back then?"

The Holy Spirit was persistent in pressing me to follow through regarding this dilemma. One night it was more than I could stand, so I left my bed to find Mom and Dad, and in tears explained I was sure I had lied that day as a 5-year old. Surely, I had not really asked Jesus to save me from my sin and make me a new creation. I was keenly aware of my sin nature at that young age.

Dad, sensing the weight of it, knelt with me in our living room, and led me in the sinner's prayer. A few months later, my Dad baptized me in a Costa Rican river, which we later found had sewage dumped in it upstream. However, I was cleaner than bleached snow.
—*Sis Moore*

James

Growing up on foreign soil we saw many things most suburbia children would never experience. I remember picking up a large Ant Eater from the middle of a busy road, and loading it into our Volkswagen Van and driving it outside of town to an animal sanctuary. Being the oldest boy, I often opted for riding along with my dad almost everywhere he went, while my younger brothers stayed home to play with their toys.

Countless nights, I would sit and hear my dad preach in outlying churches jam packed with people coming to hear what this "gringo" was going to say. There was a certain novelty to a tall North American proclaiming the Gospel in many of the tiny towns and villages we would travel to. Even more amazing to most Ticos (Costa Ricans) was that this man and his son spoke flawless Spanish.

Every trip with dad seemed like an adventure, but one with a purpose. We weren't just sightseeing; even at an early age, I was aware that we, I and my dad, were on a mission, a higher calling. The purpose was eternally important; people had to hear what my dad was saying. It felt good to know what my dad was doing was of utmost concern and urgency.—*James Moore*

Cal

I was born in Costa Rica on January 14, 1969, not quite nine months after my parents arrived in San Jose to attend language school. They had moved there from the States with my older sister and brother. Had they gone on to Peru at the end of that period of schooling, as had been planned, I would have been born in Lima, instead of San Jose.

While my parents awaited the birth of their *chiquito* (little boy), my Dad had begun to preach in the market place of San Jose. Our home was only a stone's throw from the lost souls of that busy, bustling area of the city. My parents opted to stay there, where once a week my Dad's preaching of God's Word drew crowds to a parking lot.

My own memories of being a small toddler began in our next home, located in the *Por la Sabana* area of San Jose. I always loved the walks to the ice cream shop nearby for banana ice cream, which in pleasant memory I can still taste to this day. Even now at 50, my dessert of choice is banana cream pie, banana pudding, and all things banana!

I remember getting my first haircut at the airport in Mexico City. That was in my second year of childhood. We were on our way to the States for my first trip ever to my own country. We settled into an apartment in El Paso, Texas, and I experienced snow for the first time ever while we were visiting with Grandma, my Dad's stepmother. I remember receiving my first set of Lincoln Logs there.

251

Soon we moved to Fort Worth to live near the Seminary. I remember getting to go with my Dad to see our second cousin Cliff Harris play for the Dallas Cowboys, and learning to enjoy American football as a new entertainment. We often watched the games on TV in the small duplex on Seminary Drive. I remember my Dad having shoulder surgery. Then, in November, my little brother was born. Shortly before Christmas, we moved to an apartment near where my sister would attend elementary school.

It was during that time that I met for the first time the man my Dad admired most from his days studying at the Seminary. He named me after this man, Dr. Cal Guy, the Missions Professor and our Pastor at the church in the tiny community of Retta.

Later, we drove back to Costa Rica and took my little brother with us. About the time of my sixth birthday, we moved to El Salvador. In the Capital, we lived in an upstairs apartment of the Central American Mission House. The host family's dwelling was on the ground floor. On occasion we would have various other missionaries as guests as they were passing through, on their way to minister in other locations. My memories of San Salvador include counting black beans on the island table in a small kitchen, which was 'common ground' shared with other missionaries, and walking down the walkway joining a string of hotel-like rooms along an outdoor corridor. My Mom would soak those beans in water overnight and then, while we four Moore kids enjoyed our baloney sandwiches for lunch, she would use the softened beans for making "Gallo Pinto." Gallo Pinto is still one of my favorite meals.

One particular gentleman who showed up as a regular at that mission house left an everlasting impression on me, as he pretended that a "little man" lived inside his wooden leg. He entertained all of us with conversations with that "little person" which only he could hear.

Later that year, after we found a house of our own to rent in San Salvador, I entered 'Kinder' for the first time in the only American School there. I remember struggling to learn English, since Spanish was always spoken in our home. The only English I heard was at school or when we would have visitors from the States.

I remember coming home from school, and then walking with my Mom, or sometimes with our in-home helper, Paula, to buy 'Nutella' (long before it became such a popular treat in the States). Upon returning home, I could smell the iodine in the air because Mom had brought home from the market the fresh vegetables that were to be washed with iodine before being cooked that week for our meals.

A 'sometimes' treat was the round shark steak with the bone in the middle that we all enjoyed so much. I am told it was much cheaper than other meats, since not everyone cared to eat meat from a flesh-eating fish. Trying to eat turtle eggs was a memory I am less fond of.

One of the many things that have served me well throughout my own life was being taught self-discipline by a father who had served in the military. Self-discipline was instilled in us by having us do our weekly chores such as cleaning the garage, organizing our rooms, and eventually doing our own laundry. This all led to the self-confidence I needed to start my own business at fifteen.

Through the years, I observed and assisted my dad in many business-type activities, including simple tasks like brochure or newsletter folding. These experiences equipped me to later successfully fit into leadership roles in a variety of jobs. One such job took me to Hong Kong and mainland China, as well as forty-eight states. Later I started my own electronics business, which I still have today.

After many years of experiences and travel, I returned to visit Costa Rica as an adult. It was a surprise to me that as I stepped off the airplane, I sensed peace, tranquility, home, and belonging such as I have never known in any other place on the planet.

God, in His goodness, takes care of missionary children living in a "foreign land" in His own perfect way.

—*Cal Moore*

Charles V

While being of such a young age during our time in Central America, my spotty memory jumps from playing on the tile floor near the "pila" watching my middle brother jump into the pool, fully clothed, to avoid bees at the Apartotel where we were staying—not just once, but twice—to spending time with my brothers and other children trying to catch fireflies, playing in the cul-de-sac at the Missionary house. Even though I was so young I do remember the strong sense of Family that I felt at home, in the car or wherever we were.

With three older siblings I was never far away from one of them and their caring oversight; and Mom made sure she knew where I was and who was watching. I do not recall even one night when both Mom and Dad didn't tell us "Goodnight...I love you." After the long hours of working at the Upper Room or spending the day taking care of all of us, Dad and Mom always made sure that we felt safe and loved.

As I grew older I realized how important those simple but so profound moments in a child's life are, and how they can help mold their future. For a family with four small children to safely travel and live in a "foreign" country—I know it has never been foreign to my parents—not only in the love and watch-care of our parents, but also under God's love and protection through all areas of the various countries, was truly evidence of God's plan for our father's and our family's role in the Ministry.

—*Charles B. Moore V*

My Judy

Years after completing seminary and beginning our missionary work in Costa Rica, we were back in the States; and eventually we settled in California. There, our goal of knowing God's will and following His lead would become more challenging with job changes, and with the world from a secular perspective presenting a more obscure picture of what God's will might look like. But even with four children, our lives still revolved around Dad as the leader, Mom as the homemaker, and Christ as the head of that fun, active, and loving household.

Whatever job changes or challenges or opportunities came his way, because Charles chose always to follow God's leading, we each remained content in our own place and space. Even with life-changing "skirmishes" in the world's way of thinking in those late seventies and early eighties, Charles would always lead us in God's way, however improbable or difficult that way might look at any given time.

Yes, I had my moments, hours, and days before the Lord, hoping that "the obvious" might be the answer; but typically, God showed Himself faithful in some unusual way, usually contrary to what anyone might have predicted.

It is a certainty that my own family's loving forgiveness in the midst of failure, when that inevitably would occur, contributed to an inner understanding on my part that "success is never final; and failure is never fatal."

I could not live with a man who suffers so deeply and bears it so well without having my own deep grief and outlook affected. Being privileged as I was to watch and experience that true dedication to God's leadership, and the daily need for His loving touch, unfalteringly assures me that my life with Charles is a life that I would trade for no other under God's Dear Heaven.

Our God has been found faithful at every turn, and when the doubts seem to "pile up" and want to overwhelm, in His Righteous Goodness He has NEVER, ever, failed us. His Loving Hand of Mercy is, and has always been, just around that seemingly endless corner every time, usually when least expected.

No, you cannot afford to hold your breath. No, you cannot come up with an answer that will suffice. No, you will never succeed if and when you choose another's "good" advice. The only pathway to Knowing God is to daily, truly, invite Him into the midst of your deepest dilemma, when you see "no way out."

He is the "Answer Giver" after all; your "All in All." He is the Only Wise God, and the Giver of ALL GOOD THINGS. HIS Way is the only way; you might just as well understand that from the outset. There is no other answer.

"There is therefore now no condemnation to them which are in Christ Jesus, who walk not after the flesh, but after the Spirit. For the law of the Spirit of life in Christ Jesus hath made me free from the law of sin and death.

"For what the law could not do in that it was weak through the flesh, God sending his own Son in the likeness of sinful flesh, and for sin, condemned sin in the flesh; That the righteousness of the law might be fulfilled in us, who walk not after the flesh, but after the Spirit."—Romans 8:1-4 KJV

"But the salvation of the righteous *is* of the LORD: *he is* their strength in the time of trouble. And the LORD shall help them, and deliver them...and save them, because they trust in him." —Psalms 37:39-40 KJV

Honor God. Love Him. Serve Him. There IS no Greater Joy. —*Judy Moore*

Charles V   Cal   Judy Anne   James
Judy   Charles IV
March, 2019

Three generations: Judy and Charles IV
Judy Anne and Ricardo Carrucciu and their young son Marco
James and Maribeth with Thomas and Brianna Moore
Cal and his daughter Tiffany with her husband Aaron Lusteg
Charles V with wife Michelle Moore and their son Jordan Moore

Just my Judy and me